D0207504

The Human Tradition in
Modern Europe, 1750 to the Present

The Human Tradition around the World Series

Editors: William H. Beezley and Colin M. MacLachlan

The Human Tradition in Modern Europe, 1750 to the Present

Edited by
Cora Granata and Cheryl A. Koos

ROWMAN & LITTLEFIELD PUBLISHERS, INC.
Lanham • Boulder • New York • Toronto • Plymouth, UK

D
289
. H86
2008

ROWMAN & LITTLEFIELD PUBLISHERS, INC.

Published in the United States of America
by Rowman & Littlefield Publishers, Inc.
A wholly owned subsidiary of The Rowman & Littlefield Publishing Group, Inc.
4501 Forbes Boulevard, Suite 200, Lanham, Maryland 20706
www.rowmanlittlefield.com

Estover Road, Plymouth PL6 7PY, United Kingdom

Copyright © 2008 by Rowman & Littlefield Publishers, Inc.

All rights reserved. No part of this publication may be reproduced, stored in a
retrieval system, or transmitted in any form or by any means, electronic, mechanical,
photocopying, recording, or otherwise, without the prior permission of the publisher.

British Library Cataloguing in Publication Information Available

Library of Congress Cataloging-in-Publication Data

The human tradition in modern Europe, 1750 to the present / edited by Cora Granata
and Cheryl A. Koos.
　　p. cm. — (The human tradition around the world series)
　Includes bibliographical references and index.
　ISBN-13: 978-0-7425-5410-8 (cloth : alk. paper)
　ISBN-10: 0-7425-5410-4 (cloth : alk. paper)
　ISBN-13: 978-0-7425-5411-5 (pbk. : alk. paper)
　ISBN-10: 0-7425-5411-2 (pbk. : alk. paper)
　1. Europe—History. 2. Europe—Social conditions. 3. Europe—Civilization. I. Granata,
Cora Ann. II. Koos, Cheryl A., 1966–
　D289.H86 2008
　940.2—dc22
　　　　　　　　　　　　　　　　　　　　　　　　　　　　　　　2007025397

Printed in the United States of America

∞^TM The paper used in this publication meets the minimum requirements of
American National Standard for Information Sciences—Permanence of Paper
for Printed Library Materials, ANSI/NISO Z39.48-1992.

For Jackson Koos Davis and Chris Endy

University Libraries
Carnegie Mellon University
Pittsburgh, PA 15213-3890

~

Contents

Acknowledgments

We wish to thank many people whose support, guidance, and assistance helped make this book possible. Carla Bittel, Michelle Nickerson, and Doug Yule provided invaluable encouragement and support. Chris Endy offered both his steady support and his sharp, critical eye at all stages of the project. David Igler was an important resource, generously sharing with us his experiences editing a volume in the Human Tradition in America series. We would also like to express our appreciation to graduate student Christopher Axtell for his assistance with the manuscript preparation. California State University, Fullerton, and the Center for the Study of Genders and Sexualities at California State University, Los Angeles, provided grant moneys for the student assistantships. We also owe a debt of gratitude to Rick Hopper and Scholarly Resources for their initial interest in this project. Susan McEachern, our editor, deserves special thanks for continuing their enthusiasm, for offering useful advice and suggestions, and for shepherding the project through the review and publication process with Rowman & Littlefield Publishers when they took over the series. Series editors Bill Beezley and Colin MacLachlan, as well as the anonymous readers, also provided insightful feedback that strengthened the book.

This list would be incomplete without a tribute to the late Clark Davis. We owe the genesis of this book to him, for it was he who suggested that we join forces to edit this volume and who facilitated initial inquiries with the publisher. We wish he were here to witness its completion. Clark was the consummate teacher-scholar of history; he imparted his passion for justice, humanity, and the past to all who crossed his path. We each had the distinct pleasure and privilege to call him our colleague and friend. Cheryl had the additional honor of being his wife and is the mother of his son. Our lives, and those of his friends, family, students, and the historical profession he loved so dearly, are richer for having known and loved him.

~

Introduction

CHERYL A. KOOS AND CORA GRANATA

"Rien" (Nothing).

—King Louis XVI of France, 14 July 1789

I believe in aristocracy, though—if that is the right word, and if a democrat may use it. Not an aristocracy of power, based upon rank and influence, but an aristocracy of the sensitive, the considerate and the plucky. Its members are to be found in all nations and classes, and all through the ages, and there is a secret understanding between them when they meet. They represent the true human tradition, the one permanent victory of our queer race over cruelty and chaos. Thousands of them will perish in obscurity, a few are great names. They are sensitive for others as well as for themselves, they are considerate without being fussy, their pluck is not swankiness but the power to endure, and they can take a joke.

—E. M. Forster, *Two Cheers for Democracy* (1951)

As the first quote above illustrates, Louis XVI's diary entry did not reflect the magnitude of events that pivotal day in July 1789 when an armed insurrection toppled the Bastille prison in Paris. That day, ordinary men and women took matters into their own hands and stormed the city's most imposing symbol of royal despotism. Louis' characterization of that day exposed the growing chasm between the Old Regime's perception of power, one that stemmed exclusively from the absolute monarchy and was supported by the nobility and the clergy, and the belief on the part of the monarch's subjects that they should be active participants in the political process of the nation. These people comprised a new aristocracy that ran counter to the old, an aristocracy, as E. M. Forster would call it, of "the sensitive, the considerate and the plucky." It would be their actions, their power to endure, that would propel Europe into the modern age.

This volume centers on the experiences, actions, and perceptions of the individuals whom Forster referred to as "the true human tradition." Two general themes stand out in this book, themes that highlight ordinary people as agents of historical change. Indeed, the adage "People make history and are made by history" proves an accurate assessment of the way in which the people featured in the following chapters shaped their lives and their communities large and small, and how forces beyond their control structured the degree to which they were able to do so. A first theme of the book deals with the decline of feudal, monarchical powers and the growing but competing claims for popular rights that fueled the events of 1789 and beyond. With the rise of the Enlightenment, we see how people attempted to negotiate the desire for collective and individual rights in the face of new exclusivist practices of putative "universal" ideas of liberty, equality, and citizenship. In a sense, these people were the Enlightenment's true heirs in that they took its ideas at face value and claimed them for themselves and others who were disenfranchised and marginalized by political, social, and economic entities. What stands out in this book is the ways in which ordinary people not blessed with wealth or the inherent status of noble birth sought to claim the mantle of these rights, and with that, fashioned new identities, whether individual or collective.

In chapter 1, we meet a low-level cleric turned major architect of the French Revolution who championed the inclusion of Jews and people of color, but not women. In chapter 2, a radical nationalist in the German states similarly adopted the French Revolution's ideals of liberalism and nationalism in the face of intractable absolutism. Inspired by Marxism's promise of equality, the textile workers in chapter 3 collectively fought against the ravages of industrial capitalist exploitation. On a more individual level, a pious working-class servant in chapter 4 personally challenged the social hierarchies of Victorian England in her diary. We encounter in chapter 5 an Indian nationalist who fought against British ideas of gender and race that upheld colonial authority, and in chapter 6 a "New Woman" who consciously used prevailing notions of womanhood in late nineteenth-century France to push the boundaries of acceptable behavior. In all of these chapters, we are introduced to ordinary people who appropriated in one way or another language and actions that reaffirmed their core humanity and worked to solidify their identities as individuals or groups deserving respect and better treatment.

A second predominant theme that emerges in the following chapters is directly related to the first. Along with the rise of Enlightenment ideas and competing and, at times, conflicting claims to be included in their promises, modernity brought with it the entrenchment of modern bureaucratic and totalizing states. At the same time, we see individual and group efforts to negotiate and even oppose the homogenizing and bureaucratizing efforts of modern states—whether capitalist, fascist, or communist. In their efforts to maintain a modicum of personal autonomy and expression in the face of sometimes totalizing structural and/or cultural control, some individuals confronted their opponents through open resistance. Such was the case with a group of Jewish communist youths in Nazi Germany (chapter 10). Others defied imposed state legal and social dictates. From an Italian widow who sued the Fascist state in an effort to restore her Slavic-sounding name (chapter 9), to a former Stasi spy who founded an underground Jewish culture club in East Germany (chapter 14), to Soviet peasants whose ideas about sexual practices contradicted those of the state and prevailed (chapter 8), all asserted personal, collective, and/or cultural identities to navigate life in the modern state. In some cases, as seen in the experience of a Czech rock-and-roll group, the disenfranchised and marginalized developed a distinctly antipolitical counterculture in the face of a dictatorship's totalizing efforts (chapter 13). Yet as Czech dissident Václav Havel's statement that concludes that chapter illustrates, it would be a mistake to assume that communist and fascist dictatorships possessed an exclusive lock on bureaucracy and attempts at economic, political, and social standardization. Chapter 12 looks at the United States' efforts after World War II to modernize Europe. Here we learn about the case of an Italian industrialist who, rather than become "Americanized," responded to the modernizing impulses of the United States by adapting and altering aspects of American culture to achieve his own local goals for Italian society.

In addition to addressing the broad themes discussed above, *The Human Tradition in Modern Europe* explores the common persistent topics of modern European history—liberalism, nationalism, industrialization, imperialism and decolonization, the rise and fall of communism and fascism, and Americanization. Yet it does so through lenses that most standard histories rarely use. For example, the book highlights some countries often neglected in traditional texts. We learn, for instance, of Belgium's attempts to deal with its brutal colonial past rather than those of larger imperial powers (chapter 11).

Instead of politicians and prominent cultural figures, one essay examines Czech rock musicians to probe the youth revolts of 1968 (chapter 13); another moves Russian literary memory of the Great War's eastern front to center stage and compares it with Germany (chapter 7). Chapter 12 eschews major European powers such as Germany or France to interrogate postwar economic modernization by highlighting an Italian industrialist. Likewise, instead of famous men of elite status, working-class women and men, colonizers and colonized, as well as cultural minorities, come into clear view. By shifting the historical gaze away from the usual suspects in the usual places, students of history can gain a greater understanding of the complexities and range of European historical experience and an appreciation for how those whom some may consider to be minor characters in the drama of human events have made a difference.

The individual and collective histories that we present in the following pages are not intended to be exhaustive by any means; a volume such as this can only begin to touch on the continent's rich political, geographical, social, and cultural diversity. This volume is instead designed to highlight for students and scholars alike major historical moments and broad themes through the lived and imagined experiences of representative people. By focusing on the lives of ordinary people, the scholars in this volume have recovered individuals and groups who have often been obscured by historians' broad brushstrokes. Each of the historical actors featured in these pages participated in Europe's turbulent modern past and contributed to the emergence of the world we know today.

CHAPTER ONE

~

Defining the Nation

The Abbé Grégoire and the Problem
of Diversity in the French Revolution

ALYSSA GOLDSTEIN SEPINWALL

The French Revolution, an epic event that convulsed not only France but also the entire European continent, remains to this day the model for most revolutionaries throughout the world. Unlike the American War of Independence, the French Revolution ushered in significant political change along with social revolution. It shifted the balance of power from a feudal monarchy in which the nobility claimed an inordinate amount of economic, political, and social privilege, first to a constitutional monarchy (1789–1792) and then to a radical republic (1792–1794), and also abolished noble privileges and enfranchised previously marginalized social groups. This brave social and political experiment eventually gave way to a military dictatorship under Napoleon Bonaparte (1799–1814). Yet Napoleon considered himself the embodiment of the core revolutionary values of liberty, equality, and fraternity, and many of his contemporaries shared this view. His military campaigns exported these enlightenment principles to absolutist states in central and eastern Europe, and sowed the seeds of both nationalism and liberalism.

One of the French Revolution's novel contributions to the modern world was how it struggled with the concept of creating an inclusive national identity from a population that was stratified economically, religiously, linguistically, and racially. Following from the writings of philosopher Jean-Jacques Rousseau, the architects of the French Revolution attempted to define "the will of the people" and to decide who was a citizen and what citizenship meant regarding civil and political rights. The Declaration of the Rights of Man and Citizen (1789) opened up political dialogue

1

and guaranteed basic legal rights. It also allowed varied marginalized groups in-
cluding religious minorities, people of color, and women to lay claim to its princi-
ples. What followed was the attempt to define a constitutional and legal apparatus
that would formalize these debates.

In this chapter, Alyssa Goldstein Sepinwall explores the life and writings of the
Abbé Grégoire to examine how French revolutionaries dealt with the philosophical
and political challenges of realizing a nation while dealing with a diverse population
with varied interests. She posits that Grégoire used the concept of "regeneration" to
conceive of a way in which the French could be brought together as a unitary peo-
ple. This idea, she shows, was radically inclusive on the one hand but remained ex-
clusive on the other.

The transition from monarchical to democratic government in Europe was
marked by many challenges. One of the greatest concerned how to shift from
monarchies where all people were "subjects" of a king to governments in
which the "citizens" of a "nation" ruled themselves. In territories where kings
had ruled over multiple linguistic, social, and religious groups, new regimes
struggled to define the "nation": who belonged and who did not. The difficulties that new democracies had in dealing with diversity (especially of race,
religion, and gender) are exemplified in the French Revolution, and in the
career of Henri Grégoire, a priest who would play a central role in that event.

Childhood

Grégoire was born on 4 December 1750 in the Lorraine region of eastern
France, in a countryside of rolling hills. His birthplace, Vého, was a tiny
hamlet near Emberménil, the parish seat. An only child, Henri came from
a humble background; his parents, Bastien Grégoire and Marguerite
Thiébaut, were modest artisans. Ordinarily, Henri would have been too
poor to pursue an education past the age of eight; like most people in early
modern Europe, he would have been fated to share the same station in life
as his parents. After excelling in his early education with the local priest,
however, he received a scholarship from the clergy's funds for the poor, and
was later sent to attend religious seminary. By the time of his ordination in
1775, he had already become a professor at the seminary, teaching the hu-
manities to younger students.[1]

If Grégoire's two decades of schooling detached him from the harsh realities of life for people of his background, his first job was an instant reminder. In 1775–1776, Grégoire served as a *vicaire* (a rural priest serving
several communities) in the district of Chateau-Salins. This time may have

crystallized his feelings about the oppression of peasants under the Old Regime and about the clergy's ability to alleviate their suffering. Among the many taxes in prerevolutionary France, the *gabelle* (which required peasants to buy their salt at high rates) was particularly onerous. While Grégoire served in Chateau-Salins, a poor eighty-four-year-old was imprisoned for having dared to dry some salt himself to make a thin soup; the man never saw freedom again and died behind bars. Grégoire, who administered last rites to the man, remained haunted by this incident fifty years later.

Grégoire also had ambitions outside the church, and dreamed of becoming a famous intellectual. While in seminary, he began spending time with Lorraine aristocrats, and read secular books voraciously. In 1773, he entered and won a contest held by the Academy of Nancy on the importance of poetry. He also traveled outside his parish and outside the Catholic world, making friends with influential Protestants in Alsace. He became involved in a philanthropic group in Strasbourg, which inspired him to be interested in the status of Jews. At the time, Jews suffered from humiliating legal restrictions and violent social prejudice in France. In 1778, Grégoire participated in an essay contest that asked whether their condition should be improved. Though his entry is now lost, later evidence suggests that he advocated at least limited toleration for them.

In 1782, Grégoire's ascent continued, and he was named *curé* [parish priest] of Emberménil, as successor to his former teacher. Keen to effect reform in his parish, Henri began a lifelong campaign to "improve" the inhabitants of the countryside. His efforts included the establishment of a parish library—a controversial endeavor given that many Catholic priests believed that reading the Bible was forbidden to ordinary people, while nonreligious books were a waste of their time.

Grégoire also became involved in church reform efforts, even while conservative clerics sometimes complained about his innovations. In an anonymous 1778 essay, he agreed with critics outside the church that a poor clergy could spread religion just as easily as a rich one: "Religion could subsist very well if bishops were not like princes."[2] By the end of the 1780s, Grégoire had become a leader among the Lorraine lower clergy, particularly in their efforts to share in decision making with their superiors.

Regenerating the Jews

Even as Grégoire rose in the clerical world, he continued to aspire to fame in the literary world. In 1787, he entered a new contest on the Jews, this time sponsored by the Academy of Metz, on the topic "Are there ways of making the Jews more useful and happier in France?" In his prize-winning entry, *Essai sur la régénération physique, morale et politique des juifs* (Essay on the Physical, Moral and Political Regeneration of the Jews), Grégoire laid out methods for "regenerating" the Jews of France, whom he felt had been corrupted both by Gentile persecution and by the "ridiculous" teachings of rabbis. Grégoire's use of "regeneration" would be highly influential, and it would later become a key slogan of the French Revolution, describing a process in which every feature of French society would be purged of the corrupting germs of the monarchy. The term also implied making people anew, by changing them morally, politically, and physically.

Where did this term come from? Until the mid-eighteenth century, regeneration had been a rare word with only three meanings: two theological ones (baptism and resurrection) and an infrequently used medical one (repair of injured body parts or the flesh). The word was secularized in the second half of the eighteenth century, especially in the new science of natural history, the forerunner of modern biology. In particular, the scientist Comte Georges-Louis Leclerc de Buffon's notion of the "degeneration" of species gave rise to a parallel discourse about the degeneration of the French state and culture.

Grégoire's *Essai* would give him a reputation as "the friend of the Jews." It was indeed striking that a priest was defending Jews at all, at a time when they were blamed for the death of Jesus. The text itself, however, was not a straightforward defense of Jews. On the one hand, he argued that, though the Jews were the "greatest enemies of my religion," they also were human beings. He stressed that Jews were part of the same family as Christians, and that their supposed degeneracy was not innate but resulted from their circumstances: "Any people placed in the same circumstances as the Hebrews . . . would become just like them." Recounting the long history of Jews' sufferings in Europe, the *abbé* was ashamed that the persecutors purported to be Christians: "Charity is the cry of the Gospels, and when I see Christians being persecutors, I am tempted to believe that they have not read them." At the same time, Grégoire declared that Jews shared the blame for their condition. For him, Jews had become inferior to other men not only because of Christian persecution, but also because of the "ridiculous" teachings of the Talmud. Sounding like a more straightforward anti-Semite, he warned his readers of the "alarming" speed at which Jews were "multiplying." Moreover, he called Jews usurers and portrayed them as driving peasants to immorality. He hoped that Jews would convert to Christianity if they were treated humanely: "If we encourage the Jews, they will insensibly adopt our way of thinking and acting, our laws, our customs, and our mores."[3]

Despite its negative aspects, the essay brought fame to Grégoire and to his model of integrating outsiders into society. On the one hand, this model was liberating and inclusive, for it implied that all people belonged to a single family, and that no one group was inherently defective. At the same time, "regeneration" suggested that a group was degenerate and would endanger the state if not reformed. For Grégoire, the goal of "tolerating" a group was encouraging it to lose its own culture and to adopt what he thought was the right path.

Grégoire shared the prize in the contest with a Protestant lawyer named Claude-Antoine Thiéry and a Jewish writer named Zalkind Hourwitz, who challenged the academy's question by arguing that it would be better to ask how to regenerate the Christians persecuting Jews. Just as Grégoire was beginning to attain literary fame, however, his life took a new turn. With the dawn of the French Revolution and his election to the new Estates General as a clerical deputy, Grégoire would have a chance to enshrine his ideas into law.

The Revolution Begins

Grégoire arrived in Paris in the midst of a profound political and social crisis. Louis XVI's financial problems, the result both of huge war debts and of the court's fancy lifestyle, had been rumored throughout the 1780s. In 1787, the king called an Assembly of Notables, hoping to persuade the clergy and nobility to consider changes that would allow him to repay his debts. These two groups, however, were unwilling to pay new taxes and relinquish privileges without a clearer picture of the king's finances. Meanwhile, a hailstorm and drought in 1788 destroyed much of the grain crop and led to higher prices. Though an Estates General, a formal gathering of clergy, nobles, and commoners, had not been convened since 1614, the king soon realized that calling for one might be his only option if he wished to keep the monarchy from bankruptcy. He also asked every district to send a *cahier de doléances*, a list of complaints, hoping that his subjects would pay higher taxes in exchange for reforms. Deputies to the Estates General gathered in Versailles in May 1789.

In May, the deputies could hardly have imagined that, in only a few months, full-scale revolution would break out, with the Bastille being destroyed and the monarchy being forced to accept "the will of the people." Even if they understood the financial crisis, the deputies could not fathom the monarchy's inability to maintain order. The deputies of the Third Estate, those not from noble or clerical backgrounds, soon realized that the monarchy was powerless to control them, and that they could set their own agenda.

They soon declared themselves a "National Assembly" and dictated their desires to an increasingly frustrated Louis.

In the midst of these changes, the *curé* of Emberménil might have gotten lost amid the sea of luminaries arriving from every corner of the empire. He caused a sensation from the moment he appeared, however; his forceful oratory and youthfulness made him a natural leader. He persuaded the lower clergy to join the Third Estate, a key act in the Revolution, and was one of the first to take the Tennis Court Oath. It must have been an exciting time for Grégoire. In addition to a dazzling array of organized social activities that included dining out, classes, lectures, parties, theatrical performances, and concerts, Grégoire became a particularly sought-after guest for unofficial gatherings. He was now admired by the same people whose works he had read in Lorraine. As the Estates General became a Constituent Assembly, a body designed to draft a new constitution, Grégoire became a key member of the assembly's leadership, elected first as secretary and later as president. With the famous Robespierre, he would become one of the leaders of the Jacobin Club, with broad support from the populace.

Universal Citizenship and the Declaration of the Rights of Man

During the early years of the Revolution, anything seemed possible if only humans willed it. Through political action, Grégoire and others imagined, France's problems could disappear. The drafting of the Declaration of the Rights of Man and Citizen in the summer of 1789 was a major impetus for such dreams of a utopian future. Whereas the Old Regime had been characterized by differential layers of privilege, in which a person's legal status varied depending on his or her lineage, religion, occupation, place of residence, and gender, the Declaration used a universalistic language that spoke of the rights of "all men." Why did the revolutionaries use this new language? Whereas an older body of scholarship viewed the Revolution as a preplanned effort to put "Enlightenment ideas" into practice, much of the best recent work on the Revolution has shown how these ideas were often embraced retrospectively, and that the political choices of 1789 were made in the heat of political contestation rather than as the result of long reflection.[4]

The choice of the Declaration's universalistic language was one of these practical solutions. Though it might seem that the deputies were consciously thinking of issues like the unequal status of the Jews, they used this language for narrower and more pragmatic reasons. First, they were aiming to destroy the system of privilege that had given the Third Estate fewer privileges than aristocratic and clerical elites. By choosing a language that posited that "all men" should have the same "rights," they were trying to ensure their own legal equality. Second, the decision to speak of "all men" was rooted in a desire to substitute popular for monarchical sovereignty. Drawing on an idea most closely associated with the Enlightenment thinker Jean-Jacques Rousseau, and hoping to legitimate their seizing control from the king, the deputies wanted to suggest the existence of a unified "nation" with a unitary will, speaking as one to reclaim its rights.[5]

The revolutionaries did not fully understand the consequences of their choice, however, and were surprised to discover that they did not control the meanings of their utterances. They soon faced an onslaught of petitions from groups across the land—from peasants to Jews to actors—using the assembly's new language to declare that they too were "men," and thus deserved the same rights as "all other Frenchmen." The revolutionaries faced an unexpected challenge: how to apply the universal language of the Declaration to the realities of French society. How could they create a unified nation out of a country bursting with diversity of religion, language, wealth, gender, geography, and race? How could difference be reconciled with equality, to cement the notion of a common "French" identity? These questions coincided with anxieties over the French "nation"; at the very moment when the nation needed to emerge, people worried that it did not really exist.[6] Even minor differences seemed to represent a danger to French national character.

Into the void stepped the idea of regeneration. In Grégoire's formulation, it promised to solve the problem of difference by creating a unitary people where one did not yet exist. On the one hand, regeneration was radically inclusive; it demanded that all potential members of the French nation be brought into a single family. Grégoire had not forgotten the Jews, and still believed that their integration was essential to social harmony.[7] He now broadened his concern to include people of African descent in the French colonies. While in Paris, he met abolitionists, as well as mixed-race property holders from Saint-Domingue (modern-day Haiti). He discovered that the French colonial system, which produced a huge portion of the world's sugar and coffee and fueled the French economy, had a brutal human cost. He heard about the inhuman conditions of the Middle Passage, and about the nearly half a million slaves who labored in Saint-Domingue, facing savage repression if they dared protest. He also learned of the legal and social discrimination faced even by free blacks and mixed-race people.[8]

By late fall 1789, Grégoire had decided that the colonies needed regeneration as urgently as the mainland, and he pressed his colleagues to apply the Declaration's universalism throughout the empire. Instituting racial equality, he suggested, would be one of the key components in revitalizing the colonies. When property holders of mixed race (who were called mulattoes by their opponents but preferred the term "people of color" [*gens de couleur*]) complained in 1789 about their disenfranchisement, Grégoire denounced what he called the "aristocracy of color." His demands for equality for free people of color proved too radical for the majority of the assembly, and he found himself attacked as a troublemaker by the colonists and their allies. He nevertheless remained a leader in efforts to eradicate legal racism.[9]

Grégoire was also a champion in the assembly for the common people in the French countryside. As one of the few deputies from a humble background, he was a leading advocate of the idea that the common people deserved full political rights and inclusion in the nation. In 1789, he and Robespierre were the only leading revolutionaries to object to the concept of passive citizenship, by which those who could not afford a tax would have fewer rights than those who could. The *abbé* argued that the crucial ingredient of citizenship was patriotism, not wealth.

Regeneration and Cultural Homogenization

We would misunderstand regeneration, however, if we thought it meant only crusading for kindness toward excluded groups and giving them citizenship. Grégoire's frustrations and silence regarding Jews are revealing. Despite his early attentions to the Jewish issue, he turned elsewhere after 1789; when Jews ultimately received citizenship, other revolutionaries were more involved than he. There is evidence that he was prevented from speaking during the initial debates on their citizenship, but that afterward, he voluntarily remained silent to avoid jeopardizing his other projects.[10] This would suggest that, as before the Revolution, Grégoire's interest in Jews was only one part of his larger plan for social reform. While he relished being seen as their great defender, other issues had a greater claim on him. Indeed, he wrote to a friend that the exclusion of Ashkenazi Jews (those of east European origin) was "their fault. They would like to keep their communities and a torrent of customs which conflict with our current government."[11] To him, the Ashkenazim's notion of multicultural citizenship that they could be patriotic Frenchmen while maintaining distinct religious practices was absurd.

Grégoire's comments remind us that regeneration entailed not only the granting of citizenship to oppressed groups, but also measures to change them. Grégoire applied similar ideas to nonwhites, suggesting, as he had earlier with the Jews, that a key means for their regeneration would be interracial marriage. Interracial liaisons had been made degenerate under the Old

Regime; depraved colonists had forced themselves on their slaves, and destroyed families of color. Furthermore, the legal system penalized white men for marrying women of color but not for extramarital affairs with them. Furious, Grégoire invoked a regenerated vision of interracial relationships; if such liaisons were sanctified by church and state, the colonies could display "regenerated education and purified morals." Interracial marriage would improve not only the morals of nonwhites, but also their physiques; they would benefit, he contended, from exchanging blood with Europeans. Grégoire saw the blending of the races as a key step toward national harmony: as offspring became lighter over time, prejudice would disappear because there would be no marker of racial difference.[12]

The fact that regeneration did not only entail inclusion can also be seen in Grégoire's attitude toward slaves during these years. Though he would later become a fervent abolitionist, Grégoire at this point opposed extending citizenship to slaves; to him, they did not yet merit rights. Their cause "has nothing in common with that of the [free] mulattos. . . . One must not rush into anything . . . and give complete political rights to men who do not know all their duties. This would be putting a sword in the hands of the furious." Grégoire did admit that the revolutionaries would eventually need to end slavery to be true to their principles, an idea that was too radical for many of his colleagues. He nevertheless believed that slaves needed a long period of moral regeneration before they could belong to the nation.[13]

A parallel attitude about the need for cultural change to accompany political rights can be seen in Grégoire's view of country dwellers. Even as one of the most loyal champions of their equality, the *abbé* argued that regeneration required changes in their cultural practices. He was particularly eager to wipe out local patois, by which he meant not only dialects of French, but also non-French regional languages; he also wanted to infuse peasants with learning from the cities. In 1790, prompted by riots in the southwest that he attributed to language confusion, he sent questionnaires all over France asking how the patois could be eradicated.[14] Here also, Grégoire's efforts suggested that universalism involved not only political inclusion, but also cultural "melting."

For Grégoire, difference thus appeared as a problem that needed to be solved. The *abbé* was a great believer in the universal language of the Declaration; unlike many of his colleagues, he advocated immediate political rights for nearly all men. At the same time, he saw rights as only a first step. The nation needed a unified character, and groups that were different would need to alter their customs and values. Country dwellers who spoke patois would need to speak only French; Jews would eventually need to convert;

people of color would have to intermarry and adopt regenerated French values. Fully regenerated citizens would be French speaking, Christian, enlightened, and light skinned.

Gender and Regeneration

If nonwhites, Jews, and patois speakers could change themselves into full members of the nation, there was one group that, in Grégoire's eyes, could not: women. Even as he campaigned against other kinds of generalizations about human difference, he made sweeping claims about natural differences between men and women. Like many of his colleagues, Grégoire believed that women were so far from being able to fulfill the rights and duties of citizenship that the category should be restricted to males.

Grégoire's feelings about women over the course of his life were complex and ambivalent, and he did have positive feelings toward certain individual women. The most important of these would be Mme Dubois, his closest friend and "adopted mother" until his death. Grégoire first met Mme Dubois and her husband during the first year of the Revolution; his own mother had accompanied him to Paris to take care of him during the Estates General, but she returned to Lorraine as the Revolution continued and found him a place in the Dubois' home. Grégoire called Mme Dubois "one of the most virtuous people" he knew; their bond was strengthened by the fact that Grégoire had no siblings and was not close with his extended family.[15]

Apart from exceptions such as Mme Dubois, however, Grégoire saw most women as frivolous creatures whose immorality threatened the next generation. His antifemale diatribes went beyond those of contemporaries who claimed that women had superior moral qualities but lacked intellectual ones, and thus needed to avoid politics. This kind of argument, sometimes called "separate spheres," served to exclude women from public life, but also implied that women possessed positive qualities that men lacked.

While occasionally speaking of virtuous peasant women, Grégoire more commonly denounced French women as immoral and vain. He wrote of white women in both the French colonies and in French cities that they were largely shameless, brazen, and cynical. In 1792, he blamed women for the moral degradation of children.[16] Because women's corruption threatened to affect the next generation, Grégoire spent a great deal of energy appealing to women to improve themselves. If the next generation, the first born into the new regime, was to remain untainted, he declared, women needed to rediscover their mothering instincts and instill revolutionary values in their children. His antifemale rhetoric would increase during the Revolution as he suspected that counterrevolutionary Catholics were using gullible women as tools to defeat it. Like other revolutionaries who voted in 1793 to ban women's political clubs, Grégoire contended that the Revolution could succeed only if women were prevented from influencing the national will.

Grégoire's attitude toward women shows how complicated the Revolution's notion of universalism was, and how much it depended on the homogenizing action of regeneration. Women could not transform themselves into fully regenerated citizens in the same way as patois-speaking, Jewish, Protestant, or nonwhite males; their difference was a fixed one that could not be erased by converting, adopting a new language, or intermarrying. Women could thus never be fully regenerated, and universal citizenship could not apply to them.

Grégoire's views on the issue of diversity did not go unchallenged. Members of these groups and their allies argued that they did not need any regeneration different from that of other Frenchmen. Free people of color like Julien Raimond maintained that they deserved the same "sacred rights of humanity" that the Declaration had promised to others, not any special measures for improvement. Similarly, the Jews of Bordeaux wrote Grégoire that their regeneration should be no different from that of the "entire Kingdom." Patois speakers also criticized Grégoire's belief that they needed to change their language to belong to the regenerated nation. Finally, radical women such as Olympe de Gouges contested the notion that they were unworthy of citizenship. In her famous "Declaration of the Rights of Woman," de Gouges rephrased the "Declaration of the Rights of Man" to highlight women's equality. Revising Article I ("men are born and remain free and equal in rights"), she wrote: "Woman is born and lives equal to man in her rights."[17]

In the end, though, the assembly adopted a strategy that paralleled Grégoire's; it erred on the side of wanting to know that groups were capable of being regenerated before it would grant them rights. In December 1789, the assembly offered citizenship rights to Protestants and actors, but it took two years before it accorded them to all Jews, having granted them in January 1790 only to the more assimilated Jews of the southwest. The deputies extended the limits of citizenship in May 1791 to a small portion of the *gens de couleur* (those whose parents had also been free), and to all people of mixed race and free blacks only in April 1792; they did not end slavery until 1794, however, and then only after slaves in Saint-Domingue had forced its end with an insurrection. As for peasants, the assembly maintained the "passive citizenship" category that kept them and the urban poor from equal rights until 1792. Many of Grégoire's colleagues were also enthusiastic about his idea that wiping out the patois was essential for national unity. Just as

Grégoire had hoped, the revolutionaries deemed women too unregenerable to be part of the national community. Even as the revolutionaries granted citizenship rights to long-excluded groups of men, they refused to grant women the same status.

Regeneration facilitated, however, the creation of a unitary nation of French men. As the revolutionary Camille Desmoulins noted in 1789:

> Saint Paul . . . once wrote: "Those of you who have been regenerated by baptism, you are no longer Jews, no longer Samaritans, no longer Romans, no longer Greeks: you are all Christians." It is in the same way that we have just been regenerated by the National Assembly; we are no longer from Chartres or from Monthléri, no longer Picards or Bretons, no longer from Aix or Arras: we are all Frenchmen, all brothers.[18]

In choosing "regeneration," the revolutionaries selected a path that promised to build unity, but only in effacing difference. Their model would endure for centuries, not only in France, but also across Europe, as modern democratic nations struggled to reconcile equality and diversity.

Notes

1. For a more detailed presentation of Grégoire's childhood and later career, see Alyssa Goldstein Sepinwall, *The Abbé Grégoire and the French Revolution: The Making of Modern Universalism* (Berkeley: University of California Press, 2005).

2. [Grégoire], "Considérations sur les abus de la sécularisation des biens ecclésiastiques," in *Mémoires de la Société des Philantropes* (Berne: Chez la société typographique, 1778), 174.

3. Grégoire, *Essai sur la régénération physique, morale et politique des juifs*, ed. Rita Hermon-Belot (Metz, 1789; repr., Paris: Flammarion, 1988), 67, 94, 131, 58–61, 189n8, 83–85, 95, 138.

4. See especially Antoine de Baecque, "Le choc des opinions: Le débat des droits de l'homme, juillet–août 1789," in *L'an I des droits de l'homme*, ed. de Baecque, Wolfgang Schwale, and Michel Vovelle (Paris: Presses de CNRS, 1988), 7–37; Keith Michael Baker, *Inventing the French Revolution* (Cambridge: Cambridge University Press, 1990), esp. 301–5; Timothy Tackett, *Becoming a Revolutionary: The Deputies of the French National Assembly and the Emergence of a Revolutionary Culture (1789–1790)* (Princeton, NJ: Princeton University Press, 1996), 120.

5. See especially Marcel Gauchet, "Rights of Man," in *A Critical Dictionary of the French Revolution*, ed. François Furet and Mona Ozouf (Cambridge, MA: Belknap Press of Harvard University Press, 1989), 137–50; and Baker, "The Idea of a Declaration of Rights," in *The French Idea of Freedom: The Old Regime and the Declara-*

tion of Rights of 1789, ed. Dale Van Kley (Stanford, CA: Stanford University Press, 1994), 154–96.

6. David A. Bell, *The Cult of the Nation in France: Inventing Nationalism, 1680–1800* (Cambridge, MA: Harvard University Press, 2001), 75.

7. See Henri Grégoire, *Motion en faveur des juifs* (Paris: Belin, 1789).

8. On conditions in the French colonies, see esp. Carolyn Fick, *The Making of Haiti: The Saint Domingue Revolution from Below* (Knoxville: University of Tennessee Press, 1990), 15–75; and Robert Louis Stein, *The French Sugar Business in the Eighteenth Century* (Baton Rouge: Louisiana State University Press, 1988), 17–23, 40–59.

9. See, for instance Grégoire, *Mémoire en faveur des gens de couleur ou sang-mêlés* (Paris: Belin, 1789).

10. See Ruth Necheles, *The Abbé Grégoire 1787–1831. The Odyssey of an Egalitarian* (Westport, CT: Greenwood Press, 1971), 27–33.

11. Grégoire to J. A. Balthasar, 2 July 1791, reprinted in Hans W. Debrunner, *Grégoire l'Européen* (Anif/Salzburg: Verlag Müller-Speiser, 1997), 27–30.

12. Grégoire, *Mémoire en faveur des gens de couleur*, 38–9; Grégoire, *Lettre aux philantropes sur les malheurs, les droits et les réclamations des gens de couleur* (Paris: Belin, 1790), 4.

13. *Archives Parlementaires de 1787 à 1860, 1e série* (Paris: Librairie administrative de Paul Dupont, 1879–1913), 25 (11 mai 1791): 740; Grégoire, *Lettre aux citoyens de couleur et nègres libres* (Paris: Imprimerie du Patriote françois, 1791), 11–14.

14. On Grégoire's ideas about language, see esp. David A. Bell, "Lingua Populi, Lingua Dei: Language, Religion and the Origins of French Revolutionary Nationalism," *American Historical Review* 100, no. 5 (1995): 1403–37.

15. A. Mathiez, "Une lettre de Grégoire [22 septembre 1792]," *La Révolution Française* 47 (1904): 371.

16. Grégoire, *Lettre aux philantropes*, 19; Grégoire, *Discours sur la fédération du 14 juillet 1792* (Orléans: Jacob l'aîné, [1792]), 9.

17. Mercer Cook, "Julien Raimond," *Journal of Negro History* 26, no. 2 (1941): 144; Abraham Furtado et al., *Lettre adressée à M. Grégoire . . . par les Députés de la Nation Juive Portugaise de Bordeaux* (Versailles: Baudouin, 1789), 2–3; Augustin Gazier, *Lettres à Grégoire sur les patois de France, 1790–1794* (Geneva: Slatkine Reprints, 1969), 81; Olympe de Gouges, "Les droits de la femme" (1791), in de Gouges, *Écrits politiques, 1788–1791* (Paris: Côté-femmes, 1993), 204–15.

18. Cited in Antoine de Baecque, "L'homme nouveau est arrivé: La 'régénération' du français en 1789," *Dix-huitième siècle*, no. 20 (1988): 204.

Suggested Readings

Carol, Raymond L., ed. *Two Rebel-Priests of the French Revolution*. San Francisco: R and E Research Associates, 1975.

Grégoire, Henri. *Oeuvres de l'Abbé Grégoire*. 14 vols. Nendeln, Liechtenstein: Kraus-Thomson Organization, 1977.

Grégoire, Henri. *On the Cultural Achievements of Negroes* [*De la littérature des nègres*]. Translated by Thomas Cassirer and Jean-Francois Briere. Amherst: University of Massachusetts Press, 1996.

Necheles, Ruth. *The Abbé Grégoire 1787–1831. The Odyssey of an Egalitarian*. Westport, CT: Greenwood Press, 1971.

Popkin, Jeremy D., and Richard H. Popkin, eds. *The Abbé Grégoire and His World*. Dordrecht, Netherlands: Kluwer Academic Publishers, 2000.

Sepinwall, Alyssa Goldstein. *The Abbé Grégoire and the French Revolution: The Making of Modern Universalism*. Berkeley: University of California Press, 2005.

CHAPTER TWO

~

Arnold Ruge

Radicalism in a Reactionary Society

KARIN BREUER

Once in a while in modern history, dozens of countries undergo dramatic trans-formations in the same year. One such year was 1848. While monarchies con-tinued to be the dominant form of government in Europe, they were increasingly under challenge. It became more and more difficult for these monarchs to "turn the clock back" and to reinforce absolutist ideas and practices following the spread of liberalism and nationalism during the French revolutionary and Napoleonic eras. In 1830, a Polish revolt against Russian rule was violently thwarted and France successfully overthrew an absolutist king and replaced him with a loose constitutional monarchy. In the 1840s, much of Europe was plagued by food shortages, unemployment, and high prices, all of which created fertile soil for pop-ular unrest. Political thinkers published pamphlets and essays advocating the need for social and political reform. This economic unrest and dissent combined in early 1848. Remarkably, dozens of revolutions took place within a matter of weeks of one another in places as wide ranging as Palermo, Paris, Munich, Vi-enna, Budapest, and Krakow. Thousands of people built barricades and con-fronted their kings' troops. In what became known as the "Springtime of Peo-ples," monarchs in continental Europe initially seemed to surrender their monopoly over power swiftly in the face of crowds who took to the streets de-manding more political, legal, and economic rights.

The revolutionaries were a diverse group, a factor that contributed to the even-tual short-term failure of these revolts. Many bourgeois liberal reformers sought moderate political changes. They advocated for the right of property owners, but not average people, to choose their own rulers. Socialists and republicans advocated more radical changes, such as universal male suffrage and measures to ease the conditions of Europe's working poor. In the Italian and German states, liberalism also combined with nationalism, as bourgeois revolutionaries sought to combine independent monarchies into unified, ethnic-based nations. In the Habsburg Empire, Poles, Czechs, and Hungarians sought independence from Austrian rule. For several months, newly elected assemblies declared basic civil liberties such as freedom of speech, assembly, religion, and equality before the law. However, bourgeois liberals clashed with radicals seeking broader social reforms, and they feared that the demands of ordinary workers, peasants, and craftsmen would contradict the principles of economic liberalism. Lacking military strength to buttress their efforts, these short-lived assemblies were ultimately quickly suppressed by monarchical troops. Although these revolutions initially failed, historians recognize now that they had significant long-term consequences. Hundreds of thousands of ordinary people, including workers, women, and peasants, participated for the first time in political life. In the German and Italian states, the revolutions were a testing ground for nationalistic ideas that would catapult both societies toward national unification just decades later.

In the chapter that follows, Karin Breuer examines the life and political perspectives of a prominent German revolutionary, the philosopher and publisher Arnold Ruge. As a loyalist to the Prussian state who also sought liberal reforms, Ruge held evolving political views that illustrate the diversity of revolutionary goals in this period. His personal experiences demonstrate the challenges faced by those who sought to reform their societies.

In 1826, Arnold Ruge, a philosophy student at the University of Heidelberg, was sentenced to fifteen years in prison for high treason against the German Confederation. Yet Ruge was and would remain a staunch supporter of the state of Prussia, the largest state in the German Confederation, for much of his life. He hoped the state would unify Germany and was overjoyed when Otto von Bismarck achieved this end in 1870–1871. On the surface, then, Ruge's arrest seems remarkable and contradictory. This chapter examines this apparent paradox in order to shed light on the relationship between intellectuals and the German states in the first half of the nineteenth century.

To understand Ruge's troubled relationship with the state, some political context is necessary. German political life in the pre-March era, the period between the end of Napoleon's occupation in 1815 and the March Revolution of 1848, differs from that of the contemporary world. In fact, the word "Germany" is anachronistic when applied to this time. The German nation-state did not yet exist and most government officials opposed national sentiment, which threatened to dispossess them. After all, a united Germany had no need for the scores of princes, kings, and archdukes who ruled the tiny states in central Europe. Although authorities of the German-speaking lands profited from patriotism during the era of the Napoleonic Wars, they supported the status quo after Bonaparte's defeat in order to preserve their power. Throughout the pre-March era, authorities within the German Confederation, a loose association of thirty-four central European states and four free cities, censored newspapers and suppressed associations with national or liberal goals. Thus began decades of intermittent state repression of public politics.

However, the relationship between the Prussian state, the German Confederation, and Arnold Ruge was far more complicated than the subject of nationalism. Ruge was, before and during the Revolution of 1848, at the vanguard of political radicalism. Due to social, political, and personal factors, his ideas shifted radically from liberal nationalism to democratic republicanism to socialism. Because of his articulation of progressive political and social ideals during the era preceding and including the Revolution of 1848, Ruge provides an excellent case study of the German Confederation's treatment of radicalism and its effects both on the individual and on the larger climate of the age.

This chapter serves several purposes important to the study of the pre-March era. First of all, it throws into question the notion that German national aspirations were exclusively cultural, rather than political. Indeed, Ruge exemplifies throughout the late 1830s and the 1840s a dedication to a rational and democratic political community, rather than a cultural nation based on ethnicity and language. Second, Ruge's political thought during the first half of the nineteenth century shows an individual grappling with philosophies that were relatively new to German public life: liberalism, nationalism, democracy, and socialism. Although Ruge was not a consistent thinker, his efforts to reconcile these philosophies to contemporary politics—and his choice to reject some of them—are illustrative of the factors that can shift individual political allegiances over time. Third, an examination of Ruge's life illustrates the extent of state repression during the pre-March era, which in his case, ironically, appears to have served as an instrument of radicalization. Finally, this chapter's biographical approach illustrates how both political context and one's personal life can shape ideas.

Early Life and University Studies

In 1802, Arnold Ruge was born on the island of Ruegen, a Swedish territory that would later be incorporated into Prussia. His autobiography, *In*

Earlier Times (*Aus frueherer Zeit*), portrays a happy, if relatively unevent-ful, childhood. One of Ruge's most vivid memories of his early years was that of the French occupation of Ruegen. The Francophobia and anti-Napoleonic sentiment that frequently accompanied the nascent German patriotism also gripped Ruge. When Napoleon returned from his exile on Elba, the thirteen-year-old Ruge swore an oath to kill the despot if he again subjugated the German people.[1] The invasion had not only spiritual con-sequences, but material ones. As the local economy declined, the finances of Arnold Ruge's father, a tenant farmer and agricultural manager, were badly damaged.[2] Ruge's father revealed the family's precarious financial po-sition before Arnold began his university studies. The elder Ruge explained that he hoped that Arnold would one day be able to help the family finan-cially and suggested that a practical course of study, such as the law, would be provident.[3] However, Arnold was contemptuous of learning a "trade" and opted to study philosophy and philology instead of the more lucrative professions preferred by his father.

Ruge began his studies at the University of Halle in 1821. Soon thereafter, he became acquainted with members of the Burschenschaft, an association of German students that touted "honor, freedom, and fatherland." Formed in 1815, the association did not have a uniform political agenda, but most of its members were committed to German unification. Four years later, the Burschenschaft was banned throughout the German Confederation after one of its members, Karl Sand, murdered a reactionary playwright, August von Kotzebue. Although this was an atypically violent act for the usually roman-tic and idealistic student association, it was the culmination of the revolu-tionary rhetoric of the leftist mentors of the Burschenschaft. These men, usu-ally young university professors, advocated liberalism and national unification by force, if necessary. Ruge was impressed with the agenda of the leftist Burschenschafter. Although he would later renounce the organiza-tion's romantic nationalism, it instilled in Ruge a lifelong commitment to civil liberties and broad political participation. Looking back in 1862, he wrote that "it was clear that they were not only enthusiastic about, but lived and acted for the future of the fatherland in that they cultivated and strengthened a new, noble spirit in youth."[4] Ruge joined the forbidden or-ganization and soon found himself in an inner circle of approximately fifty members who sought radical political change. As Ruge stated in a speech to leading members of the association, "The Burschenschaft has a political task. We should do more than shape convictions; we must also make a revolu-tion."[5] To the young Ruge, then, armed rebellion was a necessary precondi-tion to political change.

Influenced by radical students and professors, Ruge also joined the secret League of Youth (Juenglingsbund), which intended to foment revolution. Yet despite activist intentions and rhetoric, the League of Youth did little. In 1823, investigators of the German Confederation discovered the league and, with the help of internal denouncers, arrested Ruge in 1823 for his participation in a subversive and traitorous association. Ruge was sentenced to fifteen years' imprisonment for his activities. He served six years before being pardoned. During that time, he wrote poetry and reflected on German political life, which he characterized as backward and tyrannical.[6]

Released from prison in 1830, Arnold Ruge moved to Jena. That same year, revolution broke out in Europe. The July Revolution deposed the ultra-royalist Charles X of France, and German intellectuals, silenced by years of repression, again began to promote liberal and national goals. Arnold Ruge, however, did not participate in this wave of political activism. Instead, he procured work as a tutor and in 1832 married Louise Dueffer, the wealthy daughter of a professor at the University of Halle.[7] When traveling to Italy with his wife later that year, he met an old friend from the Burschenschaft, Gustav Bunsen, who invited him to a patriotic assembly. In responding to the invitation, Ruge replied, "It is too late. The spirits have cooled off and the authorities have established themselves again. . . . I share the aim, but it is not to be attained at the present."[8] This statement suggests that while in prison, Ruge abandoned the political idealism of his youth, opting instead to lead the life of a loyal subject. However, his writings in Hegelian philosophy would again make Ruge an enemy of the state.

Ruge's 1832 trip to Italy was eventful and tragic. While there, both he and his wife contracted cholera. Louise died that year; Arnold, bedridden and mourning, studied Hegelian philosophy for months. As a result of this study, Ruge came into contact with a group of "Young Hegelians," of whom he would eventually become a prominent member. For our purposes here, Hegel's political philosophy is important, as it helps to explain many of Ruge's assumptions early in his publishing career. Georg Wilhelm Friedrich Hegel (1770–1831) had sought to understand the relationship between individual freedom, modern society, and state power. He believed that the state gave form to social and economic life, and maintained that rational administrative rule was necessary in modern society. Thus, Hegel strongly emphasized the importance of the state and its administration, both of which he considered necessary to the functioning of individual will and civil society.

Hegel's philosophy was initially met with favor by the Prussian administration, and became the dominant philosophy at universities, which were state institutions. As increasing numbers of university-educated Prussians embraced Hegelianism, though, the movement began to fragment. A new generation of Hegelians, who came of age in the late 1820s and 1830s, came to be known as the "young," or "left," Hegelians. Inspired by Hegel's notion of the state, many of these men began their careers hoping for the development of a Prussian *Rechtsstaat* (constitutional state). Frequently these men came to advocate social and religious changes in Prussian society, however, claiming that Hegel was not sufficiently critical of the state in which he lived. Some of Hegel's young followers ultimately came to question what—if anything—should remain of the Hegelian inheritance.[9]

Ruge's interest in Hegelianism was, in some ways, a departure for the intellectual. His earlier political activity had been, after all, revolutionary and therefore more explicitly antistate. Unlike his years in the Burschenschaft and the League of Youth, Ruge no longer seemed inclined to compromise both his personal freedom and financial future for democracy. But the early years of Ruge's political engagement reveal some consistency, as well. Ruge would, throughout his life, continue to take risks to promote political views that were radical for and frequently unpopular in their time.

Journals and Persecution

Ruge's contact with the Young Hegelians led him to begin publishing journals, bringing us to another chapter of his participation in public life. By the mid-nineteenth century, print had become cheap and accessible, making reading habitual for much of the population.[10] The abundance of print helped to create a critical press that was "disrespectful of authorities" and "little inclined to religious obedience or belief."[11] Although strictly regulated by the German government, this critical new press both reflected and helped to create the emerging critical public sphere.

In 1838, Ruge and a colleague, Theodor Echtermeyer, founded the *Halle Yearbook*, Ruge's first in a series of journals. They hoped it would express the artistic and philosophical Zeitgeist to a young generation of intellectuals and that would make Hegelian philosophy matter politically and socially. In particular, it was to evaluate the historical tendencies of the German states and determine the extent to which they moved Germany in the proper direction of political and cultural freedom, openness, and flexibility.[12] As scholar Andre Spies points out, although there were fewer than five hundred subscribers, "The journal's influence was out of proportion to this small number."[13] This journal, eagerly awaited by Young Hegelians, helped to crystallize their identity as an oppositional group.[14] Following Hegelian philosophy, Ruge and Echtermeyer's journal supported Prussia, or at least an *ideal* version of the state.

One particular episode sheds light on Ruge's vision of the state and its relationship to religion. He and other contributors to the *Halle Yearbook* defended Prussia during a dispute with one of Prussia's newly acquired territories, the Rhineland. In 1837, Protestant Prussia and the Catholic Rhineland were at odds over the subject of mixed marriages, a conflict that resulted in the arrest of the archbishop of Cologne, Clemens von Droste-Vischering.[15] Ruge championed Prussia in the conflict, using the dispute to expose the state's enemies. He did not merely target Catholic apologists in the Rhineland, however, but also Protestant compatriots. In particular, Ruge's animus centered on Heinrich Leo (1799–1878), a history professor at the University of Halle with pronounced pietistic and romantic leanings. Leo, a former Burschenschafter, represented to Ruge much of what was wrong with the association with which Ruge had been affiliated in his younger days: the unrealistic and backward-looking tendencies that extolled the Middle Ages rather than create real change in the modern world. Spurning rationalism and the Enlightenment, Leo had become a staunch opponent of Hegelianism and a supporter of reactionary forces within the state of Prussia. Leo became the focus of the *Halle Yearbook*'s crusade against the "principle of romanticism" in the social and political climate of Prussia.[16] In an article published in April 1838, Ruge implied that Leo and his ilk attempted "to convert the state and its king to illiberal principles."[17] He maintained that Leo behaved like a "Jesuit" and an "inquisitor," while Leo countered that Ruge was an "atheist" and a "revolutionary."[18]

Ruge appeared to imagine that by pointing out internal enemies like Leo, he was helping the Prussian state. He highlighted his support within the pages of his journal: "I am a free citizen of a free land; I am a Prussian who knows his rights and his obligations; I hold them from my city and from my state."[19] Yet, the critique of both religion and Heinrich Leo cut too close to Prussia. Leo, a university professor, was an employee of the state. For that matter, the state itself was, in many ways, tarred by the same brush as the institutions and individuals Ruge attacked. As Ruge's own earlier experiences of investigation and imprisonment illustrated, neither Prussia nor the German Confederation refrained from illiberal and even inquisitorial practices. Whether due to a Machiavellian attempt to ingratiate himself with the censors or sincere political myopia, Ruge presented a free and liberal Prussia that was imaginary. Prussia in the 1830s was no bastion of freedom or liberalism, and Prussian identity had long been connected with religion, albeit Protestantism. Perhaps recognizing this dilemma, the Prussian minister of culture, Karl Freiherr vom Stein zum Altenstein (1770–1840), refused public support of the journal that fought in the name of the state.

The controversy between Leo and the *Halle Yearbook* became a cause célèbre of its time, with newspapers and pamphleteers taking sides on the issue. University students became involved, and this further horrified the hierarchy-conscious professors and administrators of Halle.[20] As a result, the incident affected Ruge's other career, that of an untenured lecturer of philosophy at the University of Halle. The Prussian state, responsible for hiring and promoting civil servants, passed over Ruge for the faculty appointment for which he had hoped.[21] The actions of his colleagues added to his sense of professional disappointment. Leo, along with twenty-two other professors at the university, sent a letter denouncing Ruge to Altenstein.[22] Not all supported Leo's beliefs explicitly; rather, many were as dismayed that Ruge, a mere lecturer and private instructor, boldly questioned Leo, a professor.[23] As a result, the minister censured Ruge.[24] Responding to this professional and personal betrayal, Ruge began to turn against and publicly criticize the state of Prussia.

As the conflict between Ruge and the Prussian state intensified, the political system of Prussia changed dramatically. In 1840, the Prussian king, Frederick William III (1770–1840), died. Although he had by no means been a reformer, the monarch had recognized the Prussia-centrism of Hegelianism and had been willing to tolerate even the more radical Young Hegelians. His successor's attitudes differed fundamentally. Inspired by romanticism in his youth, Frederick William IV (1795–1861) opposed the intellectual and political disposition of the Young Hegelians. Almost immediately, demands for orthodoxy increased and censorship strengthened.[25]

Given his anti-Hegelian stance, it is not surprising that the new king singled out the *Halle Yearbook* for special treatment.[26] The government ordered the magazine to move its press so it could be censored more effectively.[27] Instead, Ruge opted to close down the *Halle Yearbook*, move to the neighboring state of Saxony, and open a new journal entitled the *German Yearbook for Scholarship and Art*.

Rather than make him more cautious, Ruge's experience with censorship radicalized him. The new journal openly declared its support of constitutionalism, democracy, and the formation of a republic.[28] From his new home in Saxony, Ruge began to renounce more explicitly the state of Prussia. "Prussian Absolutism," Ruge's first article for the *German Yearbook*, situated the state's conservatism not as a momentary shortcoming, but as a result of long-standing historical forces.[29] Many of Ruge's fellow Young Hegelians disapproved of the explicitly political tone of the journal and stopped contributing articles.[30] This was not the journal's main obstacle to survival, however. Its attacks on Prussia, the most powerful state of the

German Confederation with the possible exception of Austria, did not go unheeded by Saxon and confederate authorities. First published in July 1841, Ruge's journal had already received a warning from censors by the end of that year.[31] Ruge did not back down. In an essay entitled "Press and Freedom," he wrote, "Censorship makes private thoughts, the inner, secret thoughts of individuals . . . its targets. . . . [But] censorship cannot hinder private thoughts. Thoughts are free."[32] Given his defiance, it is hardly surprising that Ruge continued to struggle with censors until the German Federal Assembly, one of the few common institutions of the confederation, voted in January 1843 to suppress the journal. This was one of dozens of such bans during the 1840s, the most famous of which was Karl Marx's *Rhenish News*, also suppressed in 1843.[33]

Disappointed, Ruge concluded that his future was not in the German Confederation. After the suppression of his second journal, Ruge wrote to Marx that "this generation was not born to be free. Thirty years of political degeneracy . . . and censor[ship of] even the secret thoughts and feelings of human beings in accordance with the dictates of the secret police, have degraded Germany and set her back politically more than she ever was before."[34] Ruge's disillusionment makes sense, given that the German states had now imprisoned him and twice suppressed his journals.

Due to the illiberal atmosphere, Ruge decided to emigrate. Like the Socialist Karl Marx and many other activist intellectuals from the German Confederation, Ruge moved to Paris, the center of European republicanism. Marx and Ruge soon became reacquainted and decided to begin another journal, this one entitled the *German-French Yearbook*. This journal aimed to create greater cooperation between French and German intellectuals. This would be no easy feat. France and the German states had again been at odds; the Rhine Conflict (1840) pitted France against the German states for hegemony in the Rhineland. After France's vague threat to invade the territory, nationalist posters, songs, and festivals reaffirmed the German identity of the Rhineland.[35] As had been the case during the Napoleonic era, many German intellectuals viewed France with suspicion. Ruge sought an intellectual rapprochement, with French and German speakers contributing journal articles in their own languages. Each area, he thought, had something to offer the other. Although politically advanced, the French were philosophically backward, while the German situation was reversed. Thus, German intellectuals could teach the French about philosophy while the French could teach the Germans about practical politics.

The editors published only one volume of the journal. Its problems were both practical and ideological. First and foremost, many French intellectuals resented the hubris of Marx and Ruge's project. They rejected the assumption that they, the intellectual descendants of Enlightenment philosophes, would benefit from German philosophy. Prominent French radicals like Louis Blanc also criticized the journal for its godless philosophy.[36]

Moreover, the two editors found little common ground either professionally or philosophically. Although both had been influenced by Hegel and now, to some extent, renounced the philosopher's work, Ruge did not embrace communism. Although a democrat and a revolutionary, Ruge simply did not grasp the determinism of scientific socialism. He considered communism to be emblematic of the problems of German philosophy: it was too abstract and divorced from political reality. That is not to suggest, however, that Ruge supported the status quo. In the preceding two years, he had written in support of democratic socialism, the conversion of churches to schools, and the right to teach atheism as part of theology.[37] Such ideas were far more revolutionary than Ruge's earlier political goals, which had centered largely on civil liberties and popular representation.

Ironically, however, the main disagreement between the two leftists was caused by financial concerns. Marx had few financial resources, while Ruge, through his first marriage, was fairly prosperous.[38] Ruge, however, was not inclined to financially support an unsuccessful journal that had been, in his eyes, co-opted by Marx and his followers. Ruge later wrote that Marx "hates me. . . . It angers him that my name was first on the title page. . . . But what is most ridiculous is that [he thinks that] I should be held to risking my property to continue the journal."[39] Due to these personal, political, and financial concerns, Ruge temporarily ended his publishing career and moved to Switzerland.

The history of Ruge's three journals, the *Halle Yearbook*, the *German Yearbook*, and the *German-French Yearbook*, reveals several themes of both this era and this chapter. First, they illustrate the growing radicalism indicative of the politicization of the ideological milieu of the German states leading up to the Revolution of 1848. The journals became progressively more politically engaged and therefore more openly subversive, in part a reflection of the increasingly revolutionary atmosphere within Europe. Second, these journals' trajectories illustrate the relationship between civil society and state repression. Perhaps the most surprising lesson here is that, rather than silencing Ruge, the repression by the Prussian state and the German Confederation actually *strengthened* his attacks. Third, it is important to note that many of the factors that influenced Ruge were not strictly political in nature. Indeed, the content and fate of the journals appear to have had a personal component, as well. While historians frequently point to political events as the key to shaping ideas and human actions, Ruge's failure to get promoted and his personality conflicts with Leo and Marx appear to have influenced him as much as the great historical events of his day.

1848 Revolution

As revolutions broke out across Europe in 1848, Ruge returned to the German states and again began to participate in public life. He viewed the revolutions in the German states, especially Prussia, as a vindication of his ideals. Ruge wrote, "The third French Revolution is European liberation; it is the greatest event of world history."[40] In a letter shortly after the outbreak of revolution, Ruge celebrated that "the king is beside himself, he is conquered, he is no longer the powerful king, but the instrument of the people."[41] He considered the events of the day to be the end of despotism and the beginning of popular sovereignty. To support the transition, he moved to the Prussian capital of Berlin and began to publish the democratic newspaper *Reform*.

Meanwhile, it seemed that the German Confederation was falling apart, as were the governments of many of its member states. Revolutionaries called for elections to a provisional government, the Frankfurt Parliament. Ruge, still a leading figure of the Left, was elected in Breslau as a delegate to this assembly, which met for the first time in May. The Frankfurt Parliament had several tasks to fulfill. It had to write a constitution and determine what kind of political system a united Germany would have. Before this, however, the delegates had to determine what, exactly, Germany was. Although some German-speaking intellectuals had professed patriotism for decades, the concept of "Germany," a state that had never existed, was understandably nebulous. Did Germany include (1) all German speakers, (2) all communities ruled by a German speaker, or (3) all member states of the German Confederation? Such questions became especially problematic in the case of the Austrian Empire, ruled by the German-speaking Habsburgs. Although Austrian affairs were generally conducted in the German language, it was a polyglot empire also inhabited by Magyars, Czechs, Poles, Romanians, Italians, and other ethnic minorities. Furthermore, its inclusion in a united Germany would necessarily create conflict with the other great German power, the state of Prussia.

For Ruge, Austria's exclusion from Germany made perfect sense. If ambivalent about Prussia, Ruge had long been consistent about his dislike of Austria. For him, Austria was too Catholic and too reactionary to play a leading role in a united Germany. Ruge's dismissal of Austria helped to marginalize him further from mainstream Germans. Controversially, he wrote a "Political Letter to the Germans" (February 1848), in which he advocated support for northern Italians wishing to throw off the yoke of Austrian rule. The majority of his fellow politicians in the assembly booed this proposal, which they considered a betrayal of fellow German speakers and proof of Ruge's unrealistic radicalism.

Indeed, Ruge was solidly on the left of the Frankfurt Assembly, as was best illustrated by his antimonarchical stance. In a call for universal male suffrage, Ruge proclaimed, "Now the only German dynasty with authority and power is the people!"[42] Ruge entered into the debate regarding the creation of a provisional central authority in June 1848. He advocated a republican president who would embody popular sovereignty rather than the monarchical principle. According to Ruge, the moderates who wished to grant a hereditary monarch executive and legislative powers were traitors. The moderate group won this political power struggle, however, and Archduke John of Austria became the temporary regent of the German empire.[43]

Ruge soon experienced another disappointment with the assembly. One of the tasks of the assembly was to deal with the question of self-determination of non-German speakers, particularly the Poles. Due to the partitions of the late eighteenth century, Prussia had acquired the Polish territory of Posen. The Polish-speaking inhabitants called for the independence of Posen and the radicals in Frankfurt supported this measure. Echoing his earlier calls for Italian independence, Ruge became a spokesman for a free Poland and a "Congress of Peoples," which would guarantee free nationalities and international peace.[44] In his "Speech on Polish Freedom" (26 July 1848), Ruge maintained that "there are nations and people who must be emancipated. They are the slaves, the serfs, and the subjugated. The Poles have been enslaved by the . . . force of despotism." The liberal majority, however, was in no way prepared to subordinate the German national principle to abstract cosmopolitanism.[45] To Ruge's dismay, the assembly voted instead to incorporate Posen into the larger German state.

Angry at the direction of the parliament and perhaps aware of his political impotence, Ruge resigned in October 1848. He spent several months in Berlin. While he was there, the parliament proposed a state with the Prussian monarch at its head, only to have Frederick William IV turn down the proffered throne. This and other events signaled the demise of the German revolutions. Ruge, considered one of the most dangerous German revolutionaries, did not fare well with the revolution's collapse. The Prussian government closed his paper and, in mid-1849, confiscated all of his property and ejected him from Prussia.[46] Ruge's next stop was the Saxon city of

Leipzig, but soon after he arrived there, that state's revolution also fizzled. In disappointment, Ruge became convinced, again, that the political failure was a result of the political apathy of the German people. Ruge emigrated to Brighton, England, where he would die in 1881. Impoverished by the Prussian confiscation of his property, Ruge struggled to make ends meet by embarking on various professions, most notably as a tutor and a daguerreotype specialist.

Ruge must have considered the year of revolutions to be one of the greatest disappointments of his life. Not only did he see the disintegration of a cause in which he believed, but his own political star fell precipitously. He began the year as one of the greatest leftist thinkers in the German states, yet by the end of the revolution he was considered an unrealistic radical and, judging by political cartoons, something of a laughingstock. This, added to the loss of his personal fortune, must have been a bitter pill to swallow. Yet his position at the forefront of German radicalism had continued to make him a target even when much of Europe was embroiled in revolution. Although Ruge attempted to remain politically active after 1848–1849, he was no longer deemed relevant by his German-speaking contemporaries.

Conclusion

This chapter has pointed to Ruge's ever-shifting politics during the pre-March era. Later in life, his ideas would continue to change. Ruge reconciled himself to Germany after Prussia's victory in the Austro-Prussian War of 1866. He rejoiced at the unification of Germany four years later, although the state was hardly democratic. What, then, does this brief and ever-changing intellectual biography of Arnold Ruge tell us about the German states in the early nineteenth century, and the practice of history in general? It should be apparent that Ruge was hardly a typical thinker of his age. During his life, he managed to alienate almost everyone—from government authorities to colleagues—who were familiar with his thoughts. Moreover, many of his experiences illustrate that his radical politics were not the norm.

Yet Ruge might also be considered representative of German intellectuals of his generation. Ruge scholar James Willard Moore suggests that Ruge's politics were typical of pre-March liberalism, for the philosopher's writings suggest an ambivalent desire for both a progressive political agenda and a strong, possibly monarchical, Prussian state.[47] Yet this, perhaps, is not the most important lesson to draw from Ruge's ideas. Instead, what might be considered most striking here is the extent to which, in an era before set political parties and their slowly changing ideologies, Ruge's political thought underwent so many rapid transformations based on personal as well as political circumstances. This is, ultimately, a reminder not to isolate ideas from the historical context that helps to produce them. To focus on only one of Ruge's writings without context would neglect the rapidly changing political and personal conditions' impact on his ideas.

Notes

1. Harold Mah, *The End of Philosophy, the Origin of "Ideology": Karl Marx and the Crisis of the Young Hegelians* (Berkeley: University of California Press, 1987), 92.

2. Oscar J. Hammen, "The Failure of an Attempted Franco-German Liberal *Rapprochement*, 1830–1840," *American Historical Review* 52, no. 1 (October 1946): 54.

3. Mah, *The End of Philosophy*, 89.

4. Arnold Ruge, *Aus frueherer Zeit* (Berlin: F. Duncker, 1862), 12.

5. R. O. Gropp, "Arnold Ruge," *450 Jahre Martin Luther Universitaet Halle Wittenberg* 2:275.

6. H. Steussloff, "Arnold Ruge," in *Die Junghegelianer, Ausgewaehlte Texte*, ed. H. Steussloff (Berlin: VEP Deutscher Verlag der Wissenschaften, 1963), 86–87.

7. Gropp, "Arnold Ruge," 275.

8. Ruge to Gustav Bunsen, quoted in *Zeit* 3:377, in Mah, *The End of Philosophy*, 99.

9. John Edward Toews, *Hegelianism: The Path toward Dialectical Humanism, 1805–41* (Cambridge: Cambridge University Press, 1980), 245.

10. Simon Burrows, *French Exile Journalism and European Politics, 1792–1814* (Rochester, NY: Royal Historical Society, 2000), 2.

11. Roger Chartier, "Book Markets and Reading in France at the End of the Old Regime," in *Publishing and Readership in Revolutionary France and America*, ed. Carol Armbruster (Westport, CT: Greenwood Press, 1993), 133.

12. James A. Massey, "The Hegelians, the Pietists, and the Nature of Religion," *Journal of Religion* 58, no. 2 (April 1978): 114.

13. Andre Spies, "Towards a Prosopography of Young Hegelians," *German Studies Review* 19, no. 2 (May 1996): 322.

14. Spies, "Towards a Prosopography," 322.

15. Jonathan Sperber, *Rhineland Radicals: The Democratic Movement and the Revolution of 1848–1849* (Princeton, NJ: Princeton University Press, 1993), 82.

16. Mah, *The End of Philosophy*, 109.

17. Gropp, "Arnold Ruge," 277.

18. James Willard Moore, "Arnold Ruge: A Study in Democratic Caesarism" (PhD diss., University of California, Berkeley, 1977), 120.

19. Ruge, quoted in Hook, *From Hegel to Marx* (New York: Columbia Press, 1993), 128.

20. Moore, "Arnold Ruge: A Study in Democratic Caesarism," 120.

21. Steussloff, "Arnold Ruge," 89.

22. Moore, "Arnold Ruge: A Study in Democratic Caesarism," 121.

23. Moore, "Arnold Ruge: A Study in Democratic Caesarism," 121.

24. Steussloff, "Arnold Ruge," 89.

25. Massey, "The Hegelians, the Pietists, and the Nature of Religion," 114.

26. Mah, *The End of Philosophy*, 113.

27. Mah, *The End of Philosophy*, 113–14.

28. Mah, *The End of Philosophy*, 122.

29. Kurt Koszyk, *Deutsche Presse im 19. Jahrhundert*, ed. Fritz Eberhard, Abhandlung und Materialien zur Publizistik series 6 (Berlin: Colloquium Verlag, 1966), 96–97.

30. Hook, *From Hegel to Marx*, 129.

31. Koszyk, *Deutsche Presse*, 94.

32. Ruge, "Die Presse und die Freiheit," in *Arnold Ruge, Werke und Briefe*, 7:68–69.

33. Moore, "Arnold Ruge: A Study in Democratic Caesarism," 192.

34. Ruge, quoted in Hook, *From Hegel to Marx*, 128–29.

35. Sperber, *Rhineland Radicals*, 114.

36. Mah, *The End of Philosophy*, 130.

37. Moore, "Arnold Ruge: A Study in Democratic Caesarism," 228.

38. Moore, "Arnold Ruge: A Study in Democratic Caesarism," 218.

39. Moore, "Arnold Ruge: A Study in Democratic Caesarism," 217.

40. Ruge, quoted in Stephan Walter, *Demokratisches Denken zwischen Hegel und Marx: Die politische Philosophie Arnold Ruges, Eine Studie zur Geschichte der Demokratie in Deutschland*, Beitrage zur Geschichte des Parlamentarismus und der politischen Parteien 104 (Duesseldorf: Droste Verlag, 1995), 347.

41. Arnold Ruge, letter from Berlin, 20 March 1848, in *Arnold Ruge, Werke und Briefe*, 7:241.

42. Arnold Ruge, "Wahl Manifest der radikalen Reformpartei fuer Deutschland," in *Arnold Ruge, Werke und Briefe*, 7:175.

43. Mah, *The End of Philosophy*, 140.

44. Mah, *The End of Philosophy*, 141.

45. Walter, *Demokratisches Denken zwischen Hegel und Marx*, 337.

46. Mah, *The End of Philosophy*, 141–42.

47. Moore, "Arnold Ruge: A Study in Democratic Caesarism," 3.

Suggested Readings

Clark, Christopher. "Germany 1815–1848: Restoration or Pre-March?" In *German History Since 1800*. Edited by Mary Fulbrook. London: Arnold, 1997.

Levinger, Matthew. *Enlightened Nationalism: The Transformation of Prussian Political Culture, 1806–1848*. Oxford: Oxford University Press, 2000.

Mah, Harold. *The End of Philosophy, the Origin of "Ideology": Karl Marx and the Crisis of the Young Hegelians*. Berkeley: University of California Press, 1987.

Sperber, Jonathan. *Rhineland Radicals: The Democratic Movement and the Revolution of 1848–1849*. Princeton, NJ: Princeton University Press, 1993.

Toews, John Edward. *Hegelianism: The Path toward Dialectical Humanism, 1805–1841*. Cambridge: Cambridge University Press, 1980.

Vick, Brian E. *Defining Germany: The 1848 National Parliamentarians and National Identity*. Cambridge, MA: Harvard University Press, 2002.

CHAPTER THREE

~

The World of Textile Work

French Industrial Workers and the Labor Movement

HELEN HARDEN CHENUT

The Industrial Revolution, while not a revolution in the traditional political sense like the revolutions of 1789, 1830, and 1848, indelibly changed the economic and social landscape of the European continent in the nineteenth century. Concurrent revolutions in technology, demographics, and agricultural production converged with the introduction of free-market capitalism to produce these significant changes first in Great Britain and then in continental Europe and the United States.

This dramatic shift from an agrarian society to the industrial factory system followed many paths within Europe and subsequently throughout the world. Key to this process, as Karl Marx described, was the emergence of class polarization between bourgeois capitalists and the industrial proletariat, so identified by its dependence on wages. Working people's way of life was thus drastically altered. People conceived of time, space, and their labor differently after the introduction of the wage economy. From the time children could join their parents in the factory, they too were expected to contribute to the family's survival. As Manchester mill owner Friedrich Engels decried, the family structure itself was "turned upside down" as women's wages undercut men's, forcing men to "sit at home" and care for children while the wife worked long hours. In reaction to the social dislocation and squalid living conditions that grew to define working-class life in the early nineteenth century and the growing conflict between the haves and have-nots, in 1848 Engels and his associate Karl Marx published The Communist Manifesto, *which gave the working class hope that they, in the Marxist view of class conflict, would eventually triumph over the bourgeoisie economically and politically. As a result, the second half of the nineteenth century would be marked by the growth of Marxian socialism as an alternative to capitalism, and this socialism would fuel the growth of labor unions among industrial workers. To this end, workers' actions against their employers, particularly strikes, became increasingly potent weapons in exacting labor reforms such as the eight-hour day and child and women labor laws.*

In this chapter, Helen Harden Chenut traces this process in the French town of Troyes during the last decades of the nineteenth century. She examines the changes industrialization wrought on the knitting industry and the workers who inhabited it. She insightfully shows how a variant of Marxian socialism empowered mill workers to counter exploitative conditions and analyzes the methods they employed to enact change.

As in many other European countries, manufacturing in France was rural and scattered in domestic production before it became urban and concentrated in factories. Mechanization and new forms of energy provided the impetus for change. Technological innovation financed by capital investment led to the possibilities of mass production and economies of scale. Under these historical conditions, the woven cotton textile industry in England was the first to mechanize through the invention of the spinning jenny and the power loom during the late eighteenth century. Over the following century the progressive integration under a single roof (the factory) of the various operations for manufacturing woven cloth made production vastly more efficient. Yet this complex process of change was never linear in its development and in many regions of Europe industrialization and the factory system long remained incomplete. There were many advances and retreats, commercial successes but also failures, in the uneven technological transformation of handloom textile workers laboring at home into factory-based machine operators.

The textile town of Troyes in the Champagne region of northeastern France became the capital of the knitted-goods industry during the second half of the nineteenth century.[1] Like other European industrial regions, industrialization was accompanied by urbanization. Between 1850 and 1900, the industry developed from domestic manufacture in the surrounding countryside to an urban factory system with an extensive outwork system of small artisan workshops in the suburbs. The introduction of new forms of energy, harnessed to more productive knitting machines, made the hand frames of rural knitters less competitive in relation to those operating in urban mills. This long process of industrialization required a significant redistribution of the population between town and country, as rural inhabitants severed contact with the land and moved to the two major industrial towns of the Aube department, Troyes and Romilly-sur-Seine. Over this period the population of Troyes nearly doubled, from 31,027 in 1851 to 53,146 in 1901, while that of Romilly increased by 40 percent. Yet some workers saw advantages in maintaining production in small family suburban workshops rather than lose their relative autonomy by entering the urban mills. Worker resistance to the factory system was, in fact, integral to the growth of industrial capitalism throughout the period. Labor grievances were expressed in various forms of collective action such as strikes, the formation of labor unions, and political organizing within socialist movements—all inspired by a series of remarkable and sometimes charismatic leaders.

Transition to the Factory System

Why did factory production become for the most part a necessity, or at the least the preferred industrial strategy? What role did labor and technology play in these changes? To answer these questions we need to examine the organization of production around 1900.

During the 1880s and 1890s, the economic recession that developed in France and in much of Europe also affected the hosiery and knitted-goods industry in Troyes. These difficult years slowed industrial growth until the end of the century. However, sheltered by high protective tariffs, manufacturers in Troyes were able to use this pause in industrial growth to introduce more modern high-speed knitting machinery and expand their markets outside of Europe. This stage of industrialization was accompanied by an influx of workers into Troyes, yet the great majority of them were still employed in relatively small urban workshops. Out of the twenty-seven textile mills producing in 1900, sixteen employed between 20 and 250 men and women workers; and only one large mill, the Mauchauffée firm, employed more than 1,000 workers.[2] Indeed, large mass-production mills would remain a rarity until after 1920. Altogether, knitted-goods production in Troyes and the nearby suburbs employed roughly eight thousand workers, a labor force in which women textile workers already outnumbered men by 1900.

Industrial competition among mill owners in Troyes and with other textile centers plagued these prewar years. Mill owners had hitherto upheld their authority in labor and industrial affairs relatively unhampered by politics and the state. But there are many examples, drawn from the 1904 parliamentary inquiry on working conditions in the textile mills, of mill owners' outright hostility toward what they regarded as state intervention in industrial questions. They refused the arbitration of strikes and imposed lockouts to break worker solidarity. Moreover, they were particularly opposed to the laws short-

Knitting-machine workshop in a Troyes mill, showing the Cotton patent knitting machines for producing fully fashioned stockings. The seated figure in the center is an older man who is training a young apprentice standing next to him, ca. 1900. (Photograph courtesy of the Archives départementales de l' Aube.)

ening working hours in the factories, strictures they felt were prejudicial to French industry in relation to foreign competitors. Their arguments were essentially the same as in 1884 when they opposed the regulation of women's and children's labor: shortening the working day meant cutting productivity and increasing the cost price of knitted goods; and regulating adult labor meant limiting individual freedom. Faced with the shorter-hours law of 1900, Troyes mill owners sought special exemptions for overtime hours when needed, and they reiterated their pleas for more protective duties.

Technological Change and Knitters' Work

The technical complexity of knitting machines and the variety of articles produced made knitting an intricate operation. Production in the Troyes mills was labor intensive, and that labor had to be skilled. As a hosiery manufacturer in 1895 explained: "Hosiery production is not limited to just knitting the raw materials used to feed the knitting frames; it involves making garments, either by cutting the knitted fabric or by fully fashioning them on the frames, seaming them and finishing them to make clothing."[3] For these reasons, labor accounted for half or even two-thirds of the production cost of an article at the end of the nineteenth century.[4] Historically, the work process was divided into several operations, assigned to men, women, and children according to their sex, age, and ability. Men had appropriated the knitting frame and the technical knowledge required to repair and adjust the machine. The mechanics of knitting technology were decidedly a masculine preserve, and the technical skills so prized for their prestige and productivity were those that developed out of the craft tradition. Customarily, women were employed as bobbin winders to prepare the raw materials, and in the various occupations of seaming and finishing knitted goods.

The most important technical transformations during this period concerned the knitters' work. Powered knitting frames now had more automatic functions, and thus produced articles with greater speed and in series. One of the most productive frames was the Cotton flatbed knitter, named after the Englishman who invented it in 1862. Displayed at the Paris World's Fair of 1867, and constructed in France beginning in 1878 by the Couturat manufacturers in Troyes, the Cotton frame would become the mass-production knitter of the modern mill. With multiple heads, it could simultaneously knit several fully fashioned articles on the same frame, so that the manufacturer could diversify his production and gain in flexibility with response to fashion changes. The leap in productivity produced by these high-powered frames provoked worker apprehension that unemployment would follow the decline in wages already evident since 1890. Testimony from workers' delegates sent from Troyes to the Paris World's Fair of 1900 evoked similar concerns. One knitter, Amédée Sèlves, expressed his apprehension in a series of existential questions: "What conclusion can be drawn from all this progress demonstrated at the World's Fair? How can we truly foresee the future miseries that will result from such progress in increased productivity? For everything has been made to produce more. As a consequence of reducing the number of productive workers, what will society do with those who are idled?"[5]

Women's work was less affected by technological innovation. The tasks assigned to them entailed using simple, manual tools or operating small machines such as seamers. The fact that many of the women's tasks were only partially mechanized led to a need for increasing numbers of "nimble fingers" to sew and finish goods. Seaming was labor intensive. The first loopers and seamers—types of small sewing machines—together with other accessory machines became progressively more reliable during this period. For the most part, these technical improvements resulted in a greater specialization, and even a rationalization, of women's tasks. Many of these tasks relied on women's aptitudes for, and competences in, sewing, embroidery, mending, and ironing—all skills acquired largely through family education.

The Precariousness of Work and Wages

Workers' testimony during this period reflected two major concerns: the precariousness of work and the extreme variability of wages. For many hosiery workers, new norms of productivity imposed by mass-production machines, and the intensification of work itself, seemed like secondary preoccupations. When mill owners requested a more flexible application of shorter-hours legislation that would allow them exemptions for overtime work, militant workers in Troyes demanded a reduction in periods of unemployment through the establishment of the eight-hour day and a minimum wage.[6]

In his testimony before the parliamentary commission of inquiry in 1904, Émile Clévy, representing the Troyes knitters' union, claimed that knitters did not work more than 225 days a year on average. Seasonal unemployment was a given in the knitted-goods industry, which followed the fashion market. But Clévy imputed the blame primarily to the organization of work and to mechanization: "In the knitted-goods industry, where mechanization has totally transformed and modernized the tools of the trade every day, unemployment is becoming more and more common. Thus certain knitting machines produce in one day what a worker operating a Paget frame only twenty years ago would have produced in a week."[7] From the worker's viewpoint there was an obvious contradiction between unemployment that resulted from the increased productivity of knitting machines, and employers' demands for overtime work at their discretion. Clearly, workers perceived that unemployment was not inevitable. Rather, they experienced it as both a mishap of mechanization, and a consequence of bad work organization under capitalism.

Workers also mounted resistance to wage reductions that resulted from idleness imposed by difficulties in executing work or in operating the machines. The uncertainty of work and wages were closely related. Workers' productivity was subject to the risks of badly functioning, unreliable machines and cheap-quality yarn that broke too easily. Wages were further reduced by the employers' policy of reducing wages for the downtime produced by broken needles or for periods of quality control, both of which were imputed to workers. All these factors—unemployment caused by technical problems, variations in the piece rates, wage deductions—contributed to the uncertain calculation of daily wages and added to the precariousness of the workers' existence.

During the debates over protective legislation for women working in industry, mill owners in Troyes had lobbied against government intervention. After the passage of an 1892 law that restricted working hours for women and children in factories, mill owners sought to have such restrictions temporarily lifted for adult women workers. Such efforts underscore the importance to the knitted-goods industry of women's work during this period. Thus, hosiery manufacturer Léon Vitoux, an unusually accommodating and benevolent employer, recognized the need to treat women workers with a particular consideration that would make factory work compatible with women's domestic duties. In a singular deposition before the parliamentary commission of inquiry concerning the textile industry in 1904, Vitoux described women's work in these striking terms: "Let us remind the legislator that, when he inscribed in the law eleven hours of industrial work for women, she must still work five more hours at home; let us remind him that the law, whose purpose is to regulate work, intends at the same time to protect women and girls. This is what I would call, if you allow me, pampering the goose that lays the golden eggs. Let us not forget that woman's condition is for our industry a question of life and death, and that we must treat her gently."[8] In the end, Vitoux had two objectives in mind: to maintain women in the mills by assigning them tasks that were compatible with their status as mothers and housekeepers; and to preserve their individual economic roles through the best possible organization of work. Thus, despite this mill owner's humanitarian concerns, it was clear that worker productivity and discipline were fast becoming the overarching goals of the modern factory system.

Mill Workers and the Labor Movement: Jules Guesde and Étienne Pédron

French socialism at the turn of the twentieth century was divided among several factions at the national and local level, all competing for worker loyalty and proposing different revolutionary or reformist strategies to gain power. The growing appeal in the region around Troyes of a strand of socialism led by Jules Guesde corresponded with the historic moment when labor unions were first fully legalized in France. Guesde and his followers seized on the Marxian notion of class struggle, and attempted to integrate into their program egalitarian elements from the French revolutionary tradition. They were among the first in France to create a structured socialist party with trained militants, party discipline, and the subordination of unions and cooperatives to party political ends. Their aim was to win political power through the ballot, first at local elections and then at the national level. For this reason they worked tirelessly to popularize and disseminate Marxist socialism.

By 1886, knitters in Troyes had founded a union that was intended from the outset to be inclusive and to integrate workers who were seriously divided along craft lines. Women were actively welcomed according to the statutes. Two workers' consumer cooperatives were also created that same year: the Sociale, founded by the Guesdists, and the Laborieuse, a more successful venture founded by metalworkers and knitters who were inspired by revolutionary syndicalism. Their desire was to build class solidarity through direct action in the mills and in the workers' community. The socialists' initial success in creating class organizations gave them a solid grassroots base, but they would need an eloquent and charismatic leader before they could attract a larger constituency. For this role, militants in Troyes were able to turn to an exceptionally talented local worker, Étienne Pédron.

Étienne Pédron (1849–1931) was a skilled watchmaker who had begun his organizing career with the Parti Ouvrier Français (POF) in Reims, just north of Troyes. He arrived in Troyes in 1889 and over the following seven years he would create the structures needed to overcome competition from other socialist groups and to train new militants. He was a gifted political organizer, a committed socialist, and a creative propagandist. All these talents helped to transform the local socialist party and to create working-class support for the POF electoral program. For the Troyes workers, he was the "wandering Jew of socialism"; for the police who tracked his movements, he was a "ferocious revolutionary."[9] As an orator and propagandist, he possessed a special charisma. One account of a workers' congress held in Troyes in 1888 described him as "tall, emaciated, with the head of a prophet and the gestures of a preacher."[10] Pédron left his mark on the labor movement through his reorganization of socialist groups in Troyes, through his tireless political meetings in towns and villages, and through the education and training of local militants. Above all, his activity as a propagandist and polemicist served the POF in its popularization of Marxist socialism. When the police raided Pédron's lodgings on 24 April 1890 and found a list of POF members as well as their strategy for neighborhood networking, they undoubtedly acted in anticipation of his involvement in the celebration of the first socialist May Day, 1 May 1890, in France.

The May Day celebration was initially promoted by the Second Socialist International in 1890 as part of an international offensive for hours reform, a movement that had broad support among French labor leaders. POF leader Jules Guesde and his party were instrumental in launching this celebration nationally. Guesde claimed that shorter hours would put an end to overproduction and to periodic or seasonal unemployment. The demand for the eight-hour day was the focus of the protest, to which Guesdist militants added the demand for a legally mandated minimum wage. This was the logic of their argument: "The eight-hour workday would benefit the working class because it would put an end to fratricidal competition for jobs among hungry workers, thereby obliging manufacturers to employ the unemployed, and thus, by the simple logic of supply and demand, the decline in the number of idled workers would inevitably lead to higher wages." The eight-hour day, they argued, would also allow time for increased leisure and family activities, for education, and for improved hygiene for all those workers whose "labor produces social wealth . . . for the needs of all society." While the argument for reform was clearly stated, the peaceful intention of the May Day demonstration was even more explicit. From the outset, the demonstration was intended to be a peaceful show of strength, characterized as both a protest and a celebration.[11] Nevertheless, the organizers cautioned workers that the state would not hesitate to intervene and employ the use of force.

Unfortunately, in Troyes the first May Day celebration led to just such a confrontation. Étienne Pédron called for a meeting at eight o'clock that evening in the Saint-Nizier market hall near the center of town; official authorization from the prefect and the mayor had been requested. At the last moment, however, the prefect banned the meeting and ordered the hall occupied by the light infantry. As the crowd gathered, workers arrived in groups organized by workshop and filled the marketplace. Finally, a dense crowd spontaneously broke out in song: "C'est huit heures, huit heures, huit heures, c'est huit heures qu'il nous faut, oh! Oh! Oh! Oh!" This was Étienne Pédron's song in support of the eight-hour day, which had already become a lightning rod for mobilization, a declaration of workers' rights. It galvanized the crowd of supporters, and some four thousand workers, carrying red flags, set out to march across town to the Faubourg Sainte-Savine in search of another meeting hall. What began as a peaceful, festive demonstration unfortunately turned into a pitched battle, as the infantry closely followed and confronted the workers in Sainte-Savine. The prefect's reports now qualified Pédron as "a violent and dangerous revolutionary" and accused Guesdist militants of fomenting disorder. Nineteen arrests were made, including those of ten textile workers on the grounds of their "rebellion and participation in an armed gathering." In fact, there is no evidence that any of the participants were armed.

Popularizing Marxist Socialism

In October that same year, Pédron followed up his action with a more typical POF political meeting, featuring Jules Guesde himself as speaker. The leaflet for the meeting appealed to men and women workers, socialists of all tendencies, union leaders, and revolutionary syndicalists to lay aside sectarian quarrels and unite behind the POF and its electoral program. The appeal was couched in terms of class conflict and stressed that a united bourgeoisie was only too happy to see a divided working class. While organized meetings of this type did not draw the same crowd as political demonstrations, they did provide the opportunity for dissident socialist groups to contradict the speaker, air their own views, and generally create trouble. Leftist political leaders developed a culture that made wide use of this kind of event to train militants in public-debating techniques, common to both the face-to-face verbal battles of working-class self-defense and the sometimes harsh exchanges of parliamentary debate. Speakers typically came prepared to face hecklers and detractors for a more lively political debate.

Thus, political meetings, organized under such circumstances, served one of the essential purposes of Guesdist political strategies, the education of the working class. Through their newspapers, reading rooms, public lectures, plays, and songs, Guesdists in Troyes attempted to popularize the principles of Marxist socialism. In 1892, Pédron founded *Le Socialiste Troyen*, a newspaper that published theoretical articles by party leaders Jules Guesde and Paul Lafargue (Karl Marx's son-in-law) as well as chronicles of party activities and accounts of life in the mills around France. Socialist publications were sold from hand to hand, but they were also available on newsstands and in a special library and reading room at the Maison du peuple (People's Hall) in the center of town.

Pédron knew how to reach workers through songs and short sketches, many of which he wrote himself. Several of his revolutionary songs were composed in Troyes and evoked mill life in stark, human terms. Drawing on the world that workers knew, Pédron contrasted the poverty and humiliation under capitalism with promises of a better world under socialism. Some songs represented a call to arms against bourgeois exploitation in the strident terms of class war, while others celebrated socialist victories at the polls, calling on the ruling bourgeoisie to respect the rules of democratic order and accept the possibility that a legitimate working-class party could govern locally with an agenda of social justice, as it did in nearby Romilly in 1895. In an age when work songs strengthened a culture of community, Pédron's compositions were significant in creating a sense of political identity and in galvanizing worker support for the POF's notion of social revolution, envisaged within the "social" republic they sought to create.[12] His song in favor of the eight-hour day depicted a system of low-wage slavery that drove mothers to work twelve hours in the mills and allowed mill owners to use repression to reduce wages even further. There was little connection, as this song depicted it, between working hours and real wages. Pédron's argument was presented in moral terms rather than in economic ones. The power of his words lay in their claim for workers' universal right to eight equal hours of work, leisure, and rest.

Pédron's plays, however, were clearly more ephemeral. Only police records survive to recount the political sketches that he performed with a small troupe, often in private cafés or back rooms to escape censorship. One such piece, called *Le combat social*, dramatized mill owners' actions in Troyes, contrasting them to what would exist in millwork under socialism, and ending with May Day's historical and political significance for worker solidarity. The police commissioner covering the performance in the line of duty found the pointed caricature of the mill owners particularly distasteful because Pédron had singled out for ridicule the best known among them, scarcely hiding their names. Popular theater of this kind was intended to educate while entertaining and was a form of propaganda more likely to reach more people than those attending strictly political meetings. Such performances often closed with the audience joining in singing. Henri Millet, a knitter in the mills who had been elected mayor of Romilly, praised Pédron's performances as artful propaganda: "[His plays] undertake the dramatization of 'the social question' which depicts so completely the drama of this fin de siècle, bringing to life, before the assembled workers, these hideous types of insatiable bourgeois and renegade workers that playwrights of every period have always carefully dissimulated. To make art an element of struggle, a revolutionary force, to oppose old melodramas where Providence and God play the principal roles, with this new artistic conception that consists of representing human life in its daily manifestations: this is an enterprise worthy of a party that expects to triumph on the sole basis of revealing truth."[13] Étienne Pédron's plays combined a special blend of caricature of the bourgeoisie and the dramatization of the experience of labor that fueled individual aspirations and formed a culture of resistance to industrial capitalism.

While Guesdist socialists and revolutionary syndicalists in Troyes shared a similar vision of the social republic they wished to create, each group advocated different means to achieve this end. Moreover, each had to mobilize and discipline a diverse, often rebellious working class to attain such goals. A majority of Troyes textile workers, with roots in rural community and family workshops, were predisposed to resistance to urban factory exploitation. But only a minority seemed to embrace Marxist socialism, which defined such resistance in terms of class struggle. Guesdist militants had hoped to convince male workers that they could create a cooperative

socialist society through the ballot and the parliamentary system. To realize these aims, Guesdists helped forge an emergent class identity through
political propaganda that prioritized and dramatized grievances of working-
class life. Gender solidarity formed one component of this strategy, although disenfranchised women workers were increasingly marginalized
from political action.[14] But in the end, Guesdists failed in their efforts to
create a disciplined political party and a worker constituency that could
ensure electoral victory over the established forces of the moderate Left in
Troyes. The subsequent shift of many Troyes knitters toward revolutionary
syndicalism revealed their desire to rebuild class solidarity through direct
action in the mills and in the workers' community. Young workers in particular had little faith in political parties or in a bourgeois-dominated republican state, and they continued to favor strikes. Other workers invested
their energies in labor unions and in the consumer cooperative, the Laborieuse, which would become one of the instruments of socialist transformation. This utopian political vision would help satisfy workers' needs for
greater workplace autonomy and control over their lives.

To be sure, at the century's end industrial and commercial capitalism continued to dominate in Troyes, as it did in the rest of France. Nevertheless, as
the bourgeois republican government in Paris attempted to integrate workers
into the political system, it was compelled to confront an emergent working-
class culture that laid claim to an alternative vision of the French Republic:
a "social republic" in which both men and women had the right to work for
a living wage and to partake in a consumer society.

Notes

This text has been excerpted from chapters 2 and 3 of *The Fabric of Gender: Working-
Class Culture in Third Republic France* (Pennsylvania State University Press, 2005).

1. The mills in Troyes produced not just knitted fabric, but also socks, stockings,
underwear, and garments of cotton, silk, and wool. Knitting, in contrast to weaving,
interloops one strand of yarn with two or more needles to create a fabric.

2. Archives départementales de l'Aube (ADA) SC 417.

3. Jules Herbin, *Rapport sur les modifications au règlement sur le travail des filles
mineurs et des femmes dans l'industrie à la Chambre de Commerce de Troyes, 6 December
1895*, Archives du Musée de la Bonneterie.

4. French National Assembly, Parliamentary Inquiry of 1904, p. 507, Archives
Nationales (AN) C 7318.

5. Testimony of M. Sèlves, secretary of the Association syndicale des ouvriers bon-
netiers, Archives Municipales de Troyes (AMT) 2F 47.

6. Testimony of M. Sèlves.

7. Testimony of Émile Clévy in Parliamentary Inquiry of 1904, p. 95.

8. Speech made before the Chambre syndicale patronale de bonneterie and deposited in the records of the parliamentary inquiry in December 1904 (AN C 7318).

9. Report of the Commissaire spécial de police in Troyes, 3 July 1895, (ADA) SC 340.

10. Quoted from L'Aube, 1–2 January 1889, in Michel Bedin, "Le socialisme dans l'Aube: Des origines à la creation de la SFIO" (DEA thesis, University of Dijon, October 1977), 67.

11. Manifestation internationale du 1er Mai, Archives du Musée de la Bonneterie.

12. A collection of his songs, Chansons socialistes, was published by the POF in Lille in 1906. See also Robert Stuart, Marxism at Work (Cambridge: Cambridge University Press, 1992), chaps. 7 and 8.

13. Report of the Commissaire spécial to the prefect, 5 July 1895. The police quote an article by Millet in a socialist newspaper (ADA SC 340).

14. While the women's suffrage movement in France was growing in numbers during the prewar period, the opposition to it increased as well. Yet working women were granted a form of limited suffrage: the opportunity to vote in elections to the local trade boards (Conseils des Prud'hommes) in 1907 and to serve on them in 1908. However, it was not until 1944 that all French women received political suffrage on equal terms with men.

Suggested Readings

Berlanstein, Lenard. The Working People of Paris, 1871-1914. Baltimore: Johns Hopkins University Press, 1984.

Canning, Kathleen. Languages of Labor and Gender: Female Factory Work in Germany, 1850–1914. Ithaca, NY: Cornell University Press, 1996.

Chenut, Helen Harden. The Fabric of Gender: Working-Class Culture in Third Republic France. University Park: Pennsylvania State University Press, 2005.

———. "The Gendering of Skill as Historical Process: The Case of French Knitters in Industrial Troyes, 1880 to 1939." In Gender and Class in Modern Europe, edited by Laura Frader and Sonya Rose, 77–107. Ithaca, NY: Cornell University Press, 1996.

Rose, Sonya. Limited Livelihoods: Gender and Class in Nineteenth Century England. Berkeley: University of California Press, 1992.

Scott, Joan. The Glassworkers of Carmaux. Cambridge, MA: Harvard University Press, 1974.

The Stevensons and servants in 1866, three years after the family's Grand Tour. Cunningham, wearing a dark apron, stands to the left of Robert Louis Stevenson. (Photograph courtesy of The Writers' Museum, Edinburgh, Scotland.)

CHAPTER FOUR

~

Alison Cunningham

Victorian Leisure Travel, Religious Identity, and the Grand Tour Journal of a Domestic Servant

MICHELE STRONG

As did the European working class of the nineteenth century, the middle class cemented its existence as a new social class in the wake of the Industrial Revolution. England emerged as the epicenter of these social and economic changes in the late eighteenth and early nineteenth centuries. There, the nascent middle class used the philosophies of economic and political liberalism to consolidate its power. These theories, as articulated by Adam Smith and John Stuart Mill, among others, championed individual rights in the form of a free-market economy that functioned without government interference (economic liberalism) and democratic participation in government (political liberalism). (It is important to note that these definitions differ dramatically from current American understandings of liberalism.) With the perceived excesses of the French Revolution and new revolutionary movements in 1830 as a potent reminder of working- and middle-class discontent, the British parliament passed the Reform Bill of 1832, effectively enfranchising middle-class males. With newfound political muscle backing industrial and politically liberal interests, the new, nonaristocratic middle class enshrined its economic and social philosophies in the English law and politics throughout the nineteenth century.

The British middle class also dominated the country's social and cultural life during this period. Queen Victoria and the period of her rule, 1837–1901, embodied the English middle class's cultural values in what has come to be known as "Victorianism," which would be marked by a noted emphasis on domesticity, the ideology of separate spheres and the gendered division of labor, and religiosity. As *the middle class evolved into a new "moral" elite, it would display the trappings of its wealth that would distinguish its members from the working class in particular. Flaunting their wealth and cultural capital through domestic and international travel, "dignified" sporting events, fashionable attire, and sizable staffs of household servants showed others their newfound status and solidified their economic and cultural standing.*

In this chapter, Michele Strong illustrates the complexities of class, religion, and gender in this period. Using the travel journal of Alison Cunningham, a pious working-class Scottish servant to a notable middle-class Scottish family, Strong demonstrates that the middle class had a monopoly on neither religion nor morality. The memoir gave "Cummy" a way in which to testify to her own faith and to contrast the middle-class values of her employers with her own.

On a January afternoon in 1863, a Scottish servant named Alison Cunningham and her employer, Thomas Stevenson, could be seen entering the Paris morgue. Stepping through its double doors and into a high-ceilinged exhibition room, they joined a queue of curious tourists and ordinary Parisians, who, like them, had come to inspect the morgue's most recent arrivals, either homicides or suicides who had likely been fished out of the Seine river that very morning. When their turn came to view the corpses, the duo approached three broad windows and peered through the glass panes. Displayed for identification in a brightly lit gallery were two men propped up on black marble slabs so as to face their audience, their lifeless bodies temporarily preserved under a thin blanket of cold running water. Cunningham shifted her gaze from one nameless corpse to the other, her eyes lifting momentarily to register the men's "dirty looking clothes" hanging on a rack from the ceiling above them. It was "a dreary sight," she later remarked, one that "was long ere I could get . . . out of my mind."[1]

Cunningham recorded her impressions of the morgue, and many more tourist attractions, in a journal that she kept during a European tour with the Stevensons. For this reason, it has become a valuable primary-source document. Historians have mined her journal for details about elite leisure travel and biographers have used it to learn more about Thomas Stevenson, a wealthy member of Edinburgh's professional elite; his wife, Margaret Stevenson, a socialite and semi-invalid; and their young son, Robert Louis Stevenson (RLS), who later became the famous author of *Treasure Island* (1883). The irony, of course, is that scholars have largely neglected to analyze Cunningham's journal to learn more about the author herself.[2]

Some Stevenson biographers have predictably dismissed Cunningham's journal as "homely" or "boring," a fate it shares with many working-class writings for their supposed lack of "complexity." Yet, a close textual analysis of Cunningham's journal can offer students and scholars a rare glimpse into how a domestic servant creatively responded to "leisure" travel. The purpose of this chapter, therefore, is to approach Cunningham's travel journal as a "complex text," one in which the author made choices about how to represent people, places, and events; determined what details to include or exclude; and developed a strategy that helped structure her narrative in a meaningful fashion. As we will see, although Cunningham navigated this textual terrain by drawing on a number of literary conventions associated with travel writing, it was the genre of "spiritual autobiography" that lent thematic coherence to her narrative and established the ultimate meaning of her tour. As a devout Protestant, Cunningham saw her trip abroad not only as a novel way to go to work each day, but as a spiritual journey that she likened to the Exodus in the Old Testament. Viewed in this way, Cunningham's tour of the morgue appears to have been just the first stop on a bumpy road to spiritual salvation.[3]

Victorian Leisure Travel in Europe: Motives and Itineraries

In cultural terms, the Victorian era, which conventionally dates from Queen Victoria's accession to the throne in 1837 to her death in 1901, is known for its highly ritualized manners, its middle-class morality, and its ornate decorative design; but the Victorian era also produced new forms of consumer culture, such as leisure travel, which made tourism as accessible to the masses as serial installments of a Charles Dickens novel. London's Great International Exhibition of 1851, for instance, did more than establish Britain as the undisputed leader of the industrialized world: it created a new ethos of rail travel as a form of "leisure," inspiring millions of Britons to ride the country's vast railway network to join the festivities in London. Thomas Cook and other travel entrepreneurs profitably fostered this ethos by organizing cheap day trips or package tours of short duration to British and continental destinations. In the 1860s, however, leisurely continental travel, which took months rather than weeks to complete, was still the prerogative of well-to-do consumers like the Stevensons.[4]

Reaping the rewards of the Industrial Revolution, the upper middle classes could afford the time and expense of an extended tour abroad. Indeed, they appropriated the seventeenth-century Grand Tour from young, male aristocrats and redefined the Tour to suit their tastes, resources, and schedules. While young aristocrats, England's future rulers had traditionally loitered up to three years abroad adding the final touches to their educations by visiting Europe's principal cities, the Stevensons, for example, spent "a season"—the winter months—on the Continent and traveled with their family; this arrangement was a recognizably Victorian trait reflecting the idealization of the "home" as a self-contained unit and fortress against the immorality of the public sphere. The Stevensons' entourage included their thirteen-year-old son, RLS; his twenty-year-old cousin, Bessie Stevenson, who, like many single women, traveled under the "protection" of relatives; and Cunningham, who had her hands full reproducing the comforts of "home" abroad as a "maid of all work," and functioning as a symbol of the Stevensons' elite status, since nothing indicated wealth and class better than a well-trained servant.[5]

Similarly, the Stevensons, like most wealthy travelers, would have professed a number of reasons for taking a Grand Tour. Restoring Margaret Stevenson's health topped the family's agenda. She had begun to show signs of consumption by "spitting up blood," and the sunny Riviera promised invalids like her temperate climates, if not always cures, at new health resorts that dotted the coast. The Grand Tour also afforded the whole family opportunities for rest and recreation, cultural refinement, and the distinction of having "done the Tour." In perfect conformity with their social set, the Stevensons traveled in first-class steamboats, coaches, and trains; lodged at elegant inns and luxury "Grand Hotels"; and visited culturally elevating tourist sights from the Tuileries Gardens to St. Paul's Cathedral. In between Paris and Rome, they also sojourned on the Riviera and lingered in a British holiday enclave at Mentone, where they rented a large villa. All in all, they traveled five months before returning to Scotland in May via the Brenner Pass, exhausted and, as Cunningham noted, exceedingly happy to be home.[6]

As for Cunningham, we know more about her own motives for traveling abroad than is usual for servants of the Victorian era by virtue of RLS's celebrity. After RLS's death in 1894, Alison Cunningham (1822–1913) became a minor cult figure. Stevenson fans made pilgrimages to sit at her feet, they produced and bought postcards stamped with her image, and one even wrote a small biography of her life and "vocation" as a domestic servant. Consequently, we know that when she arrived at the Stevensons' home in 1851 to nurse their infant son, she was thirty years old, "comely," and well educated for her class. Most importantly, she was an experienced nurse with sterling credentials as the daughter of respectable artisan weavers and as a member of the evangelical Scottish Free Church. A staunch Presbyterian, Cunningham firmly believed in predestination; zealously observed the Sabbath as a day of rest; viewed the theater, cards, novels, and the opera as the devil's work; and advocated temperance. With these qualifications, Cunningham was a welcome addition to the domestic staff, especially since the Stevensons had dismissed RLS's previous nurse for taking their only child on a bender at the local pub.[7]

From RLS's perspective, however, Cunningham fulfilled two other essential qualifications: she possessed a nurturing disposition and a lively imagination. Because RLS suffered from a chronic respiratory illness that required Cunningham's vigilant attention, she became his childhood companion as well as his nurse. RLS gratefully recounted the late-night story sessions she conducted to soothe the pain and fear that kept him from sleep and even attributed his own love of language and literature to Cunningham's gifted storytelling. According to her biographer, Cunningham filled his mind with "scripture passages, tales of bible heroes, stories of Scots Reformers and covenanters, and legends of pirates and smugglers, witches and fairies." Best of all, she sometimes entertained RLS by acting out the stories, or singing and dancing with the drama and flair of a trained actor—even though she claimed that she had never stepped into a theater, as Free Church strictures demanded.[8]

These glimpses into Cunningham's life history can tell us much about why she joined the Stevensons on their Grand Tour. In addition to fulfilling the terms of her position (it was her job to assist her employers whether at home or abroad), she genuinely cared about RLS and his welfare. Furthermore, as a voracious reader, she wanted to see with her own eyes the tourist sights, such as the ruins of Pompeii, that she had learned about "long ago." Finally, she wanted to use her journey as a means by which to express her most salient identity as an evangelical Christian. Cunningham charts this ambition in her journal by weaving together the Stevensons' worldly itinerary and her own spiritual journey in a single narrative that articulates the wide range of her experiences and emotions. And yet, the result, if we are to believe her, was an "ill-written Journal."[9] Why would Cunningham paint such a gloomy picture of her journal, which was a significant literary achievement for a woman of her social position and education? A glance at the gender, cultural, and class structures in Cunningham's life will offer some clues.

"This Ill-Written Journal"

Craven Hotel, London
January 4, 1863

> My Dear Cashie, My first entry in my Journal begins on Sunday. I just thought I would like to talk a little with you to-day, with pen and ink, in London at Last. How strange I feel in this great City![10]

When Cunningham packed for her journey, she tucked a small blank book into her travel bag and assumed a new role as a travel writer. A gift from her closest friend, Cashie, the journal, with its thin, pale blue leaves and marbleized, pressboard cover, was just a little larger than a prayer book, yet small enough to fit in an apron pocket. With a mandate from Cashie to "write a little every day," Cunningham intended to fill its pages with her impressions of Europe for friends and family left behind in Scotland. If the fragment of Cunningham's "first entry" is any indication, she was eager to begin.[11]

Cunningham approached her role as a travel writer with the dedication of a professional journalist. Almost from the start, she composed a "petit bit" every night, often when ill or exhausted, and even on the Sabbath, for which she suffered small pangs of conscience. In adopting her writer's regimen, Cunningham also narrated her journey using textual conventions associated with contemporary travel literature that she would have encountered in many different literary mediums, from missionary tracts to travel adventure stories in her favorite weekly paper. Consciously or unconsciously, she emulated their styles in her own writing.[12]

For instance, much like Murray's *Handbook for Travellers* series, Cunningham peppered her journal with statistical information, noting the heights of mountains, the populations of cities, and the distances between destinations. Cunningham also captured the exotic dress, manners, and customs of the "natives" with an ethnographer's eye for visual detail and ear for sound, narrating, for example, "the clank, clank" of "fearfully thick wooden shoes, painted at the toes" on Lyon's cobbled streets. Similarly, Cunningham contributed to the ocean of Protestant travel writing that ridiculed Catholicism and the piety of cardplaying, snuff-taking priests. Just as typically, however, Cunningham expressed her appreciation of "affecting" Catholic art and architecture, and even adopted the persona of a romantic travel writer, describing a gondola ride through magical Venetian canals and bidding a fond farewell to Italy with a quote from Byron's *Childe Harold's Pilgrimage*.[13]

Evidently, Cunningham had come to feel the same kind of creative delight in writing that she conveyed in dramatizing stories in RLS's nursery. If nothing else, she seems to have indulged a transgressive compulsion to put pen to paper, even bending Sabbath strictures to write about worldly subjects. It comes as something of a surprise, therefore, to find in her closing entries that she repeatedly laments her "ill-written journal," complaining of inkblots, forgotten names, rambling thoughts, and needless repetitions that marred its pages. Summing up her frustrations, Cunningham decided that her journal was not only "ill-written" but that "it has not been written in the spirit I would have wished, as I shrink from giving publicity to my feelings."[14]

What should we make of Cunningham's literary self-loathing given her obvious commitment to duplicating the conventions of travel writing? While her comments sound suspiciously like the self-effacing prefatory statements found in women's published works (another literary convention), this should not obscure the fact that Cunningham wrote her journal, as she put it, at a "great disadvantage," a common complaint of working-class authors.[15]

As a working woman with a limited education and little leisure time for intellectual pursuits, Cunningham could not hope to imitate the seemingly effortless and polished prose of published travel journals. Moreover, her experience as a servant on the Grand Tour simply did not fit the middle-class "leisure" model of a travel narrative. After all, Cunningham saw much of Europe from the top of careening coaches in inclement weather and through the filmy windows of smoky second-class traveling cars; she came in contact with foreign "others" in markets and kitchens, and at the common dining tables of hotels and inns; and she rose early in the morning to fill water basins, blacken shoes, and mend clothes before she descended servant stairs to stroll the Tuileries Gardens or to tour the Vatican. These disjunctures, therefore, between existing literary models and her material reality—the "disadvantages" of her class position—ultimately produced a different kind of narrative than she had hoped for, validating her own condemnation of her "ill-written journal."[16]

And yet, we would not do justice to Cunningham's journal if we accepted her verdict and thought no more about it. To do so would ignore the strength of her religious identity and her creative imagination. Cunningham may have lacked the education and social position to write a middle-class travel narrative, but she did possess the experience, and thus the authority, to write a gripping personal narrative of sin, wandering, and redemption.[17]

"A Trial of No Ordinary Kind": Cunningham's Journey through the Wilderness

As an ardent Protestant, Cunningham had probably written in a religiously confessional mode since childhood, keeping a daily diary for spiritual self-examination. On several occasions, for example, Cunningham reminds herself that even though "it is a relief to do so" she must refrain from revealing her inner thoughts "as if I were writing a Diary . . . in case any other person may happen to see it." Clearly, she wanted to use her journal like a diary to express the intensity of her emotions, but she also wanted to write in a way that was suitable for a public audience. The purpose, content, and structure of spiritual autobiography allowed her to strike this balance.[18]

First, in terms of purpose, evangelicals used the spiritual autobiographies of famous religious divines, as well as those of friends and family, as "instruments" to convert others. The evangelical function of spiritual autobiography made it permissible to share one's spiritual struggles and convictions with a wider discursive community. Cunningham, for example, rejoiced to receive a letter from a friend at home who "[felt] as if on the verge of the eternal world . . . happy girl!" Candidly longing for the "grace to act like her," Cunningham presumably hoped that her journal would hold the same power to inspire others. Additionally, the scriptural signs and symbols that spiritual autobiographers used to tell their stories obviated the need for explicit detail typical of diaries, since most readers would be familiar with the larger meaning of references taken from the Bible. Finally, the form of spiritual autobiography fit naturally with that of a Grand Tour. Both modes of travel charted a journey, a series of events occurring in time and space with a beginning, middle, and end, even if they ultimately pointed to different destinations. It made perfect sense, then, for Cunningham to underpin her Grand Tour with a divine purpose.[19]

Specifically, Cunningham conferred religious significance to her Grand Tour by representing the journey as a contemporary manifestation of the biblical Exodus and herself as a spiritual Israelite. She drew inspiration for this approach from the popular Baptist preacher John Bunyan. In his autobiography, *Grace Abounding* (1666), Bunyan maps his spiritual evolution from sin to salvation. This structure paralleled the Exodus narrative, which spiritual autobiographers used to trace their religious conversions. As literary critic Linda Peterson explains, "The autobiographer's description of his unrepentant ways corresponds to the Egyptian bondage; the dramatic conversion, to the flight from Pharaoh and the crossing of the Red Sea; the period of confusion or backsliding, to the wilderness wandering; and the final peace, to the entry into Canaan."[20]

The parallel to the Exodus was deliberate. Autobiographers created this neat fit between their own spiritual journeys and that of the Israelites by using a method of scriptural interpretation called biblical typology. This method "treated Old Testament persons, events and things (types) as prefigurations of Christ or some aspect of his ministry (antitypes)." Theologians, therefore, viewed correlations between the Old and New Testaments as prophetic of reality. Christian grace in the New Testament, for instance, fulfilled the prophecy of the Old Testament. Thus, "the Passover is turned into the Holy Communion, circumcision into Baptism" and "Moses and the Prophets into Christ and His Apostles." In the eighteenth and nineteenth centuries, evangelical ministers, such as the ones Cunningham would have listened to in Edinburgh, urged their parishioners to interpret events in their lives through biblical typology, stressing that "types" could be fulfilled in the reality of each person's lived experience, just as they were in the days of the New Testament. Thus, part of the ordinary Christian's goal was to identify correlations between the scriptures and his or her personal experience. Cunningham was more than equal to the task.[21]

Less than a week into her journey, Cunningham began to construct her Exodus narrative and, within it, her identity as a spiritual Israelite. Likening her band of travelers to the "way-faring man mentioned in the Song of Solomon," she wrote with some weariness: "We turn aside to tarry for a night, and are gone in the morning." And so they were. In their race to get to the Riviera, they traveled from Edinburgh to Nice in thirteen days, "pitching their tents" in a new city almost every night. This whirlwind of change quickly thrust Cunningham alone into the "wilderness," where she encountered "snares," or what Bunyan called "temptations of doubt," which tried her spiritual endurance with two chief challenges to her faith: her "cold dead heart" and the "school of [physical] affliction."[22]

For evangelical Christians, the phrase "cold dead heart" referred to a numb or stony indifference rather than fiery passion toward one's faith. Cunningham began to experience this condition on the Riviera when carnival revelries converged with the Sabbath. Cunningham, you will remember, fervently revered the Sabbath as a holy day of worship and a holy day of rest. And yet, she began to accept and, conceivably, even to enjoy, some of the "gaiety" around her when carnival was under way and seemingly turned the world upside down.[23]

Carnival marked a period of holiday excess in the Catholic calendar when rules were suspended and social hierarchies overturned before the austerity of Lent. Adults indulged their "carnal" appetites, riotous boys played pranks on their elders, and for a few hours the rich played at being poor and the poor at being rich, all wearing masks that allowed such behavior to go on with impunity. At first, Cunningham found such "disgraceful" antics repulsive. But it was not long before Cunningham reported a shift in her response to such "wickedness," writing: "I do not feel that sorrow which I ought to do. I see such doings on God's Holy Day. I might show in many ways my abhorrence of it if my heart was in a right state." Alarmed, Cunningham prayed to have her religious ardor restored to her, plaintively asking for "a heart going out in deep, heart-felt love to Jesus."[24]

In this state of spiritual distress, Cunningham lacked the insight necessary to interpret "the Word" made manifest, typologically, in the world around her. Her "cold dead heart," she declared, had become a "trial of no ordinary kind." But, her "temptation of doubt" was an expected and even desired part of her spiritual journey. Just as the Israelites had faltered and then recovered their faith in the wilderness, Cunningham's "backsliding" into temptation would be followed by the promise of salvation. Cunningham demonstrated this promise in her journal when she experienced a flurry of typological divinations (i.e., correlations between the biblical past and her own experience) soon after carnival.[25]

The Mediterranean landscape encouraged travelers to draw biblical associations and Cunningham was no exception. Olive trees reminded her of the "prosperity of the Christians" in Hosea 14:6; the Mediterranean's "tideless sea" prefigured the New Jerusalem in Revelation 21:1–5, and a shepherd with his flock stood as a "beautiful emblem of Jesus and his people" in John 10:27. It was the sight of the Alps, however, that soothed her most. As Cunningham wrote shortly after arriving in Mentone, the view of the Alps prompted thoughts of Moses "going up the Mount and entering the cloud to meet with God."[26]

Here, at last, was a sign that could restore her "deep heart-felt love to Jesus." Moses as "redeemer, lawgiver, and intercessor" prefigured the more perfect Christ. Just as Moses led the Israelites to Canaan, Christ would lead his followers to eternal salvation. Cunningham hoped to be among them. While her "cold dead heart" had put the strength of her convictions to the test, she and her readers very well knew that these struggles were part of the "fight and battle," as she put it, "of even trying to look up, in genuine saving faith to be enabled to do it always!"[27]

As a projection of her spiritual anxieties, Cunningham's "fight" in the wilderness also became a "battle" to accept physical affliction as a necessary step toward a new, broken, and thus contrite heart. When the Stevensons took the villa at Mentone, Thomas Stevenson warned Cunningham that she would "not be . . . nearly so comfortable" as she had been at the Grand Hotels in Cannes or Nice, especially because he "expect[ed] every thing as usual." Cunningham's housekeeping duties thus began at dawn and ended only around midnight. This schedule would not have troubled Cunningham ordinarily, but she had caught a chill sitting on the outside of a carriage in the bitter cold "as usual," so that her chest had become very "sore." Despite throwing a Shetland shawl around her shoulders, which Margaret Stevenson mocked as her maid's "flag of distress," Cunningham could not seem to "get a warm." Moreover, Cunningham then began to experience painful headaches and a frightening ringing in her ears that made her feel dizzy and faint.[28]

As Cunningham's symptoms persisted, they gave rise to more typological musings. Resting one afternoon, she gazed out of her bedroom window and described an alpine landscape that prefigured eternity, declaring that "everything looks so beautiful that one would almost suppose it to be a type or emblem of that city beyond the river of death." As Cunningham longed for the city of God, her physical suffering made her spiritual struggle more intense. She pleaded for a "heart burning with love to Jesus" and asked to be "enabled so to rise above all these little things, or rather that they may be so sanctified to me that, like St. Paul, I may glory in them." Believing that it was through "these little ills" that she was assured of God's love in the wilderness, she exclaimed: "He knows I need the rod, but O how gently does he apply it!"[29]

These emotional confrontations with her faith fortified Cunningham's spiritual resolve. Like Moses and the Israelites who experienced the "miracle of the manna," Cunningham's faith in "Christ as savior" gave her the confidence to take her readers farther into the wilderness. Thus, when the Stevensons decided to resume their tour at the end of March, Cunningham gladly prepared to venture deep into the heart of Catholic Italy. Indeed, reaching Rome in mid-April and staying a week, Cunningham exuberantly declared that she could "hardly believe I am really in Rome, the seat of the Popes." At the very center of Catholic Christendom, Cunningham scoffed at Rome's ancient greatness. While Rome had once been "the Mistress of the World," she declared, "it is now a poor, priest-ridden city." The comment suited the tenor of the occasion. Marking the apex of her journey, her thoughts now turned north toward home. For if Rome, to her mind, was effete, and its priests, monks, and friars mere "idle men too holy for work," then Scotland was the "New Jerusalem," a robust, Protestant nation populated by God's "chosen people."[30]

"The River": Cunningham's Journey Home

Quitting Rome in late April, Cunningham yearned for Scotland, knowing that "if I were home, I would think more of it than ever." Although the Stevensons had left the "seat of the Popes," there was still a good distance to travel before they could put Catholic Europe behind them. Crossing the border northward into Austria and then Germany, they passed through towns and hamlets studded with crucifixes, many painted with red splotches "to represent the blood" of the "Crucified One." Visually overwhelmed in this "land of darkness and gross superstition," the travelers counted more than two thousand crucifixes within four hours. A little over a week later, on Cunningham's fortieth birthday, they pulled into Nuremberg, Germany, a Protestant enclave.[31]

In Nuremberg, Cunningham felt that Providence had given her the gift of a spiritual oasis. It was a refuge from the barrage of Catholic imagery that had assaulted her Protestant sensibilities since first setting foot on the Continent, and it was a place where she could celebrate her birthday with some serenity by contemplating this world and the next. A walk through a local churchyard proved to be just the place for a reverie. Noting that the "tombstones are not like ours, but great, huge stones laid flat on the top of the grave," Cunningham "saw into one grave through a chink of the stone, and it appeared to be hollow." Struck by a typological perception, Cunningham remarked that "the thought immediately came into my mind of a cave and a great stone laid upon it. Would the tomb of Jesus be like this, I thought? I thought it might."[32]

What better birthday gift could Cunningham have received than this typological correlation, which linked her personal experience of the churchyard to the scriptures? And with thoughts of the Resurrection that the tomb invited, what better prefiguration of her own rebirth as she made her way back to Scotland? If these connections were not clear to her readers, later entries referring to the Second Coming and the millennium drove the point home.

Cunningham spent her last continental Sabbath in Cologne knowing that she would soon return to "my own loved land with a heart filled with gratitude to God for the precious privileges [a Protestant Sabbath] which we as a nation enjoy." In anticipation, she pleaded to "hear the gospel now as for eternity!" As for the "multitudes" left behind on the Continent "perishing for lack of knowledge [of the scriptures]," Cunningham declared that "the mighty arm of Jehovah shall not always be stayed. There is a day coming when He shall arise out of His place, and make His voice to be heard by the inhabitants of the earth." Such rapturous allusions to the millennium brought her to the shores of Britain on a wave of righteousness that warmed her "heart" once more. Weary of "traveling and sight-seeing," she took comfort in knowing that their journey would soon end, just as the "end of all things come!" She prayed, "O may the Lord grant it may find us watching for His coming."[33]

Cunningham left her readers with little doubt that the "end" was near when she arrived at the port city of Calais. Like the Israelites who had longingly peered across the river Jordan into Canaan, she reported that on a clear day in Calais, one could "see to the other side of the river and behold our own land," which "only makes the yearning for home all the more intense." The river Jordan prefigured the English Channel (which Cunningham first refers to as a "river"), pointing to the end of her journal, if not, quite yet, her spiritual journey beyond the wilderness and toward eternal salvation.[34]

"The New Jerusalem"

Delivered across the river Jordan to the New Jerusalem with a heightened awareness of her own need for grace, Cunningham predictably praised Scotland in her last entry, remarking that her time abroad had been "good" for her, as "no blessing is prized as it ought to be, till we are deprived of it." It was a lesson that she shared with her readers, even though she deplored the many "mistakes" in her "ill-written journal." As a text manipulated toward a specific end, Cunningham's journal testified to her spiritual progress and could serve as a tool, much like spiritual autobiography, to convert others. Cunningham therefore succeeded in overcoming the "disadvantages" she faced in her role as a travel writer by interpreting many events through a typological lens.[35]

When taken on its own terms, therefore, Cunningham's journal must be seen as more than a "homely" account of a domestic servant's travels or the trivial scribbles of a secondary figure in RLS's life. It is Cunningham's literary and intellectual invention. She invested her journal with all the creative energy that she had used in conjuring ghosts, pirates, and fairies to stir RLS's imagination; and she used her tourist experiences, from the morbid spectacle of the Paris morgue, to the typological Resurrection in a Nuremburg churchyard, to express her deep religious faith and the essential meaning of her Grand Tour abroad.

Notes

For Lloyd Kramer. Thanks to David Anderson, Anene Ejikeme, Chris Endy, Cora Granata, Brandon Hunziker, Linda Salvucci, and to Elaine Greig and the late Robin Hill at the Writers' Museum, Edinburgh.

1. Alison Cunningham, *Cummy's Diary*, ed. Robert Skinner (London: Chatto and Windus, 1926), 8–9; Vanessa R. Schwartz, *Spectacular Realities* (Berkeley: University of California Press, 1998), 45–88.

2. John Pemble, *The Mediterranean Passion* (Oxford: Clarendon Press, 1987), 107, 281; Marjorie Morgan, *National Identities and Travel in Victorian Britain* (Houndmills: Palgrave, 2001), 53, 195–96, 206.

3. Skinner, preface to *Cummy's Diary*, ix; Hunter Davies, *The Teller of Tales* (London: Sinclair-Stevenson, 1994), 11; Carolyn Steedman, *The Radical Soldier's Tale* (London: Routledge, 1988), 21.

4. Hugh Cunningham, *Leisure in the Industrial Revolution* (London: Croom Helm, 1980), 157; Piers Brendon, *Thomas Cook* (London: Secker & Warburg, 1991).

5. Pemble, *Mediterranean*, 23, 77, 85; Morgan, *National*, 141–43, 151.

6. Pemble, *Mediterranean*, 84–95, 51–110; Lord, Charles Guthrie, interview with Cunningham, 1908, Writers' Museum; Cunningham, *Cummy's*, 182.

7. Davies, *The Teller*, 5–6; Guthrie, "*Cummy*" (Edinburgh: Otto Schulze & Company, 1913), 4, 5–9, 11, 17–19; Blantyre Simpson, *Robert Louis Stevenson's Edinburgh Days* (London: Hodder and Stoughton, 1898), 88, 91; Andrew Drummond and James Bulloch, *The Church in Victorian Scotland* (Edinburgh: St. Andrew Press, 1975), 24.

8. Graham Balfour, *The Life of Robert Louis Stevenson*, vol. 1 (New York: Charles Scribner's Sons, 1901), 32, 43; Guthrie, "*Cummy*," 8–9.

9. Cunningham, *Cummy's*, 116, 182.

10. Cunningham, *Cummy's*, 1.

11. Cunningham, *Cummy's*, 182, 190; Cunningham, Manuscript Journal, postscript (1908), 168–69, Writers' Museum, Edinburgh.

12. Cunningham, *Cummy's*, 20, 51, 78, 15, 64.

13. Cunningham, *Cummy's*, 147, 184, 11, 46, 130, 108, 148, 150–52, 158, 164, 167; Shirley Foster, *Across New Worlds* (New York: Harvester Wheatsheaf, 1990), 16–17, 58, 60, 41–42.

14. Cunningham, *Cummy's*, 182.

15. Foster, *Across*, 18–21; Cunningham, Manuscript Journal, postscript, 168–69. For "disadvantages," Regina Gagnier, *Subjectivities* (New York: Oxford University Press, 1991), 41–54, 141–42.

16. Pemble, *Mediterranean*, 23; Morgan, *National*, 151.

17. Gagnier, *Subjectivities*, 45–46, 150; Billie Melman, *Women's Orients* (Ann Arbor: University of Michigan Press, 1992), 169.

18. Cinthia Gannett, *Gender and the Journal* (New York: State University of New York Press, 1992), 110; Cunningham, *Cummy's*, 33, 37–38, 64–65, 158.

19. Roger Sharrock, *John Bunyan* (repr., Westport, CT: Greenwood Press, 1984), 56; Gannett, *Gender*, 133–37; Cunningham, *Cummy's*, 28–29.

20. Linda Peterson, "Biblical Typology," in *Approaches to Victorian Autobiography*, ed. George Landow (Athens: Ohio University Press, 1979), 238.

21. Peterson, "Biblical," 236–37; Landow, *Victorian Types, Victorian Shadows* (Boston: Routledge & Kegan Paul, 1980), 22–23, 59; quoting John Keble, *Sermons*, 2:426–27; Billie Melman, *Women's Orients, English Women and the Middle East, 1718-1918: Sexuality, Religion, and Work* (Ann Arbor: University of Michigan Press, 1992), 167–69.

22. *Cummy's*, 10, ed. Note; Jer. 14:8, 80; Sharrock, *John Bunyan*, 63.

23. Ezek. 11:19, 36:26–27; Ps. 15:17; *Cummy's*, 2, 15, 30, 143, 168, 181.

24. Peter Burke, *Popular Culture in Early Modern Europe* (New York: Harper & Row, 1978), 178–204; Cunningham, *Cummy's*, 28, 43, 40–41, 32–33, 38.

25. Sharrock, *John Bunyan*, 54, 63–64; Cunningham, *Cummy's*, 40–41.

26. Pemble, *Mediterranean*, 113–28, 123; Cunningham, *Cummy's*, 93, 53, 56, 60–61, 52–53, 37.

27. Cunningham, *Cummy's*, 37; Landow, *Victorian*, 22–27, 25.

28. For parallel anxieties see Sharrock, *John Bunyan*, 65; Ps. 51:17; Cunningham, *Cummy's*, 33, 47, 50–51, 74, 47, 52, 76, 64, 97.

29. Cunningham, *Cummy's*, 48–49, 54–55, 60.

30. Cunningham, *Cummy's*, 130, 134; Arthur Herman, *How the Scots Invented the Modern World* (New York: Crown, 2001).

31. Cunningham, *Cummy's*, 145, 172, 168–69, 176.

32. Cunningham, *Cummy's*, 177–78.

33. Cunningham, *Cummy's*, 181–82.

34. See Bunyan's own "crossing" in Sharrock, *John Bunyan*, 64; Cunningham, *Cummy's*, 187.

35. Cunningham, *Cummy's*, 190.

Suggested Readings

Bell, Ian. *Dreams of Exile: Robert Louis Stevenson*. Edinburgh: Mainstream, 1992.

Berbineau, Lorenza Stevens. *From Beacon Hill to the Crystal Palace: The 1851 Travel Diary of a Working-Class Woman*. Edited by Karen Kilcup. Iowa City: University of Iowa Press, 2002.

Briggs, Asa. *The Age of Improvement, 1783–1867*. London: Longman, 1959.

Hulme, Peter, and Tim Youngs, eds. *The Cambridge Companion to Travel Writing*. Cambridge: Cambridge University Press, 2002.

Landow, George P. *Victorian Types, Victorian Shadows: Biblical Typology in Victorian Literature, Art and Thought*. Boston: Routledge & Kegan Paul, 1980.

Valenze, Deborah. *The First Industrial Woman*. Oxford: Oxford University Press, 1995.

Withey, Lynne. *Grand Tours and Cook's Tours: A History of Leisure Travel, 1750–1915*. New York: William Morrow and Company, 1997.

Suggested Visual Sources

Dyce, William. "Christ as the Man of Sorrows (c.1860)." National Galleries of Scotland.

CHAPTER FIVE

~

Strategies of Inclusion
Lajpat Rai and the Critique of the British Raj

ROBERT A. McLAIN

As with most historical developments, late nineteenth-century European imperialism did not occur in a vacuum; it did, however, significantly change in form. While the "old" western European imperialism of the fifteenth through eighteenth centuries consisted of sending settlers primarily to the Americas and subjugating aboriginal populations, independence movements and political turmoil at home cemented imperialism's decline in the late eighteenth and early nineteenth centuries. The Industrial Revolution combined with new ideologies of race and nationalism to reinvigorate the imperial enterprise for Great Britain and France. Newer nations such as Germany, Belgium, and the United States also began a quest for empire.

While the need for raw materials to supply new industry was significant, the "new imperialism" of the late nineteenth century was also a product of racialized nationalism, which applied social Darwinian theories of the "survival of the fittest" to the formation and functioning of nation-states. This new variant of nationalism positioned the "races" of European nations not only against peoples of color in Africa and Southeast Asia, but also in juxtaposition to one another. As a result, Great Britain, France, Germany, and even tiny Belgium (under King Leopold's leadership) raced to acquire as much land and population as possible as evidence of national strength and character. As Rudyard Kipling set forth, the "white man's burden" mandated the economic, cultural, and political subjugation of "lesser" peoples as part of a civilizing mission. All too often this "civilization" came about through violence rather than benevolence.

Great Britain, with its extensive dominions dating back to the earlier period of imperialism, remained the most dominant imperial power in the new race for empire. By the mid-nineteenth century, it had cemented its control over India; by the century's later decades, it controlled significant portions of Africa and South Asia. Truly, as was said at the time, the sun never set on the British Empire. Like other empires, Great Britain's was not immune to challenges from its imperial subjects. Colonized peoples throughout Asia and Africa would begin to appropriate Western concepts of nationalism and liberalism and would begin to work for independence. Robert McLain explores the writings and life of Lajpat Rai, an early critic of the British Raj (British rule in India). McLain argues that the categories of gender and race are indispensable for analyzing the increasingly contentious relationship between Indian nationalists and the British civil service administrators.

Historians of England's imperial moment have, in recent years, begun to acknowledge that British rule in India rested on ideas as much as on the coercive power of the state. Indeed, by the late nineteenth century, British colonial administrators had constructed an image of India and its peoples based on the paired notions of racial and gender inferiority. In turn, these concepts became the chief conceptual guarantors of continued British mastery in South Asia, undergirding its military power as well as its monopoly on the higher-level political positions in the colonial government.[1] This chapter will first examine how imperial conceptions of race and gender developed within India, and then consider how the radical nationalist leader, Lajpat Rai (1865–1928), forcefully used liberal British political ideology to critique a distinctly illiberal Indian Civil Service (ICS), the administrative elite of approximately 1,200 Britons who oversaw the affairs of more than three hundred million Indians.[2]

Although less familiar than nationalist icons such as Mohandas K. Gandhi, Rai nonetheless warrants further historical attention in that he proved to be one of colonialism's most incisive critics as well as the leader of one of northern India's most important Hindu revivalist/reform movements, the Arya Samaj. Moreover, Rai provides an eminently suitable vehicle for exploring how race and gender intersected with colonial politics during a crucial, yet neglected, period in the Indo-British relationship, the Great War of 1914–1918. During the war India fielded well over one million troops for Britain and its allies as they struggled to defeat Germany, Austria-Hungary, and the Ottoman Empire. Nationalists like Rai sought to erode existing notions of racial and gender inferiority within the empire by leveraging their country's service to the Allied cause. In their estimation, India's sacrifices clearly demonstrated a level of loyalty and political development commensurate with self-rule. A few British authorities agreed. Speaking in Parliament in August 1917, Secretary of State for India Edwin Samuel Montagu declared as his goal the "increasing association of Indians in every branch of the administration and the gradual development of self-governing institutions with a view to the progressive realisation of responsible government in India."[3] Montagu's ultimately successful plan called for an expanded electorate in India and provincial legislatures to oversee domestic functions such as education and agriculture. Yet, change would not come without a fight. The ensuing debate over the "Montagu Reforms" played itself out during the last two years of the war and resulted in a bruising exchange between imperialistically minded Britons on the one hand and South Asian nationalists on the other. During this debate, Rai made some of his most cogent and damning ideological assaults on the ICS.

The theories of race and gender that supported the British Raj are complex, but may be grasped more easily by outlining their contours. Briefly, rules of caste had divided India into distinct social groups long before the English first arrived in the early 1600s. At the top of the caste hierarchy stood the Brahmans, a religious and professional elite. Just below them were the Khsatriya, or warrior class, followed by the Vaisya, who generally filled mercantile or agricultural jobs. At the bottom of the caste pyramid lay the Sudra, who took on menial employment. Meanwhile, a fifth group stood outside of the caste system, the so-called untouchables, who had no status under Hindu belief and who performed jobs considered unsanitary, such as leather tanning and the cleaning of latrines.

The British, keen observers that they were, quickly gravitated toward the Brahmans to help them develop their linguistic and cultural knowledge of the region, particularly in the late 1700s when a series of military clashes between various Indian rulers and the British East India Company led to the latter's direct control of large swaths of territory. With this increased interaction came debate among English administrators: should they run the country according to existing customs, or should they refashion India by "civilizing" it in a manner akin to England? The dispute rested on more than how to govern: rather, it turned on a divergence of opinion over the relative merits of Indian civilization itself. So-called Orientalists tended to see value in India's rich cultural legacies, while their Anglicist opponents saw South Asian society as morally bankrupt and far inferior to that of Europe.

By the mid-1800s the battle between the Orientalists and their opponents had come to a head. Addressing the problem in 1835, Thomas Babington Macaulay, a member of the East India Company's governing board, argued that the country's linguistic diversity meant that English alone should become the primary governing language. This meant not only that English should become an instrument of rule, but also that the Raj should develop an English-educated indigenous cadre that would "form a class who may be interpreters between us and the millions whom we govern; a class of persons, Indian in blood and colour, but English in taste, in opinions, in morals, and in intellect."[4] Within a generation, the British educational system in India had produced a relatively small, albeit growing and intellectually active Westernized elite, particularly in the populous northeast province of Bengal. For the most part, these "educated Indians" filled low-level clerical positions because racial prejudice barred them from the upper ranks of government service. But herein lay the irony: Macaulay's plan *had* created a class trained in the English manner, yet its members would become the core of the anticolonial movement. The educated elite often read the best of Greek, Roman, and English literature while at the same time learning to admire quintessentially English democratic principles. How then, they asked, could the British love liberty so much and at the same time exclude perfectly qualified "natives" from the halls of governance?

This line of questioning would seem to place the British in a quandary, yet they parried the challenge by anchoring their belief in "native" inferiority to pseudoscientific concepts of biology, anthropology, and climate. As far as colonial officials were concerned, "educated" Indians like Lajpat Rai could by no means replace the white official. According to prevailing beliefs, the indigenous male had suffered too long from the effects of a blistering hot climate and too many years of peace and racial mixing. This had supposedly led to a loss of manliness and the "effeminization," or "emasculation," of the "educated" Indian. In the analysis of British observers, the effeminate "natives" were much like English women who wanted the right to vote. Both, the British experts presumed, suffered from an overreliance on the senses and emotion that precluded them from exercising political responsibility, either through voting or by serving in office. Imperial faith thus placed the Englishman at the pinnacle of manliness; only the colonial administrator and soldier, the "man on the spot," could remain cool enough under both literal and figurative fire to govern wisely.

Colonial conceptions of masculinity received further sanction from military experts in the form of the so-called martial races. In this formulation the Sikhs and Muslims of the Punjab region, along with the Gurkhas of Nepal, had escaped the ruinous effects of the subcontinent's southerly reaches. This allowed them to retain a hardy manliness that made them ideal soldiers for the Indian army. Nevertheless, martial-races authorities agreed that the supposedly wild and childlike nature of the "fighting classes" prevented them from assuming control of the country. Moreover, Indian army experts concluded that only the paternalistic hand of the British officer could ensure that the ordinary Indian soldier performed effectively on the battlefield. Likewise, Anglo officials frequently claimed that a British withdrawal would only result in chaos; the marital races would ransack the country and murder the "educated" classes if given an opportunity. As should be clear from this inelegant symmetry, the martial races stood as a nearly perfect counterpoise to the "educated" Indian. Colonialism in India had thus built its ideological edifice by sifting "natives" and Britons into categories of "effeminate" and "masculine."

Such a rhetorical move proved crucial to overcoming the striking inconsistency of a "liberal" state clutching "democratic" values while at the same time carrying out an explicitly imperialistic policy. Even so, colonial theories of inferiority could assume an air of undeniable authority when backed by a racism rooted in supposedly "objective" science of late nineteenth-century "New Imperialism."[5] As scholar Uday Mehta has shown, this allowed for "strategies of exclusion," by which the dominant colonizing power could champion universal values such as "liberty" while forbidding the full participation of the empire's subjects in the political process.[6] The significance of this sleight of hand was certainly not lost on nationalists, who by the late 1800s and early 1900s had begun to use the very values they had learned in English schools to punch holes through the firmament of British rule.

What makes this last strategy so compelling for our purposes is that no one delighted in pointing out the contradictions of empire as much as Rai. A lawyer by training, he wrote with a clarity and persuasiveness that defied the stereotype of English-mangling "educated" Indian "babu."[7] For several years Rai had helped lead the Arya Samaj, a Hindu reform movement with deep roots in northern India. Formed in 1875, the Arya Samaj advocated a purified form of Hinduism that rejected caste divisions and Brahman dominance. While these principles coincided to some degree with earlier reform movements, the Arya Samaj differed in that it sought to move away from Western influence, not embrace it. Instead, their slogan, "Back to the Vedas," indicated a belief that the misinterpretation of early Hindu religious scriptures had led to the adoption of faulty practices such as caste. This meant that one not need look westward for the reform of Indian society, but rather backward into the country's own history and a millennial "golden age" of power and unity.

Rai's Arya movement seemed especially dangerous to British officials, not least because of its rapid growth in northwestern India's Punjab Province, an area that provided 60 percent of the recruits for the army despite having only

7.5 percent of the colony's total population.[8] This led provincial governor Michael O'Dwyer to see the Arya Samaj as harboring a potentially cobralike lethality for British rule. The Indian army served as the basis for British power on the subcontinent; if the subcontinent rebelled there would be little hope of maintaining control. O'Dwyer also recalled that Rai had been briefly exiled to Burma in 1907 for attempting to turn the militarily minded Sikhs against the Raj. The threat appeared even more acute during the Great War, as England had come to rely heavily on the colony to bolster its forces in the fight against Germany.[9] Not surprisingly, Rai chose to avoid arrest and leave India for the United States so long as hostilities continued.

Rai used the relative safety of America to churn out a prodigious and wide-ranging series of critiques against the British Raj. He frequently assailed what he saw as the "political, physical, and economic emasculation" caused by foreign rule, the lack of education in India, and the drain that colonialism placed on India's economy. His pamphlet, Open Letter to the Right Honorable Edwin Samuel Montagu, represents his most direct assault on the ICS and its claim to be the only entity that truly "understood" India and its unique needs.[10] Indeed, Rai's work provides a compelling example of the complexities of anticolonial resistance: like many of his fellow nationalists, he quoted extensively from British periodicals and government sources to mount his attack. This strategy of inclusion provided a ready defense against sedition charges. After all, the nationalists were merely repeating what British authors themselves had said. Nonetheless, Rai's "open letter" to Montagu, a similarly titled piece addressed to Prime Minister David Lloyd George, and a number of Rai's own books, found their way on to a list of material banned by ICS censors.[11]

What then, was the specific nature of Rai's critique? First and foremost it was a full-bore attack on the mythology of an impartial and dispassionate civil service, the group with the most to lose should the Montagu Reforms reach fruition. For years the ICS had cultivated an image of starkest contrast to the educated Indian. The "imperial man on the spot" was imbued with a strong faith in the racial superiority and ruling qualities of the Englishman. It was precisely this ethos that allowed for a ready set of exclusionary responses whenever the possibility of ceding political power arose. Among the most commonly used tactics was to contrast British "efficiency" with Indian slothfulness and credulity. Indeed, the term "efficiency" had a clear meaning in colonial vernacular. It signaled the ability to act quickly and decisively in the face of crisis and to fairly balance India's diverse caste, religious, and regional interests. It also meant a calm refusal to succumb to emotion and panic. Efficiency also related closely to the notion of "prestige," itself a coded word indicating a sense of awe to be instilled in "native" subjects, as well as the need to never lose face. Only by preserving and protecting "prestige" could a few hundred Britons control the huge colony. In effect, the terms "efficiency" and "prestige" allowed the ICS man to cloak his authority with a mantle of masculine legitimacy and, more crucially, preserve the ideological continuity of the Raj.

Claims of "efficiency" did not matter to Rai. On the contrary, he systematically and brusquely rejected ICS folklore by declaring that the greatest danger to British rule came not from more Indian responsibility via the Montagu scheme, but from an ICS that had no oversight and thus abused its power. The sole purpose of the ICS, argued Rai, was to "safeguard and protect the interests of the British capitalist and British manufacturer." Great Britain had declared that it was fighting against "Prussian autocracy, Prussian bureaucracy, Prussian militarism, and Prussian Junkerism," yet in India "all these monstrosities exist in an extraordinary degree and every effort to dethrone them is vehemently opposed by persons who want the world to believe that they are fighting to establish democracy."[12]

Rai's key passage, however, denounced the Indian government for the negligence of its Middle Eastern campaign against Germany's allies, the Turks. In April 1916 an army of more than thirteen thousand men, including approximately ten thousand Indian troops, had surrendered to the Turks at Kut, in Mesopotamia (Iraq). Two-thirds of the British soldiers and nearly three thousand Indians eventually died in captivity, adding to the more than 1,600 troops who had perished within the confines of the town during the siege. The campaign, taken on by a reluctant Indian government under pressure from London, had resulted in the largest surrender of British forces since that of Cornwallis at Yorktown during the American Revolution.[13] The "Mespot" scandal, charged Rai, had revealed "the fundamental weakness of the Government of India—its irresponsibility." Furthermore, it belied the shibboleth, "repeated ad nauseum, in season and out of season, that the Indian services, Civil and Military, were the acme of perfection and that they should be absolutely trusted in Indian affairs."[14] For too long, argued Rai, the ICS had been able to dodge criticism from both nationalists and its detractors in the British parliament. The ICS thus had no accountability to the people and it felt no compulsion to rule in a truly competent manner. And as far as Rai was concerned, the Kut debacle showed the utter bankruptcy of "efficiency" as an inherent trait of the ICS administrator.

Nor did Rai's invective stop there, for it fully recognized the hardening of racial attitudes that had occurred within the Raj in the latter half of the nineteenth century. Since that time, he charged, there had arisen a class of civil and military servants with an "ethical code of their own, which brooks no interference or control from without." Rather, the Anglo civil servants had come to see themselves as a special breed, "so many gods, with their goddesses at their side, who form an oligarchy whose interests and comforts and prestige dominate all activities of Government in India."[15] Rai wondered aloud why, given this defect, "must the [provincial] governors always be Englishmen? Do you [Montagu] really think sir, that men like Sir Michael O'Dwyer . . . are such superior beings that no Indians of that calibre could be found the length and breadth of India?"[16]

Rai had a valid point. India had a population of over three hundred million people, yet one could count on one hand the "natives" with real responsibility. Rather, the government of India divided its administration into separate branches. It was fairly simple for the "educated" classes to obtain clerical jobs, or positions in isolated rail and postal stations, but one could reach the higher levels of service, the so-called covenanted branch of the ICS, only by means of an exam administered in England alone. This was a daunting proposition: the "native" would have to incur a months-long and very expensive journey to London just to have the remotest possibility of obtaining a covenanted post. The supposed mental barrier raised by the educated Indian's effeminate nature thus had as an additional obstacle the physical obstruction of a several-thousand-mile oceanic voyage. The British officials could also rely on another measure of manliness to deter the ambitious babu, the "riding test," in which ICS candidates had to prove their horsemanship skills. The logic was that the district officer had to be able to reach remote areas when needed. Unsurprisingly, this put Indians, many of whom had never ridden, at a distinct disadvantage.

In retrospect, Rai's work seems more sarcastic than subversive. Yet, the problem lay not so much with the text itself, but in the changed political circumstances of the Great War. The conflict led authorities to see a heightened threat in antigovernment material—an essay that censors would have passed over in an earlier period could earn one a trip to jail during the conflict. Indeed, in peacetime one could discern the contingencies and limits of colonial power much more readily. Authorities anxiously sought to prevent sedition, but they did not apply restrictions so rigidly as to create an outright backlash. The war cast aside censorship policies despite the nationalist strategy of drawing on British sources to pass judgment on the Raj. As the argument ran, troublemakers like Rai too often fell victim to their own effeminized and metaphysically clouded "Oriental" mind. This might well lead the slippery "educated Indian" to create political unrest among a numerically huge and ignorant peasantry that, although normally sturdy and reliable, might be too "credulous," too "emotional," and too "inflammable" if subjected to a public reading of a seditious text.[17] Still, Rai's commentary found widespread agreement, even in the thinning ranks of the more moderate nationalists like Mohandas K. Gandhi. Likewise, even some Britons puzzled over the contradictions between the word and the deed of imperial rule. The editor of the *Westminster Review*, J. A. Spender, commented precisely on this phenomenon in a letter to his friend Sir Harcourt Butler, the education member for the Indian government. Having perused material deemed "seditious" by authorities, Spender could only "wonder what the government of India can think to be legitimate criticism. Perhaps you haven't the materials for a decent Indian press, but you won't get it on . . . terms" that saw even well-meaning criticism as a danger.[18]

A few members of the ICS tacitly agreed with Rai. As early as 1902, Indian government officials at the highest levels exhibited wildly divergent public and private opinions as to the efficacy and attitudes of their organization. The correspondence of Lord Curzon as Viceroy (1898–1905) and Lord George Hamilton, the secretary of state for India, clearly shows a yawning gap between reality and the carefully constructed ICS mythology that Rai would later attack. Hamilton expressed a deep concern over the gulf between Britons and Indians and the increasing tendency of the former to openly express their distaste for India and anything to do with it. Writing to the viceroy, Hamilton laid out his views rather bluntly:

> I cannot help feeling the truth of the contention that India is exploited for the benefit of the Civil Service, and that the statutory rights which they have obtained from long possession of a monopoly of government in India, and the increasing difficulty of in any way ousting them from their position, or of stirring them up to the activity and interests in the governed shown by their predecessors is an increasing danger.[19]

Curzon's reply to Hamilton also bears repeating. Curzon, known as one of the most conservative of India's governors, opined that too many civilians were "indifferent," "incompetent," and "dislike[d] the country and the people." Furthermore, they had "no taste for their work." The decline among officials of "interest in India as Indian and in Indian people as our fellow subjects whom we are called upon to rule" posed the gravest threat according to Curzon. "In the long run," he concluded, "unless we can arrest this inclination, it must be most injurious, and one day may be fatal, to our dominion in this country."[20] Curzon and Hamilton would never have expressed their doubts publicly. Official and military Indian administrators considered the preservation of British "prestige" too important. Still, the comments are significant in that one of the most imperially minded viceroys in the history of the Raj privately corroborated Rai's sentiments of a few years later, going to the heart of the contemporary historical debates over the legacy of British rule in India and the tendency to see it as generally benign or exploitative and racist.

The dual motives of protecting the Raj *and* the organizational status of the ICS go far in explaining the relentless use of racial and gendered stereotypes by imperial apologists. The debate over the Montagu plan, however, differed in that it escaped the confines of India in a way that past political battles had not. The war had helped create a truly transnational public sphere by way of a large and active press. British and Indian opinion leaders paid close attention to one another's work and frequently did battle via their respective journals. The controversy's expanded parameters generally worked to the advantage of the ICS, for they could rely on a powerful ally in London to help coordinate their lobbying efforts, the Indo-British Association (IBA). The IBA stands as one of the most unique political pressure groups in imperial history, for its membership drew almost exclusively on retired ICS and Indian army officials who had returned to the metropole. The guest list of its raucous first meeting, held in London in late 1917, reads like a Who's Who of British India. At the head of the gathering sat Lord Sydenham, the former governor of Bombay and conservative member of the House of Lords. No fewer than four former provincial lieutenant governors and commissioners also participated, along with C. E. Buckland, author of *Biography of India*, and former Indian army Commander in Chief Sir O'Moore Creagh. And unlike their colleagues still in government service, the retirees from the IBA had nothing to lose: they could criticize the Montagu Reforms with impunity. And so they did. The tone of the dispute took on a distressingly familiar quality insomuch as it relied on mockery of "educated" nationalists to make its points.

Rai came in for direct abuse as the chief representative of the effeminized Indian menace. The pseudonymous author Zeres, acting as the IBA's mouthpiece in the British press, declared that Rai was like all Anglicized "natives"—nothing more than "an exotic development of British occupation." More pointedly, these people were essentially an "artificial" creation of Macaulay's policy that derived their "prestige" from the "reflected glory of the dominant race."[21] Misplaced Western idealism had "done absolutely nothing to uplift the effeminate races," despite the latter's tendency to see "salvation in Western Mimicry."[22] In addition, the "Young Indian" Rai had lost "all sense of proportion" by wrongly "vilifying the race to whom he owes his immediate existence."[23] Rather, Rai and his ilk lacked the backbone to rule, being nothing more than "sheltered clerkly men who have never seen danger."[24] More exactly, handing over political power to the nationalist "mimics" would amount to "filling a child's Christmas stocking with matches, paper, and gunpowder."[25] Macaulay's well-intentioned plan had apparently created not-so-pale imitations of the Britons themselves.

Zeres called Montagu to task as well, arguing that the "present bright idea—namely, the substitution of the tophat for the turban" rested on the assumption that "what must be good for an English garden must be equally good for an Indian jungle."[26] Montagu's Jewish ancestry made him too inviting a target, for Zeres and other opponents of reform readily pointed to his "Oriental" background as making him naturally sympathetic to India. This had led the secretary of state to fundamentally misunderstand the land and its people. Instead, "educated India," to whom "our own radical emasculates are always so irresistibly attracted" had duped Montagu, "the British M.P. shod in the elastic sided-boot of awful seriousness, and bearing salvation in a Gladstone bag." Furthermore, Zeres argued that "India will never listen to the blandishments of the 'good, kind' Liberal Reformer, for she has known hotter kisses from the firmer lips of stronger men. Our . . . Montagus will never blot out her passionate memories of three thousand years of blood lust."[27] The best possible government for India was the one it already had, a more balanced British version of Eastern autocracy backed by the hint of force.

Zeres's imposition of English masculinity on a feminine India is indeed striking. The country was "passionate" and full of "blood lust" to a degree that suggested the inability of the "native" subject to control his credulity and emotions. Meanwhile, "radical emasculates" like Montagu had let their own built-in effeminacy get in the way of their better judgment. They were theorists rather than men of action. They had little in common with the Anglo army officer operating on the turbulent frontier with Afghanistan, or with the ICS official who traveled from village to village dispensing even-handed imperial justice. It was in fact up to the young army officers, the "unhappy masculine Cinderellas" who had been disappointed at having to remain in India while fighting raged in Mesopotamia and France, to stay behind and lessen the pride of "educated Indians" like Rai.[28]

How then do we more broadly read the onslaught by Zeres and the many like-minded writers who sought to counter the efforts of Indian nationalists to assert autonomy? First, their labors were in a sense a struggle for the hearts and minds of the British public, or at least the relatively small number that took an interest in colonial affairs. At the heart of this fight lay the question of how far India had advanced along the path to regeneration, and how successful

England had been in fulfilling its mission to resurrect a once-great civilization. Indians argued that they had come far enough to strike out on their own, while imperialists foresaw years, if not centuries, of continued tutelage. Second, the actions taken by the ICS and IBA strongly suggest the need to reconsider the popular iconography of the colonial administrator as the relatively impartial deliverer of progress and justice. One of the few studies of the ICS as a bureaucracy has demonstrated just how avidly outgoing administrators labored to preserve the mythology of the "imperial man on the spot" through articles in metropolitan journals and magazines. A 1906 piece from *Blackwood's Magazine*, for instance, evokes the themes of "efficiency" and "impartiality" in terms remarkably similar to those used during the Montagu debate.[29]

In the end, the need to protect the prestige of the Raj via the image of the British imperial man contributed greatly to the rancor of the 1917–1918 debates. It also led Indian nationalists to conclude that the Raj would grant concessions only under extreme pressure. Seen from a more contemporary perspective, one could argue that Zeres had anticipated Benedict Anderson's later argument that communities and collectivities "imagine" the nation into existence via print culture.[30] Anglo-India had in fact caught the nationalists in the midst of envisioning independence in the immediate future, rather than as a vague and distant goal. In its confusion, Anglo-India could think only to depict national desire as a product of a delusional, and certainly feminine, flight of fancy. The problem lay in the fact that the conflict had threatened to render their longtime reliance on appeals to "native" effeminacy into an overnight anachronism. By 1919 and later, it became more apparent that the constant alliteration of "emasculated," "educated," and "effeminate" might fail to defeat Indian claims to greater postwar autonomy. Small wonder, then, that the Anglo-Indians and their conservative allies, aware that political change was an impending reality rather than a pipe dream, would react so violently.

Notes

1. Mrinalini Sinha, *Colonial Masculinity: The Manly Englishman and the Effeminate Bengali in the Late Nineteenth Century* (New York: St Martin's Press, 1995), 1–2.

2. The term "Raj" derives from the Sanskrit word for "king" but is generally used to refer to the period of British rule in India.

3. S. D. Waley, *Edwin Montagu* (New York: Asia Publishing House, 1964), 136.

4. Cited in Rai, *Unhappy India* (Calcutta: Banna Publishing, 1928), 45.

5. For a brief overview of the tenets of fin de siècle imperialism see Matthew G. Stanard's "Imperialists without an Empire: *Cercles Coloniaux* and Colonial Culture in Belgium after 1960," chapter 11 in this volume.

6. Uday Mehta, "Liberal Strategies of Exclusion," in *Tensions of Empire: Colonial Cultures in a Bourgeoise World*, ed. Frederick Cooper and Ann Laura Stoler (Berkeley: University of California Press, 1997), 59–86; Eileen P. Sullivan, "Liberalism and Imperialism: J. S. Mill's Defense of the British Empire," *Journal of the History of Ideas* 44, no. 4 (October 1983): 599–617.

7. The term "babu" had originally been used as a term of respect. Britons in India used it sarcastically to refer to "educated" Indians.

8. Sumit Sarkar, *Modern India: 1885–1947* (New Delhi: Macmillan), 74–76; Derek Sayer, "British Reaction to the Amritsar Massacre, 1919–1920," *Past and Present* 131 (May 1991): 136.

9. The Indian army consistently maintained a mix of Indian and British troops to fill its ranks; however, the white soldiers represented only about one-third of the overall forces.

10. Rai, *Young India* (New York: B. W. Heubsch, 1916), and *The Political Future of India* (New York: B. W. Heubsch, 1919).

11. N. G. Barrier, *Banned: Controversial Literature and Political Control in Northwest India, 1907–1947* (Columbia: University of Missouri Press, 1974), 234–36.

12. Rai, *Open Letter to the Right Honorable Edwin Montagu*, in *Lala Rajpat Raj Writings and Speeches*, ed. Vijaya Chandra Joshi (Delhi: University Press, 1966), 1:288.

13. Byron Farwell, *Armies of the Raj* (New York: W. W. Norton, 1986), 261–63.

14. Rai, *Open Letter to Montagu*, 282–83.

15. Rai, *Open Letter to Montagu*.

16. Rai, *Open Letter to Montagu*, 295–96.

17. Robert Darnton, "Un-British Activities," *New York Review of Books*, 12 April 2001, 86.

18. J. A. Spender to Harcourt Butler, 19 February 1914, Butler Papers, MSS EUR. F 116/46, India Office Library.

19. Cited in Bradford Spangenberg, *British Bureaucracy in India: Status, Policy, and the ICS in the Late Nineteenth Century* (Columbia, MO: South Asia Books, 1976), 4–5.

20. Spangenberg, *British Bureaucracy in India*, 2.

21. Zeres [pseud.], "Tophat or Turban?" *Blackwood's Magazine* 203 (June 1918): 738–39. See also Zeres's "India Revisited: A Recent Record of Candid Impressions," *Blackwood's Magazine* 202 (November 1917): 571–600.

22. Zeres [pseud.], "Tophat or Turban?" 740, 744.

23. Zeres [pseud.], "Tophat or Turban?" "Young Indian" is an allusion to one of Rai's wartime publications.

24. Zeres [pseud.], "Tophat or Turban?" 749.

25. Zeres [pseud.], "Tophat or Turban?" 740–41.

26. Zeres [pseud.], "Tophat or Turban?" 748.

27. Zeres [pseud.], "Tophat or Turban?" 742–43.

28. Zeres [pseud.], "India Revisited," 595.

29. Cited in Spangenberg, *British Bureaucracy*, 4–5.

30. Benedict Anderson, *Imagined Communities* (New York: Verso, 1996), 24–25.

Suggested Readings

Cohn, Bernard. *Colonialism and Its Forms of Knowledge*. Princeton, NJ: Princeton University Press, 1996.

Jones, Kenneth. *Socio-religious Reform Movements in British India*. Cambridge: Cambridge University Press, 1989.

Metcalfe, Thomas. *Ideologies of the Raj*. Berkeley: University of California Press, 1997.

Sinha, Mrinalini. *Colonial Masculinity: The Manly Englishman and the Effeminate Bengali in the Late Nineteenth Century*. New York: St Martin's Press, 1995.

Spangenberg, Bradford. *British Bureaucracy in India: Status, Policy, and the ICS in the Late Nineteenth Century*. Columbia, MO: South Asia Books, 1976.

Wolpert, Stanley. *A New History of India*. Oxford: Oxford University Press, 1999.

CHAPTER SIX

~

Colette

The New Woman Takes the Stage in Belle Époque France

PATRICIA TILBURG

After a century of unprecedented social, cultural, and political change brought on by industrialization, technological innovation, and nationalism, fin de siècle (turn-of-the-century) Europe was a place of vibrant possibility as well as tumult. Politicians appealed to their newly enfranchised male constituents with promises of empire and social peace for societies wracked by divisive labor and capital disputes and economic boom and bust cycles. Women increasingly embraced liberalism and its promises of political and social freedom. The Pandora's box that was the French Revolution held out the promise of liberty and equality beginning in 1789; while women were not included in this vision, many throughout the nineteenth century appropriated these ideals as well as those of the new middle class that led the march toward universal suffrage. To this end, women throughout Europe demanded legal reform in the arenas of marriage, child custody, and work, as well as educational reform that would give them access to public education. To the consternation of many, they also sought the right to vote.

Between the 1880s—the beginning of what contemporaries and historians alike call the Belle Époque (the Beautiful Epoch)—and 1914 when World War I began, there emerged a cultural icon, the New Woman, or la femme nouvelle, which became the object of much social and political attention. The New Woman was a product of half a century of reforms that gave women increasing access to the public sphere. While primarily middle class and thus of a social status that allowed her to acquire advanced education, she became emblematic of this age and her influence *spread beyond class boundaries. As women delayed marriage to seek education and careers, politicians, industrialists, and social commentators became obsessed with la femme nouvelle. Many conservative critics saw her as the primary culprit behind declining populations (especially in France) and thus a danger to national security and expansionist imperial ambitions.*

While many critiqued the New Woman, even more embraced her. In rejecting or postponing Victorian domesticity, she provided an alternative to a life as the "angel of the house." Men and women alike wrote fiction glamorizing and promoting her life and adventures, including the popular French writer, Colette. In this chapter, Patricia Tilburg examines Colette's life and writings. She argues that Colette, a product of nineteenth-century reform herself, pushed the boundaries of acceptable gender behavior that was emblematic of her time and in doing so was a significant force in the redefinition of femininity and female gender roles.

Late in her life, French film director and actress Musidora reminisced about the popular literature of her teenage years:

> It was in 1906 that the young girls of the era lent each other *Claudine at School*, slipped it open under the pages of [a textbook] . . . in case the teacher questioned them. . . . We did not comment on the literary classics, but instead underlined our favorite passages from *Claudine at School*. The young language was so new, the characters so lively, so like us, that we were all left delirious with enthusiasm.[1]

The novel in question was the first work of fiction by a woman who would become a canonical French writer and cultural icon: Sidonie-Gabrielle Colette. By 1906, Colette's irreverent fiction, which dealt gleefully with adultery, homosexuality, and even incest, was only one of many transgressive aspects of her public persona; she also was separated from her first husband, living with a cross-dressing woman, and headlining vaudeville shows in which she appeared scantily clad. Seemingly a poor exemplar of French womanhood, how did this sexually liberated bohemian come to speak for a generation of French women? Colette's astonishing popularity among the girls of the turn of the century was indicative of a cultural sea change in France and Europe in this period—a change in norms of femininity that found its greatest expression not only in Colette's fiction but in her career as a music-hall performer.

While Colette struggled in this period to establish a degree of professional and personal autonomy still rare for most middle-class women, the bounds of ideal femininity were being expanded on all sides by a surprising newcomer to the European social scene: the sometimes anxiety-provoking *femme nou-*

velle, or New Woman. As the nineteenth century crashed to an end, such women were beginning to seek out higher education, challenge traditional patterns of courtship and marriage, enter professions historically closed to women, and join increasingly vocal movements for women's political emancipation. As the New Woman became a common type in European popular culture in novels such as George Gissing's *The Odd Women* (1893), Marcelle Tinayre's *La rebelle* (1905), and H. G. Wells's *Ann Veronica* (1909), European women experienced real changes in their legal status and educational and professional options at the turn of the century. In 1907, for example, the same year Colette's husband Willy sold all rights to his wife's *Claudine* novels without her consent, a law was passed giving married Frenchwomen control of their earnings. The mounting visibility of the New Woman coincided with the increasing presence and scrutiny of women in the urban workforce. By 1906, women made up some 37 percent of industrial workers in France.[2]

The most visible New Women were those who took to the streets of European capitals appealing for women's political rights, most notably the vote. But such political campaigns were not the only means by which women reinvented norms of feminine behavior at the turn of the century. While contemporaries may have seen a flamboyant writer/actress as being incompatible with her reform-minded bluestocking sisters, and Colette herself sometimes referred to feminist action with amused condescension, her life and work in this period nonetheless made claims for sexual, financial, and social autonomy that harmonized with the demands of the New Woman.[3]

Though generations of pioneering women and gradual reform stood behind them, the New Women of the fin de siècle witnessed a remarkable acceleration of changes in feminine roles, from fashion to educational opportunities to notions of sexual pleasure. Each European woman (and man) had to find ways of managing this revolution in everyday life that accompanied the turning of the century. In so doing, they could not act outside of the mental horizons of their time, but rather worked from within their society's normative belief systems including religion, family traditions, local customs, and cultural biases.[4] As historian Jo Burr Margadant writes, "No one 'invents' a self outside of notions available to them in a particular cultural setting, and accepted feminine models for women in public life were few and circumscribed in nineteenth-century France."[5] Thus, women like Colette, who transgressed traditional sexual and social standards, could not simply discard the cultural codes with which they had been raised, but were obliged to adapt the languages of their time to suit novel circumstances.

Throughout her years as a music-hall performer, Colette drew on the potent cultural resources of her girlhood in the new French public school system to effect a reimagined femininity that found honor not in sexual virtue, piety, or motherhood, but in paid manual labor. Her negotiation of conflicting feminine models provides a window into how others might have enacted their own versions of the New Woman in this period and how a teenage Musidora could see so much of herself in Colette's fictional alter egos. In examining Colette's transformation from provincial schoolgirl to bohemian femme nouvelle, it becomes evident that in many ways this writer was not simply an anomalous eccentric, but a woman of her time.

Sidonie-Gabrielle Colette was born on 28 January 1873 in the rural village of Saint-Sauveur-en-Puisaye in the Burgundy region of France. Her father, Jules Colette, was a dashing war hero and tax collector; her mother, Sido, was a charming young widow who married the captain shortly after her first husband drank himself into an early grave in 1865. Gabrielle, called "Minet chéri" (darling kitten) by her mother, was the indulged youngest child of the family. Thanks to the inheritance Sido received from her first husband, Gabrielle's childhood was markedly upper middle class, as the family enjoyed luxuries such as a private carriage, a piano, and servants.[6] By the time Gabrielle reached school age, however, poor management of Sido's fortune resulted in a significant diminution of the family's wealth. As a result, Gabrielle was sent to public school, alongside the daughters of farmers and artisans, from the time she was six until she was seventeen, a relatively extensive girls' education in this period.

Gabrielle Colette was thus part of the first generation of girls educated under the sweeping instructional revolution of the 1870s and 1880s, which secularized, modernized, and nationalized French schools. Just three years before her birth, the Second Empire of Napoleon III fell during a humiliating war with Prussia, and was replaced by a democratic republic. The leaders of this precarious new Third French Republic, seeking to forge a population of reasonable, engaged citizens, conducted a thoroughgoing campaign against irrationalism and Catholic influence, with the freshly built secular school at the center of the political battlefield. Such conflicts captivated much of European society in this period, but only in France did a secularized state attempt such an uncompromising implantation of a laical moral system in the course of just a decade by way of a new public school system.

The architects of the Third Republic venerated the cross-class public school, and staked much of their political capital on its ability to reshape French society. Primary education became the subject of passionate debates from the corridors of power in Paris to provincial villages. Saint-Sauveur's municipal council, of which Captain Colette was a member, approved a massive reconstruction of the village's public schools in 1882, and established a superior primary education program for girls in the same period. While regional officials believed that such a program would be wasted on this rural town, the council of Saint-Sauveur persevered, stressing the necessity of practical training for their daughters.[7]

Fearing that educated women might just as easily become castrating viragos as sensible helpmeets, republican officials combined conservative social conditioning with forward-looking pedagogy in their schools. While female students learned to be rational, productive citizens, they were also made aware of their social duties by way of a curriculum that stressed traditional gender roles. This meant promoting the nineteenth-century feminine ideal: the domestic angel who protected her family from the corrosive influence of industrialism with the strength of her maternal and wifely love, virtue, and domestic orderliness.

But the new curriculum also inadvertently offered possibilities for women to articulate new respectable public identities outside of marriage and motherhood. Along with tried-and-true clichés of patriotic maternity, girls like Gabrielle Colette learned that an honorable life was one dedicated to physical, wage-earning work. One moral instruction text used in Colette's school linked work to the evolution of man from bestiality and claimed, "Work is a necessity. If no one worked, no one could live."[8] This republican ideal of work most specifically involved engaging in a métier, a trade requiring training and skill. A reading primer used in Colette's school told students that because "every creature is on the earth to work," they should devote themselves to "performing with zeal your métier as a student."[9] The curriculum's critique of idleness went beyond an exhortation to keep busy, extending to a veritable culture of work, in which identity was defined through one's occupation and the successful earning of one's living.

Though female students were taught values of domestic order and feminine virtue, they were also urged to occupy themselves with useful (paid) manual labor, possibly outside the home. One instructional text offered children practice in letter writing, including sample letters from working women to employers who owed them money. Such lessons treated female students as future productive workers who would one day direct their own economic lives.[10] Textbooks often elevated the hardworking lower-class girl by reproaching the moral failings of the bourgeois lady, too attached to luxury and leisure.

Though hard work assuredly was not a new concern in education, such lessons had the power to upset traditional hierarchies of gender and class when first brought to bear on a mass population of children of both genders and across the social spectrum. Rural towns like Saint-Sauveur built schools for their daughters as a means of inoculating them to the temptations of the city, but also insisted that schools provide girls with a practical professional formation that could unsettle traditional notions of women's social role. Though she hailed from a bourgeois family, for eleven years Gabrielle Colette imbibed lessons of métier, manual work, and financial aptitude intended for her peasant classmates—lessons that would facilitate her rebellion from bourgeois feminine norms in the tumultuous years that followed.

In May 1893, twenty-year-old Gabrielle married a notorious writer some fourteen years her senior, Henry Gauthier-Villars. Willy, as he was known in Paris, hailed from a prosperous publishing family and was a well-known figure on the Parisian cultural scene. Gabrielle met Willy during childhood trips with her father to Willy's family's Parisian bookshop, and secretly corresponded with him as a teenager. After their marriage, she moved to Paris with her new husband and, with her thick provincial accent and long braids, became a colorful accessory on Willy's arm at theater openings, operas, salons, and balls. Colette, as Willy had taken to calling his bride, dutifully performed the role of the socialite wife by keeping a scrupulous household account book, hosting dinner parties, and weathering Willy's numerous infidelities. In 1900, Colette became one of a stable of ghostwriters employed by Willy to produce marketable novels under his name. Her first book, *Claudine at School* (1900), a semiautobiographical account of her years in Saint-Sauveur, was a best seller that spawned a series of novels featuring the precocious heroine Claudine. Soon, Colette gained a reputation as an author in her own right, mingling in circles with cultural luminaries such as Marcel Proust, Claude Debussy, and Rachilde.

In 1906, having separated from the philandering Willy and in need of funds, Colette embarked on a lucrative if scandalous career as a music-hall performer. From 1906 to 1913, while she and the renowned mime Georges Wague toured France in a series of vaudeville shows in which Colette sometimes appeared half-nude, she chronicled the backstage life of the music hall in stories, novels, lectures, and interviews. The most famous of her vaudevillian fiction was a semiautobiographical novel, *The Vagabond* (1911), which follows a season of touring by a divorced writer turned performer named Renée Néré.

In taking the stage, Colette renounced many essential components of the middle-class feminine ideal. Wage labor outside the home was anathema to the ideal of the bourgeois woman; that this work should be scantily clad stage performance only deepened suspicion that such a woman was immodest. Popular fiction relished the image of the music hall in general as a sphere of moral and physical laxity, the opposite of the snug and orderly home tended by the middle-class housewife. Actresses and dancers invariably were portrayed as slovenly and promiscuous, thoroughly incapable of the kind of domestic hygiene and thrift required of a respectable matron.

Colette presented the public with a very different kind of music hall. In 1913 at a fashionable theater in Nice, an audience that had gathered to hear Colette divulge "sensational details" of her music-hall life was disappointed, according to a journalist:

> Mme Colette Willy revealed nothing at all . . . she tried to demonstrate that the music hall was quite simply a place whose atmosphere was moral and hygienic and where one could live tranquilly . . . that the men [of the music hall] are all honorable, the women never wicked.[11]

The audience's surprise was reasonable. While any bourgeois woman endangered her good standing by taking the stage, Colette's reputation was jeopardized further by her failed marriage, her relationship with a woman, and her onstage nudity. Cutting off her famously long hair in 1902, well before the short-cropped bob became fashionable for women, exercising with weights and even boxing on a regular basis, Colette was at the forefront of a new liberated style that blurred traditional gender distinctions. Yet more radical and more historically interesting than her short hair or muscles was Colette's reformulation of childhood lessons of honest work as a means of social rebellion. In fictional works, interviews, and letters, she proposed a theatrical world not of lust and depravity, but of earnest labor and thrift. In rendering her music-hall and literary careers in this way, Colette reconciled her unconventional lifestyle with culturally shaded notions of work and moral soundness, and in the process, radically redefined honorable feminine conduct around labor.

Yet Colette also consistently articulated the attractions of middle-class respectability and domestic order throughout this period.[12] Her conflicted treatment of work, marriage, and domesticity demonstrates both her discomfort with the transgression of social norms she was attempting and the forceful cultural codes that organized this discomfort. This process can be seen as emblematic of the kind of mental figurations many women were working through during this stormy period of social transition, as they attempted to recast notions of respectable feminine behavior.

Though most of Colette's letters to friends and colleagues were quite brief, they often contained some mention of her work during the day on which she was writing. In letters to Wague in the fall of 1908, she wrote: "All I ask this winter is to work . . . I'm dog-tired," "Today we had a dress-rehearsal for five and a half hours straight."[13] Even when on vacation, Colette took time to re-port on her work habits. While renovating her beach house in Brittany one summer, she breathlessly wrote to a friend: "I'm dropping you a line, between urgent, manual tasks."[14] In 1913, she wrote to Georges Wague: "I plan to re-lax for eight days, by working on my novel."[15]

Such references often described work (whether literary or theatrical) not simply as a financial exigency, but as a moral imperative. In June 1912, dur-ing a month in which newspaper assignments took her all over France, Co-lette wrote to a friend: "I have worked well these days, against myself and to-ward my preservation."[16] Her fictional characters Renée Néré and Brague, a fictionalized portrait of Georges Wague, seek out short-term assignments to avoid "the idleness which demoralizes out-of-work actors, diminishing their powers and making them go to pieces."[17] Renée admits to being seized by "an active passion, a real need to *work*, a mysterious and undefined need."[18]

Taking up a thick thread in republican pedagogy, which insisted on the importance of practicing a métier, Colette regularly framed her work as a trade, whether writing, performing, or completing household tasks.[19] One journalist marveled at Colette's particular formulation of performance as craft: "A mime proud of her métier and speaking of raising it to the dignity of an art, there is something that is really surprising."[20] Colette's fictional heroine Renée emulates her music-hall colleagues' professionalism, and re-sents that bourgeois acquaintances refer to her as "a woman writer who has turned out badly," rather than as an actress: "a polite refusal . . . to grant me any rank in this career that I have nevertheless chosen."[21]

Colette accentuated the affinity of performance and honest labor in her fiction by likening music-hall performers to other respectable professionals, referring to performers as "government clerks" and "workers in the same fac-tory."[22] In one story, she equates female performers with their sisters in the urban workforce: "They jump on a bus, a tram, the underground, pell-mell with all the other employees—milliners, seamstresses, cashiers, typists—for whom the day's work is over."[23] In this way, Colette depicted the music hall not as a gay retreat from the world of reputable labor, but rather as an ex-treme version of that world. When Renée's upper-class lover Max in *The Vagabond* questions her choice of profession, she answers: "What would you have me do? Sewing, typing, or the street? The music hall, that is the métier for those who have never learned one."[24] With this passage, Colette empha-sizes the narrow options afforded women without professional training in this period—low-income, unskilled jobs or prostitution. By labeling music-hall performance as honorable labor, the author challenged and expanded con-temporary definitions of respectable feminine work.

Unlike some formulations of artistic occupations that focused on creative vocation, Colette regularly avowed that, first and foremost, performance and writing were a means of "earning one's living," as she repeatedly
phrased it. "I am guided," she wrote a fellow author in 1907, "by the insane
ambition to earn my living myself, as much in the theater as in literature."[25] For Colette, "earning one's living" demanded a shrewd financial
ability that countered the common notion of bourgeois women as blissfully
isolated from the marketplace. In one letter to Wague, Colette included a
proposed budget for a show, demonstrating that she was aware of all financial details of her productions, from the cost of sets to copyright fees.[26] She
possessed an acute understanding of her celebrity as a valuable commercial
asset, sometimes managing her own publicity and contract negotiations. In
a letter to Wague in 1909, she described negotiations with two theaters: "If
the Alhambra cannot pay me as much as the Gaîté-Rochechouart, so much
for the Alhambra. It's an outfit which should be able to pay. . . . When I
have a name with proved box-office value, why should I contract myself
never to get more than five louis?"[27]

The characters of Colette's music-hall fiction are also financially shrewd.
German acrobats discuss stock investments during rehearsal, and a veteran
performer is lauded because he earns "whatever he chooses" and wisely in-
vests his money.[28] Having fled the bourgeois idleness of her first marriage,
Renée is transformed by her exposure to such frugal performers: "The music
hall . . . turned me also, despite my astonishment at finding myself reckon-
ing, haggling and bargaining, into a tough but honest little business-
woman."[29] When she is counseled by a friend to accept the financial and social security offered by a wealthy lover, Renée replies incredulously: "You
want me to upset my newly recovered peace, to make me exchange the keen,
invigorating, natural care of earning my own living for a care of a different
kind?"[30] In a fascinating inversion of traditional gender norms, Colette here
characterizes financial self-sufficiency, rather than the care of an upstanding
male suitor, as the "natural" state for a woman.

In paying tribute to the workingwomen of the music hall, Colette contested the bourgeois woman's position as moral paragon of French society.
Renée refers to middle-class women as "yawning housewives in their
camisoles" who "rise late to shorten empty days," and explicitly links her own
physical strength and her "tired and happy muscles" with "a savage defiance"
and "disgust" for the bourgeois milieu where she once "lived and suffered."[31]
Renée would rather be a harem concubine than a bourgeois wife, "a sort of
nurse for a grown-up . . . trembling lest Monsieur's cutlet should be over-
done[!]"[32] Through her protagonist, Colette turns on the republican call to

virtuous wifehood, depicting marriage as a wearying endeavor that reduces women to a moral level somewhere below sexual slaves.

Renée estimates that her paid manual work sets her above not only bourgeois women, but also above bourgeois men like her lover Max. Max judges Renée on the basis of a traditional notion of middle-class female honor (sexual purity and separation from the sphere of production), and hence interprets her music-hall work as disreputable. He is appalled when he learns that Brague and Renée will economize on tour by sharing a suitcase, calling the idea "contemptible and sordid!" Renée concludes that Max's inherited wealth is to blame for his misplaced shock: "Where could he, the spoilt child, have learnt that money, the money one earns, is a respectable, serious thing which one handles with care and speaks about solemnly?"[33] Though an affluent landowner, Max does not practice a trade, an idleness Renée finds indecent: "He has no métier. . . . He gives himself entirely to love, day and night, like . . . like a prostitute. . . . This baroque idea that, of the two of us, he is the courtesan, causes me an abrupt gaiety."[34] While contemporaries most naturally might have compared Renée to a courtesan, given her seminude performances and upper-class admirers, Colette gleefully twists this formula in her novel—the distinguished bourgeois becomes an indolent prostitute, and the music-hall dancer his industrious moral superior. The ethical yardstick of this contest is labor. Thus, New Womanhood involved not simply rejecting traditional norms of feminine conduct, but transforming norms using an appropriated language of work and honor.

Though Colette was skeptical about the moralizing benefits of marriage, her fictional music hall is a realm in which domestic tasks are sanctifying activities when performed by productive female workers. Her nomadic performers are more levelheaded homebodies than fun-loving bohemians. While the chorus girls of most popular fiction entertain themselves by seducing wealthy admirers, Colette's dancer Bastienne finds pleasure in domestic tasks: "Her stay-at-home, domesticated little dancer's soul, yearns for no furs." Joyfully engaging in her "favorite chore," hand washing her infant daughter's clothes, Bastienne reflects that life "means dancing in the first place, then working, in the humble and domestic sense of the word given it by a race of thrifty females."[35] Bastienne, an unwed stage performer with lovers, conforms to republican dicta on work and domestic order while subverting standards of acceptable feminine behavior. Such an attention to domestic orderliness in Colette's fiction and life was, in part, a way for the author to mitigate social unease about female wage labor.[36]

Because of its connections to orderly métier, Colette found moral regeneration in music-hall work. In 1909, she described her troupe's delight upon arriving at a well-kept theater in Marseille: "Once again, the atmosphere of the music hall has restored to me a light, docile, innocent soul, the tranquil soul of a novice, of a regimented female factory worker."[37] She has the fictional Renée similarly declare that her music-hall career has been a "moral convalescence" that has left her with a "purified" heart. She has "become an old maid again with no temptations" and her dressing room a "cloister."[38] Work is the agent of this cleansing revitalization.

Contemporaries took note of the startling, new view of the music hall presented by Colette in her fiction and lectures. After hearing her speak at a working-class university, one reviewer noted: "Only in the music hall has the sense of the intangible and the sacred been preserved. To believe Mme Colette Willy, the artists of the music hall have a love of their work and give themselves to it entirely. They have healthy bodies and intact souls."[39] Thus, some understood that Colette's vision of the music hall as a realm of honest labor was connected to a sacral, if secular, notion of moral soundness. During a 1924 lecture on the music hall, Colette told the audience that while for them "these memories are nothing, a little image in passing," for her, they "took on the force of a spiritual state."[40]

While Colette offers *The Vagabond* as homage to the moralizing and liberating power of labor, she was also mindful of its bleaker aspects. Her heroine Renée reflects during a bout of fatigue on tour:

> When I was small they said to me: "Effort brings its own reward," and so, whenever I had tried specially hard, I used to expect a mysterious, overwhelming recompense, a sort of grace to which I should have surrendered myself. I am still expecting it.[41]

While Colette maintained a comparable attachment to childhood exhortations to work, she recognized the potential hollowness of such lessons for exhausted working men and women. Throughout her music-hall fiction, honorable stage work is accompanied by hunger, fatigue, and social alienation. More than once she describes music-hall performers as "exiles" who have chosen a life of dignified artistic expression and labor at the price of tremendous hardship. Renée notes this aspect of the touring life: "We grow thin with weariness. . . . We change music halls . . . with the indifference of soldiers on maneuvers."[42] Emphasizing the dark corollary of the republic's idealized call to manual labor, such descriptions also underscored the challenges that awaited women who sought to construct a life outside the bounds of respectable femininity through work.

Though Colette never completed a day of manual wage labor during her long life, she also spoke a language of honorable métier that enabled her to efface the differences between the labor of seamstresses and factory workers and her professional experiences. To some degree, she seems to have exploited the figure of the working-class woman for her own psychological (and commercial) advantage. While the language of triumphal labor offered some middle-class women an effective means of reimagining feminine norms, it also obscured the jagged inequities of a modernizing capitalist economy.

While her fictional doppelganger Renée chooses autonomy over marriage at the end of *The Vagabond*, soon after the publication of the novel Colette turned from the path she laid out for her protagonist. In 1910, she began a tumultuous affair with Henry de Jouvenel, a wealthy newspaper editor. Less than a year after the two married in 1912, Colette wrote to her friend Léon Hamel:

> Since you left, my life has been made up of hard work and facile vanities. . . . Luncheon with the President and his wife at Brive (Madame Poincaré is charming and wants a blue cat). Culinary expositions, a dinner, with myself as hostess, for eighty-seven guests. . . . And during all this time I have been trying to find a synonym for *avid*. . . . At present I am sociable, attentive to conversation, very nice, and futile. . . . The day before I finished *L'entrave* [*The Shackle*]. . . . I worked six hours. The last day, eleven hours.[43]

Colette, the bohemian femme nouvelle, now seems to correspond to a feminine ideal of ornamental idleness and frivolity that she normally eschewed. Though still attentive to work, she is tellingly unable to find a particular word, as if her productivity has been stunted by her new conjugal role.

The novel Colette refers to in the letter above, *The Shackle*, was a sequel to *The Vagabond*, and, according to most critics, a fictionalized account of her relationship with Jouvenel. The conclusion of this novel finds Renée Néré submitting to the charms of a seductive womanizer named Jean, and choosing a domestic life over métier. Decades later, Colette noted her dissatisfaction with this ending, "the inadequate corridor through which I desired my diminished heroes to pass . . . the fine but empty tone of an ending in which they do not believe."[44] The difficulty Colette experienced in writing *The Shackle* points to the fierce tensions inherent in the kind of social reinvention she was attempting. If the secular moral system had provided a powerful rhetorical framework to shore up new public identities for women, it also failed to provide a satisfying synthesis of its contradictory maxims. Never wholly embracing the role of the sequestered bourgeois wife, Colette still had the greater part of her literary career ahead of her when she and Jouvenel divorced in 1925. Her life and work in the decades that followed reflected the same attraction to the moral rewards of labor and domestic order.

In achieving the transition from domestic angels to modern New Women, Frenchwomen like Colette called on the mental resources supplied to them by the secular moral system of the new republic. What endeared Colette to a wide French public over time was, perhaps in part, her imaginative attempt to reconcile the tangled threads of this powerful, if flawed, moral system. Her readers intuitively agreed with her fictional celebrations of exhausted music-hall showgirls as the moral superiors of bourgeois housewives because they too were immersed in a moral structure that associated honor with labor. This affinity between Colette and her reading public offers one example of the way in which the boundaries of respectable femininity could be redrawn in this period by political and cultural discourses that unwittingly challenged traditional assumptions about the relationship between gender and work.

Notes

A version of this chapter appeared as "Earning Her Bread: Métier, Order, and Female Honor in Colette's Music Hall, 1906–1913," *French Historical Studies* (Summer 2005): 497–530. All translations are the author's unless otherwise noted.

1. Musidora, "Les beaux visages de France: Colette," lecture ca. 1945–1951, reprinted in Patrick Cazals, *Musidora: La dixième muse* (Paris: Henri Veyrier, 1978), 182–83.

2. Robert Gildea, *France, 1870–1914* (New York: Longman, 1996), 27.

3. Patricia O'Hara points out the lack of affinity between female music-hall performers and "New Women" in Victorian England. "'The Woman of To-Day': The *Fin de Siècle* Women of *The Music Hall and Theatre Review*," *Victorian Periodicals Review* 30, no. 2 (1997): 141–56.

4. This methodological approach to cultural history began with Lucien Febvre. See *The Problem of Unbelief in the Sixteenth Century: The Religion of Rabelais* (Cambridge, MA: Harvard University Press, 1982).

5. Jo Burr Margadant, *The New Biography: Performing Femininity in Nineteenth-Century France* (Berkeley: University of California Press, 2000).

6. See Judith Thurman, *Secrets of the Flesh: A Life of Colette* (New York: Ballantine Books, 1999).

7. For details of these debates see the Archives Départémentales de l'Yonne, 46 T 13.

8. Auguste Burdeau, *Instruction morale à l'école: Devoir et la Patrie* (Paris: Picard-Beinheim, 1884), 88–89.

9. Caumont, *Lectures courantes des écoliers français* (Paris: Ch. Delagrave, 1884), 12–13.

10. Clarisse Juranville, *Premiers sujets de style avec sommaires raisonnés* (Paris: Larousse et Boyer, 1869), 26–28.

11. Henri Giraud, "Mme Colette Willy parle de l'Envers du Music-Hall," *Le Petit Niçois*, 10 February 1913.

12. For a similar approach to French artists, see Jerrold Seigel, *Bohemian Paris: Culture, Politics, and the Boundaries of Bourgeois Life, 1830–1930* (Baltimore, MD: Johns Hopkins University Press, 1999).

13. Letters to Georges Wague, 1 September and 14 November 1908, in *Letters from Colette*, trans. Robert Phelps (New York: Farrar, Straus and Giroux, 1980), 12.

14. Letter to Léon Hamel, 15 July 1914, in *Lettres de la vagabonde*, ed. Claude Pichois (Paris: Flammarion, 1961), 104.

15. Letter to Georges Wague, January 1913, in *Lettres de la vagabonde*, 87.

16. Letter to Léon Hamel, 26 June 1912, in *Lettres de la vagabonde*, 68.

17. Colette, *The Vagabond*, trans. Enid McLeod (London: Secker and Warburg, 1954), 100–101.

18. Colette, *The Vagabond*, 91.

19. I am indebted to Debora Silverman's "Pilgrim's Progress and Vincent van Gogh's Métier," in *Van Gogh in England: Portrait of the Artist as a Young Man* (London: Barbican Art Gallery, 1992).

20. Joseph Gravier, "Un entretien avec Colette Willy: Académicienne sans fauteil," *La Presse Sportive et Littéraire* (Lyon), 24 December 1910.

21. Colette, *La vagabonde* (Paris: A. Michel, 1926), 17.

22. Colette, *The Vagabond*, 185; "The Hard Worker" (1913), in *The Collected Stories of Colette*, trans. Anne-Marie Callimachi (New York: Farrar, Straus and Giroux, 1983), 129.

23. Colette, "The Strike, Oh, Lord, the Strike!" in *Collected Stories*, 146.

24. Colette, *La vagabonde*, 144.

25. Letter from Colette presumably to Claude Farrère, ca. 1907, in *Sido: Lettres à sa fille—précédé de lettres inédites de Colette* (Paris: Des Femmes, 1984).

26. Letter to Georges Wague, 1908 or 1909, #36–37, BNF NAF 18708, vol. 3.

27. Letter to Georges Wague, 29 April 1909, in *Letters from Colette*, 15.

28. Colette, *The Vagabond*, 96, 184.

29. Colette, *The Vagabond*, 27–28.

30. Colette, *The Vagabond*, 86.

31. Colette, *The Vagabond*, 172, 32.

32. Colette, *The Vagabond*, 149, 146–47.

33. Colette, *The Vagabond*, 167.

34. Colette, *La vagabonde*, 142.

35. Colette, "Bastienne's Child," in *Collected Stories*, 151.

36. O'Hara notes a similar rhetorical effort by those who wrote about English music-hall actresses. See "'The Woman of To-Day.'"

37. Colette Willy, "Marseille," *La Vie Parisienne*, 10 July 1909.

38. Colette, *The Vagabond*, 157, 82, 62.

39. Georges Martin, "Une interview de Colette Willy," *La Renaissance Contemporaine*, 10 January 1913.

40. Colette, "Des deux côtés de la rampe," 9 February 1924.

41. Colette, *The Vagabond*, 120–21.

42. Colette, *The Vagabond*, 204.

43. Letter to Léon Hamel, 16 September 1913, in *Letters from Colette*, 37–38.

44. Colette, *The Evening Star: Recollections*, trans. David Le Vay (London: Bobbs-Merrill, 1973) 137.

Suggested Readings

Berlanstein, Lenard. *Daughters of Eve: A Cultural History of French Theater Women from the Old Regime to the Fin de Siècle*. Cambridge: Cambridge University Press, 2001.

Bock, Gisela, and Allison Brown. *Women in European History*. Malden, MA: Blackwell, 2001.

Bridenthal, Renate, and Susan Mosher Stuard. *Becoming Visible: Women in European History*. Boston: Houghton Mifflin, 1998.

Clark, Linda. *Schooling the Daughters of Marianne: Textbooks and the Socialization of Girls in Modern French Primary Schools*. Albany, NY: State University of New York Press, 1984.

Colette. *The Collected Stories of Colette*. Translated by Anne-Marie Callimachi. New York: Farrar, Straus and Giroux, 1983.

Colette. *The Complete Claudine*. New York: Farrar, Straus and Giroux, 1976.

Collette. *The Vagabond*. Translated by Enid McLeod. New York: Farrar, Straus and Giroux, 2001.

Ehrenpreis, David. "Cyclists and Amazons: Representing the New Woman in Wilhelmine Germany." *Women's Art Journal* 20, no. 1 (Spring–Summer, 1999): 25–31.

Gardner, Vivien, and Susan Rutherford, eds. *The New Woman and Her Sisters: Feminism and Theater, 1850–1914*. Ann Arbor: University of Michigan Press, 1992.

Margadant, Jo Burr, ed. *The New Biography: Performing Femininity in Nineteenth-Century France*. Berkeley: University of California Press, 2000.

Richardson, Angelique, and Chris Willis, eds. *The New Woman in Fiction and in Fact: Fin-de-Siècle Feminisms*. London: Palgrave, 2001.

Roberts, Mary Louise. *Disruptive Acts: The New Woman in Fin-de-Siècle France*. Chicago: University of Chicago Press, 2002.

Silverman, Debora. "The 'New Woman,' Feminism, and the Decorative Arts in Fin-de-Siècle France." In *Eroticism and the Body Politic*, edited by Lynn Hunt, 144–63. Baltimore: Johns Hopkins University Press, 1991.

Smith, Bonnie. *Changing Lives: Women in European History Since 1700*. Lexington, MA: D. C. Heath, 1989.

Thurman, Judith. *Secrets of the Flesh: A Life of Colette*. New York: Alfred A. Knopf, 1999.

~

CHAPTER SEVEN

"All Quiet" on the Don and the Western Front

Mikhail Sholokhov and Erich Maria Remarque Respond to World War I

KAREN PETRONE

The 1914 start of World War I, or the Great War as it is commonly referred to in Europe, signaled the true beginning of the twentieth century, a century marked by bloody, even genocidal, conflict. The culmination of geopolitical and cultural tensions that had been decades if not a century in the making, the Great War was truly a global war. While its primary participants were the major powers of Europe (Germany, Austria-Hungary, and the Ottoman Empire comprising the Triple Alliance, and Great Britain, France, and Russia making up the Triple Entente), its reach extended into the Middle East and beyond because of imperial ambitions and the European powers' use of colonial troops from the South Pacific, India, North America, and Africa. The United States' entry in 1917 would further globalize the reach of the conflict.

The assassinations of Austro-Hungarian Archduke Franz Ferdinand and his wife at the hands of Serbian nationalist Gavrilo Princip in Sarajevo were merely the spark that lit a powder keg fed by the alliance system, an international arms race, and concern about preserving and defending national honor. Millions of soldiers and civilians were the victims of the carnage that ensued. After four years of devastating trench warfare, nearly an entire generation of young men would be dead or wounded physically or mentally. While the western front has received the lion's share of historical attention, the eastern front between Germany, Austria-Hungary, and Russia was equally if not more deadly. There the war spawned the Russian revolutions of 1917 and led to the establishment of the Soviet Union. The cataclysm that *swallowed up Europe between 1914 and 1918 led to World War II and the Cold War, and indelibly shaped the rest of the twentieth century and beyond.*

In this chapter, Karen Petrone explores the memory and legacies of the Great War by comparing Germany's and the Soviet Union's most influential postwar novels, Erich Maria Remarque's All Quiet on the Western Front *and Mikhail Sholokhov's* Quiet Flows the Don. *She places these works about the nature of the war and its human toll at the center of debates about militarism and pacifism in both countries.*

In 1928 two European novels exploring the tragedy of the soldier at war were published in serial form. One of these is perhaps the most famous of all World War I novels: *All Quiet on the Western Front* (*Im Westen nichts Neues*) written by thirty-one-year-old Erich Maria Remarque, a German who had seen frontline combat in World War I and been wounded.[1] *Quiet Flows the Don* (*Tikhii Don*), perhaps the most influential Soviet novel of its time, is usually considered a novel of the Russian Civil War, but a substantial part of the first two books of the novel describes warfare on the Russo-German front in World War I. The author Mikhail Sholokhov, who was only twenty-three years old at the time of publication, was too young to have fought in World War I himself, but he conducted extensive interviews with veterans in preparation for writing the novel. Sholokhov also experienced warfare firsthand when he joined the revolutionary side in the Russian Civil War (1918–1920) as a teenager and fought for the Bolshevik "Reds" against the "White" armies seeking to restore the overthrown Russian monarchy.

Each of the novels follows the fate of a young man as he experiences the day-to-day events of war, some mundane and some too horrifying for words to adequately describe. Remarque's hero Paul Bäumer and Sholokhov's protagonist Grigorii Melekhov negotiate the trials of warfare and trace the impact of events on their own lives and senses of self. While Bäumer volunteers along with three friends at the beginning of the war, Melekhov joins the cavalry shortly before the war in fulfillment of his four years of obligatory military service. Though these two youths are fictional, the novels were written in a realistic, even documentary, style and have been widely understood by readers and critics to have conveyed the "truth" of war to their readers.[2] Sholokhov not only conducted extensive historical research, but he also included actual historical figures in the novel. The fictional biographies of Bäumer and Melekhov allow modern readers two different kinds of insight into the history of World War I. The novels were both written to reveal the nature of violence during World War I and its effect on the soldiers who on a daily basis were required both to face death and to kill the enemy. Second, the two novels, appearing within months of each other in 1928 and gaining instant popularity, also shed light on Europe's preoccupation with the World War I experience in the late 1920s, and show how the memory of World War I became a key factor in debates on pacifism and militarism in the late 1920s.

The Russian and German empires both collapsed under the weight of World War I, as did the Austro-Hungarian and Ottoman empires. For Russia, the war began reasonably well with a successful advance into German territory in East Prussia and early patriotic fervor among the population. This advance was stopped in late August 1914 by the humiliating defeat of the Russians at the Battle of Tannenberg. Unfortunately for the tsarist empire, the Russian monarchy was incapable of providing effective overall strategic leadership for the army; it was also unable to adequately supply the army in the critical first year of the war, when up to a quarter of the troops were sent to the front unarmed and instructed to pick up weapons from the dead.[3] By the late summer of 1915, the Russian army was in retreat and the empire's western territories of Poland and Lithuania were under German occupation. Although by spring 1916 conditions in the Russian army had improved enough for the Russians to mount a major offensive that was temporarily successful, the economic and political strains of fighting the war toppled Tsar Nicholas II in March 1917. Six months later, the world's first Communist government came to power in the Bolshevik October Revolution. The Russian war effort, while calamitous for Russia, was also damaging to Germany. The German Empire could not sustain war on two fronts and in November 1918 revolution broke out. The defeated German emperor Kaiser Wilhelm II abdicated in November 1918. The Nazis would later accuse the revolutionary home front of stabbing the German army in the back and undermining the tremendous sacrifices that the German army had made.

Remarque and Sholokhov wrote their novels under substantially different conditions. The Weimar Republic in Germany granted freedom of expression and Remarque's novel did not undergo censorship before it was first published. It sold more than a million copies in the first year and was made into a critically acclaimed American film in 1930. After members of the Nazi Party provoked violence at movie theaters, the film was banned in Germany. When the Nazis came to power in 1933, *All Quiet on the Western Front* was among the first books that Nazi Enlightenment and Propaganda Minister Joseph Goebbels publicly burned for its "literary betrayal of the soldiers of the First World War."[4] For in the novel, the ultimate fate of Remarque's fictional soldier is a tragic and ironic one. Having survived the vicissitudes of war for several years, Bäumer is killed in October 1918, only a few weeks before the armistice "on a day that was so quiet and still on the whole front that the army report confined itself to the single sentence: All quiet on the Western Front." When he dies, "his face had an expression of calm, as though almost glad the end had come."[5] Bäumer is isolated from everyone around him, and there is no positive meaning to be taken from his suffering.

Sholokhov, on the other hand, had to submit to the strictures of Soviet censorship that became even more severe in the late 1920s when Joseph Stalin consolidated his power. While Soviet censors permitted the release of the first two parts of the novel set in the years 1912 to early 1918, publication of the third part was halted because of Soviet critics' dissatisfaction with the representations of the two sides in the Civil War. Books I and II, however, were an immediate popular success and were reprinted in book form in five large editions of over 100,000 copies each between 1929 and 1931. The novel was also made into a film in 1931.[6]

Quiet Flows the Don highlights the wartime activities of the Cossacks of the Don region. The Cossacks, a warrior caste of mixed ethnic background, gained land and privileges from the Russian tsars in the seventeenth and eighteenth centuries in exchange for their military service. Grigorii Melekhov is a brave Cossack warrior who wavers between devoted service to the tsar and revolutionary ideas. In the World War I section of the novel, he vacillates between revulsion at the violence he has perpetrated and a full commitment to his duty as a Cossack warrior to pitilessly kill the enemy. Melekhov begins the Civil War on the side of the Reds, but he returns home and joins the Whites after he witnesses the Red leader Podtyolkov massacring unarmed White officer POWs. Many readers of the first two parts of the novel expected Melekhov to switch sides again and become a committed revolutionary and a Soviet hero.[7] When the final installment of the novel finally cleared censorship in 1940, it turned out that they were wrong. Melekhov, tragically, cannot reconcile himself to the Soviet regime, and in the last scene of the novel, he returns home to his children even though he knows this means certain arrest and execution by the Soviet government. Both fictional heroes illustrate how war destroyed the lives of European men.

All Quiet on the Western Front is generally recognized as one of the most significant pacifist novels that emerged from World War I. Yet the novel also emphasizes the powerful influence of the front experience on German soldiers. Historian George Mosse points out that Remarque's novel, although antiwar, celebrates the virtues of military masculinity; even a left-wing journal (*Die Weltbuhne*) described the book as "pacifist war propaganda."[8] In a similar vein, literary critic Wolfgang Natter argues that Remarque, like Ernst Junger and other German nationalist writers, "radiates generational conflict, a sense of alienation between front and *Heimat* [homefront], and a distrust of the leadership behind the front, all the while extolling the virtues of 'comradeship.'[9] The novel, while antiwar, defines the soldier at the front as the quintessentially masculine hero, and as superior to civilians. It glorifies the comradeship of war while rejecting the war itself.

The image of the soldier in *Quiet Flows the Don* is also inextricably linked to notions of wartime honor, the definition of appropriate targets of wartime violence, and the obligation of a soldier to kill. The novel explores traditions of honor connected to the Cossack ethos and the codes of the tsarist officer corps and shows how the revolution modified these precepts. By illustrating the horrifying results of wartime violence, the novel reveals the uneasy construction of the Soviet warrior ethos. On the one hand, the Soviet government rejected the "imperialist" war that senselessly forced German and Russian proletarian brothers to kill one another. Yet the Soviet government and its leaders disdained pacifism as well; they embraced the use of violence and advocated the merciless destruction of class enemies. The face of war depicted in Sholokhov's novel is thus a multivalent one, sharing attributes with tsarist and European heroic and patriotic literatures that glorify war and honor heroic sacrifices, with European antiwar literature that questions the morality of war, and with a native Russian tradition of pacifism.

Quiet Flows the Don in Dialogue with Tsarist War Propaganda

Sholokhov's approach to wartime heroism was, in part, a response to tsarist discourse of World War I. In mid-August 1914, just days after the war began, the Russian press glorified the first individual Russian hero of the war. In a decidedly uneven skirmish with German cavalry on 12 August 1914 (twenty-seven Germans against four Cossacks), the Russian Cossack Koz'ma Kriuchkov single-handedly killed eleven Germans in battle while suffering no fewer than sixteen wounds. One popular print explained that Kriuchkov upheld the "military glory of the Russian Cossacks," when "the Germans struck with lances and first he repulsed them with his rifle, when his rifle gave out, then he began to fell them with his saber, and then he wrested a lance from a German and put it to use."[10] Kriuchkov's fame spread far and wide "in circus and variety shows, in the movies, and particularly on postcards and *lubki* (popular prints)" that depicted him skewering "German soldiers like kebab on his lance."[11] Kriuchkov was an icon of Russian national masculinity and the first and most potent emblem of the death-dealing capacity of a Russian military that fought bravely and showed no mercy to enemies. The brutal realities of 1914–1915 weakened this enthusiastic celebration of war and it gave way to a more sober and reflective discourse on the sacrifices of war.[12] Though short lived, the militaristic discourse of the early war had a profound impact on later memory of the war, as Soviet ideologues found that tsarist bravado and heroes like Kriuchkov made an easy target for Soviet propaganda.

Soviet references to Kriuchkov were uniformly negative and sought to debunk the tsarist fantasy of Germans skewered on Kriuchkov's lance. Sholokhov focused on the origins of the myth to contest the tsarist narrative of Kriuchkov's superhuman achievements and redefine the nature of heroism in World War I. However, Sholokhov's treatment of Kriuchkov contains ambiguities that may have undermined these goals.

Sholokhov uses details from his interviews with Mikhail Ivankov, one of the other three Cossacks involved in the famed skirmish, to challenge Kriuchkov's status as hero.[13] Sholokhov shows Kriuchkov to be a sadistic noncommissioned officer (like Remarque's Himmelstoss) who "had just received his corporal's stripes" and who enjoys whipping the new recruits with his belt buckle "for every trifling offense."[14] Rather than exemplifying heroism, Kriuchkov illustrates the arbitrary authority of tsarist functionaries who brutally discipline the bodies of rank-and-file soldiers. Sholokhov further contends that because Kriuchkov is the "squadron commander's favorite" he receives the Cross of St. George after his exploit while his comrades "were left in the shade." Then, "the hero was transferred to divisional headquarters, where he loafed till the end of the war."[15] Sholokhov depicts Kriuchkov as a fraud who has betrayed notions of wartime camaraderie by allowing himself to be elevated above his comrades.

Sholokhov's description of the skirmish emphasizes that Kriuchkov does not accomplish his exploit single-handedly. When four Cossacks are sent out to intercept a German patrol, the Germans surround the Cossack Ivankov and the others race to assist him. Describing how Kriuchkov saves Ivankov's life, Sholokhov echoes jingoistic tsarist rhetoric, showing how Kriuchkov kills a German with his lance before the German can draw his carbine to shoot Ivankov. Then, "about eight dragoons surrounded Kriuchkov, trying to capture him alive. But he reared his horse and, swinging his body from the waist, fought them off with his sabre. When it was knocked out of his hand, he snatched a lance from the nearest German and wielded it as if at exercises."[16] Sholokhov concedes that Kriuchkov is a brave warrior who fights vigorously against the Germans. His tone then abruptly changes as he describes how the combatants are "brutalized by fear" as they "stabbed and hacked at anything they saw." Both sides panic and take flight after the Cossack Astakhov shoots the German commanding officer.[17]

In this episode, Sholokhov emphasizes the dehumanizing influence of war; the narrator declares that the soldiers are "overcome by animal fear, had charged and battered one another, striking blindly and maiming themselves and their horses." This description of the transformation of men into animals is similar to Paul Bäumer's narration of battle at close quarters in *All Quiet on the Western Front*. Bäumer says, "We have become wild beasts . . . we can destroy and kill, to save ourselves, to save ourselves and to be revenged . . . crouching like cats we run on, overwhelmed by this wave that bears us along, that fills us with ferocity, turns us into thugs, into murderers, into God only knows what devils."[18] Both novels depict their protagonists as losing the human capacity of moral judgment in the chaos of battle. Sholokhov's narrator claims this directly when he states that after the skirmish both sides have "ridden away morally crippled."[19]

On the one hand, Sholokhov's outright rejection of frenzied killing in battle could be read as pacifist. The similarity to Remarque shows this scene's kinship to European pacifist writing. One contemporary Soviet reviewer criticized this particular passage because Sholokhov had stooped to "mechanical imitation" of the famous Russian writer Leo Tolstoy. The critic claimed that Sholokhov had adopted Tolstoy's style by casting moral judgments, and that he had also embraced Tolstoy's ideology, a component of which was the rejection of violence in any form.[20] Thus the pacifist moments in Sholokhov's novel could be related to the contemporary European context as well as Russian literary traditions.

Yet other aspects of Sholokhov's treatment of Kriuchkov contradict these pacifist elements. Kriuchkov wielding his lance "as if at exercises" and his quick intervention to save Ivankov's life demonstrate his composure. This description conflicts with the narrator's later assertion that animal fear has motivated the battle. Sholokhov thus presents multiple and contradictory ideas about the morality of war. Just as Remarque extols the romance of comradeship as he criticizes war, Sholokhov reveals the war's injustices as he demonstrates the continuing appeal of tsarist rhetoric glorifying battle.

Grigorii Melekhov, Sholokhov's protagonist, wins the Cross of St. George under very different circumstances from Kriuchkov. Severely wounded in a battle with Hungarian hussars, Melekhov regains consciousness on the battlefield and is returning to his unit when he encounters a wounded officer: "Grigory helped the officer to his feet and they walked on together. But with every step the wounded officer leaned more heavily on Grigory's arm. As they climbed out of a hollow he seized Grigory's sleeve and said through chattering teeth, 'Leave me here, Cossack. I'm wounded in the stomach.'"

Melekhov disobeys this order. After the officer faints, "Grigory carried him, falling, pulling himself up and falling again. Twice he abandoned his burden, only to go back and pick it up, and then struggle on, as if in a waking dream."[21] Melekhov doggedly pushes himself to the limits of his strength in order to save another, becoming a war hero who does not shed blood to earn his medal. A similar scene showing Bäumer's heroism in *All Quiet on the Western Front* is based on Remarque's real-life experience of carrying a wounded friend on his shoulders to a dressing station while under fire.[22] However, unlike Melekhov's act, which earns Melekov recognition for saving a life, Bäumer's efforts are futile: "'You might have spared yourself that,' says an orderly. I looked at him without comprehending. He points to Kat. 'He is stone dead.'"[23] In Remarque's ironic narrative, even the noblest expressions of bravery and comradeship are powerless against the devastation of war.

In contrast, Melekhov's winning the Cross of St. George suggests that the war could be a breeding ground for heroism as the true hero mitigates the effects of the violence around him. Yet Sholokhov depicts wartime honors as a double-edged sword; Melekhov's reward for bravery and human decency ultimately leads him away from the revolutionary rejection of the war and toward the perpetration of more violence. Receiving the Cross of St. George renews Melekhov's willingness to perform his duties as a Cossack warrior. Sholokhov depicts tsarist military honors in ambiguous ways, revealing them as being at times unjust and at other times well deserved, at times repulsive and at other times seductive.

After consciously debunking Kriuchkov's superhuman ability to kill Germans, Sholokov transforms Melekhov into the model Cossack, endowing him with mythic strength to save life and extraordinary devotion to authority. While harshly criticizing the bloodthirsty celebration of the unworthy Kriuchkov, Sholokhov foregrounds the existence of heroism, loyalty, devotion, and cross-rank solidarity in the tsarist army. Sholokhov's depiction of war makes the class-blind Melekhov and other aspects of the tsarist military appealing. Both Remarque and Sholokhov evoke the romance of certain elements of war even as they reveal its horrors.

The Act of Killing

World War I literature often highlighted the anguished personal memories of soldiers provoked into killing because of the madness of war. Sholokhov's depiction of World War I also includes such themes as the loss of innocence, the horror of killing, and the remorse of the killer. Sholokhov's work is, however, unusual in the Soviet context, being one of very few early Soviet works that devotes serious attention to the moral costs of war and soldiers' guilt after killing the enemy.

Melekhov's initiation as a killer was one of the first scenes that Sholokhov wrote. In an early draft, Sholokhov's protagonist "saw the enemy soldier through a wood eating blackberries, and shot him while he was engaged in this innocent activity."[24] In the published version, Melekhov's murderous acts occur in the context of a battle. His reaction to his first kills shapes his wartime moral philosophy.

In his first cavalry battle, Melekhov kills an Austrian with a lance blow "so powerful that the lance went right through him, burying half its length in his body. Grigory was unable to withdraw. He felt the convulsions of the falling body coming up the shaft."[25] Melekhov thus is trapped in a desperate coupling with his dying victim. Not sated by his first kill, Melekhov becomes "inflamed by the madness that was going on all around him" and next slaughters an unarmed man. "Their eyes met. The Austrian's were flooded with the horror of death. . . . With half-closed eyes, Grigory swung his sabre. The long, swinging stroke split the skull."[26] Horrified by his action, Grigorii dismounts in confusion and stares at the man he has killed. The dead Austrian is "holding out a dirty brown palm, as if for alms. Grigory looked into his face. It seemed to him small, almost childlike, despite the drooping moustache and the stern twisted mouth, tortured by recent suffering or perhaps by the joyless life it had known before."[27] Grigorii honestly and directly confronts his begging, childlike victim in an attempt to come to terms with his own violent actions.

Grigorii is transformed by these experiences of killing. After he sheds blood, he has "a nagging inward pain" and is disturbed by nightmares in which he relives these episodes:

> Often on the march and while resting, asleep or dozing, he dreamed of the Austrian he had cut down by the iron railing. Time and again he relived that first encounter, and even in his sleep, pursued by memories, he felt the convulsion that the lance had transmitted to his right hand; when he awoke, he would try to banish the dream by pressing his eyes until they hurt.[28]

When his brother arrives at the front, Grigorii confesses his distress: "My conscience is killing me. At Lesznjow I stuck my lance right through a man. That was in battle. It was the only thing to do. But why did I cut down that other one?"[29] Despite his anguish and misgivings, Melekhov gives his utmost effort to every battle and does not avoid fighting. Although he hates the war, his duty as a Don Cossack overrides his personal disillusionment. Thus,

Sholokhov defines Melekhov as a warrior hero who continues to follow orders and kill armed men on the battlefield.

Melekhov gives voice to the anguish of the warrior with blood on his hands, revealing the inner thoughts of a guilty soldier who reluctantly continues to do his duty. Melekhov's guilt prompts him to define the just warrior as one who kills the enemy in battle but protects the lives of unarmed prisoners and civilians. He defines acceptable wartime violence in a way that corresponds to the ethos of the tsarist and European officer corps.[30] Melekhov's attitude also reflects the Cossack warrior ideal, if not actual Cossack practice.[31]

Melekhov's acknowledged trauma at perpetrating gratuitous violence shows that he believes in an honor code, even though he fails to live up to it in his first battle. In Melekhov's unit, however, there is a Cossack named Alexei Uriupin who glories in killing both the armed and the unarmed. When Melekhov is heartsick with guilt, Uriupin mocks him for having a "sniveling" soul.[32] Uriupin tells Grigorii, "Cut a man down boldly. He's soft as dough, a man is. . . . Don't think about what it's all for. You're a Cossack. It's your duty to cut people down without question. It's sacred work to kill a man in battle. God pardons one of your sins for every man you kill, just the same as for a snake."[33] Uriupin's brutality, his misanthropy, and his articulation of the idea that killing is God's work all stand in contrast to Melekhov's belief that the only just killing is that of an armed enemy. Melekhov, however, expresses anguish at having killed not only the unarmed Austrian, but also the armed man whom he kills in battle. Melekhov is tormented by a killing that is "just" according to Russian Orthodox and Cossack codes; he is repelled by the act of killing itself.

Melekhov also shows distress because he is repeatedly unsuccessful at intervening when injustice is being committed against unarmed civilians and prisoners of war. Melekhov's notions of honor and his defense of the weak extend even beyond the battlefield. Melekhov is the only Cossack who vainly attempts to stop the gang rape of a Polish housemaid by the other Cossack recruits.[34] He also wants to kill the brutal Cossack Uriupin to revenge a young Austrian prisoner of war whom Uriupin has shot in cold blood. Grigorii attempts to shoot Uriupin but misses. Grigorii threatens to try again, but Uriupin sneers, "Bullshit! You won't kill me," and he is right. Grigorii does not make a second attempt, thus revealing his hatred of the act of killing.[35]

As the war continues, Melekhov loses these scruples. Sholokhov writes: "At last the pain of human compassion that had tortured him in the first days of the war seemed to have gone forever . . . Grigory's heart had become impervious to pity." Now Melekhov "knew that when he kissed a child it was hard for him to look into those clear eyes." Melekhov understands that "his row of crosses and his promotion" has come at the cost of his humanity.[36]

The notion of just and unjust killing plays a pivotal role once more in the novel at the crucial moment when Melekhov rejects the Bolsheviks after witnessing them massacre unarmed White officers. Melekhov's notion of honor means that any unarmed prisoner, no matter what his class, deserves protection and fair treatment. Melekhov has long suppressed the notion that killing itself is wrong but still defines proper and improper killing in consonance with prerevolutionary codes of honor. Early Soviet critics of Sholokhov's work attacked him because of Melekhov's compassion for all classes: "This sickly-sweet potion of religious-tasting and hypocritical all-forgiveness and of the vilest kind of humanism is clearly an expression of the influence on Sholokhov of inimical class forces."[37] Tsarist codes of military honor clashed with the Soviet dictum to exterminate class enemies.

The negative portrayal of Koz'ma Kriuchkov's "exploit" and Grigorii's agony at having become a killer suggest that certain elements of *Quiet Flows the Don* have an antiwar flavor, and were consistent with other European antiwar views. Any ambiguity about the morality of war is particularly striking in the Soviet context, where the rejection of armed conflict and "humanism" were often ridiculed. To probe the extent to which *Quiet Flows the Don* contains antiwar tropes, it is instructive to compare the scene of Grigorii's first kill with a similar scene in *All Quiet on the Western Front*. Remarque's description of the horror of killing bears a striking similarity to Sholokhov's. Paul Bäumer is lying in a shell hole when a French soldier falls on top of him. He explains, "I do not think at all, I make no decision—I strike madly at home, and feel only how the body suddenly convulses, then becomes limp, and collapses. When I recover myself, my hand is sticky and wet."[38] Sholokhov and Remarque give explicitly erotic undertones to killing at close range. They both focus on the frenzied passion of the moment of killing and the victims' vulnerability to the warriors' thrusts in an acknowledgment of the protagonists' complete loss of self-control when faced with the danger of combat.

After Bäumer and Melekhov are released from the grips of their passion, both men also carefully examine their victims. Bäumer's victim is still alive and Bäumer tries to alleviate the suffering. After the soldier dies, Bäumer, like Melekhov, describes the face of the individual whose life he has taken and imagines what that life might have been like. However, unlike Melekhov, Bäumer explicitly asks his victim for forgiveness and explains, "Comrade, I did not want to kill you. If you jumped in here again, I would not do it, if you would be sensible too."[39] Bäumer then makes a promise to fight against a future war if he should survive: "I will fight against this, that has struck us both down; from you—taken life and from me—? Life also."[40] Remarque and Sholokhov each describe how war takes life from both the perpetrators and the victims of killing. Melekhov explains to his brother, "I feel like a man who's been not quite killed."[41] Yet despite this realization, Grigorii continues to fight bravely and to kill when necessary. When, however, Melekhov falls to the ground after being seriously wounded in battle, Sholokhov has him think: "'It's all over!' The soothing thought slithered through his mind."[42] In contrast to Bäumer's reaction, Melekhov's remorse does not lead him to reject war or to promise his victims that he will work to achieve pacifism. Both warriors are exactly alike, however, in their acceptance of death as a release from the torments of war.

The scene between Bäumer and the Frenchman is similar to another scene in *Quiet Flows the Don*, where the Russian worker Knave views his German enemy through the lens of class conflict. When he finds an unarmed man in a German dugout, Knave holds him at bayonet point and then, "uttering a strange throaty sound, something between a cough and a sob, he stepped toward the German. . . . 'Run!' German! I've got no grudge against you. I won't shoot.'"[43] Knave shakes the German's hand and then frees him. Both men identify themselves as Social Democrats and the German says, "In the coming class battles we shall be in the same trenches."[44] While Bäumer's promise to the dead Frenchman constructs a universal brotherhood against war, Knave's release of the German worker defines a new war waiting to be fought. On the whole, Sholokhov's novel reflects on the ways in which war destroys the humanity of the warriors, and differentiates between just and unjust behavior in wartime, but few scenes of the novel could actually be called pacifist. In most of its reflective moments, the novel accepts the need for war. By repeatedly raising questions about the human effects of war in the hypermilitarized Soviet context, however, the novel broke new ground in memorializing the pain and trauma of war.

While most Soviet works created a sharp ideological division between the tsarist and Soviet periods, *Quiet Flows the Don* valorized at least some aspects of the World War I experience. Sholokhov incorporated myths of World War I honor and heroism into the fabric of Soviet culture, articulating the notion that valor and honorable behavior in battle were positive masculine traits. The memory of World War I thus introduced a prerevolutionary military ethos and tsarist definitions of military masculinity into Soviet culture.

The cultural milieu of the late 1920s allowed for the creation of a warrior who was sensitive to the stain of blood on his hands and whose identity was transformed by his role as a killer. This acknowledgment of the costs of war was, however, relatively short lived. In the 1930s, depictions of fear and remorse in battle were censored, and in later versions of Sholokhov's novel, Melekhov became an antihero. As censors pressured Sholokhov to paint Grigorii in an increasingly negative light, Sholokhov made Grigorii betray his own code of honor. In revenge for his brother's death in Book III of the novel, Grigorii orders the slaughter of unarmed Red prisoners.[45] Thus, paradoxically, Sholokhov's positive vision of the military honor code remained constant even as both the Reds and the Whites disregarded it.

Sholokhov's detailed depiction of the horrors of war and the striking similarities between his and Remarque's representations of World War I show Sholokhov's kinship with European pacifist writers coming to terms with World War I in the 1920s, even if Sholokhov's antiwar sentiments were muted. Like Remarque, Sholokhov also celebrated concepts of honor reminiscent of traditional military writings. Sholokhov showed sensitivity to the horrible costs of war but only in an ambiguous and fragmentary way did he challenge the necessity of fighting. Soviet memory of World War I thus communicated positive notions of heroism and valor while also acknowledging the tragedy of the warrior.

Remarque's and Sholokhov's works show the complicated nature of European response to World War I. Even the most avowedly pacifistic works revealed the attraction to the life of the soldier-hero, and a work that ostensibly embraced Soviet militarism contained both paeans to prerevolutionary honor and pacifist elements. At the end of the 1920s, European intellectuals remained conflicted about the nature and morality of war.

Notes

I would like to thank Michael David-Fox and the participants of the Harvard-Maryland Workshop on Transnational Histories (May 2003) for their comments on an early draft of this essay. I am also grateful to Choi Chatterjee, Barbara Clements, Kenneth Slepyan, and the volume editors for their thoughtful advice.

1. Hilton Tims, *Erich Maria Remarque: The Last Romantic* (New York: Carroll & Graf, 2003), 18.

2. On the reception of *All Quiet on the Western Front* see Modris Eksteins, *Rites of Spring: The Great War and the Birth of the Modern Age* (New York: Anchor Books, 1990), 285–99.

3. Nicholas V. Riasanovsky and Mark D. Steinberg, *A History of Russia*, 7th ed. (New York: Oxford University Press, 2005), 392.

4. Charles W. Hoffmann, "Erich Maria Remarque," in *Dictionary of Literary Biography*, vol. 56, *German Fiction Writers, 1914–1945*, ed. James Hardin (Detroit: Gale Research Company, 1987), 227.

5. Erich Maria Remarque, *All Quiet on the Western Front*, trans. A. W. Wheen (New York: Ballantine, 1982; original copyright of English translation 1929, 1930 by Little, Brown), 296.

6. Herman Ermolaev, *Mikhail Sholokhov and His Art* (Princeton, NJ: Princeton University Press, 1982), 20–21. The film made substantial changes to the novel and did not receive critical acclaim. See *Tikhii Don: Metod. razrabotki* (Moscow: Souizkino, 1931), 8–10.

7. See I. Mashbits-Verov, "Tikhii Don," *Novyi Mir*, no. 10 (1928): 229.

8. George Mosse, *The Image of Man* (New York: Oxford University Press, 1996), 114.

9. Wolfgang G. Natter, *Literature at War, 1914–1940: Representing the "Time of Greatness" in Germany* (New Haven, CT: Yale University Press, 1999), 71.

10. "Geroiskaia bor'ba kazaka Koz'my Kriuchkova s 11 nemtsami" (Odessa, 1914), Hoover Institution on War, Peace, and Revolution Poster Collection, RU-SU 162.

11. Hubertus F. Jahn, *Patriotic Culture in Russia during World War I* (Ithaca, NY: Cornell University Press, 1995), 24.

12. See Jahn, *Patriotic Culture in Russia*, 62–63; Ben Hellman, *Poets of Hope and Despair: The Russian Symbolists in War and Revolution 1914–1918* (Helsinki: Institute for Russian and East European Studies, 1995), 191.

13. A. B. Murphy, V. P. Butt, and H. Ermolaev, *Sholokhov's Tikhii Don: A Commentary in 2 Volumes* (Birmingham, UK: Birmingham Slavonic Monographs No. 27, University of Birmingham Central Printing Services), 1:59

14. Mikhail Sholokhov, *Quiet Flows the Don*, trans. Robert Daglish, ed. Brian Murphy (New York, Carroll & Graf, 1996), 227. This text is the best version of the novel available in English or in Russian. See Barry P. Scherr and Richard Sheldon, "Westward Flows the Don: The Translation and the Text," *Slavic and East European Journal* 42, no. 1 (Spring 1998): 119. See also Remarque, *All Quiet on the Western Front*, 23–27, 45–50.

15. Sholokhov, *Quiet Flows the Don*, 243. Ermolaev points out that Kriuchkov actually returns to the front and continues fighting. See Ermolaev, *Mikhail Sholokhov and His Art*, 216–22.

16. Sholokhov, *Quiet Flows the Don*, 242.

17. Sholokhov, *Quiet Flows the Don*, 241–42.

18. Remarque, *All Quiet on the Western Front*, 113–14.

19. Sholokhov, *Quiet Flows the Don*, 243.

20. I. Mashbits-Verov, "Tikhii Don," 234.

21. Sholokhov, *Quiet Flows the Don*, 296.

22. Tims, *Erich Maria Remarque*, 17.

23. Remarque, *All Quiet on the Western Front*, 290.

24. Murphy, Butt, and Ermolaev, *Sholokhov's Tikhii Don*, 59.

25. Sholokhov, *Quiet Flows the Don*, 221.

26. Sholokhov, *Quiet Flows the Don*, 221.

27. Sholokhov, *Quiet Flows the Don*, 222.

28. Sholokhov, *Quiet Flows the Don*, 244.

29. Sholokhov, *Quiet Flows the Don*, 247.

30. See Ernst Junger, *The Storm of Steel: From the Diary of a German Storm-Troop Officer on the Western Front* (New York: H. Fertig, 1975); Paul F. Robinson, "'Always with Honour': The Code of the White Russian Officers," *Canadian Slavonic Papers/Revue canadienne des slavistes* 41, no. 2 (June 1999).

31. Judith Kornblatt, *The Cossack Myth in Russian Literature* (Madison: University of Wisconsin Press, 1992), 5.

32. Sholokhov, *Quiet Flows the Don*, 263.

33. Sholokhov, *Quiet Flows the Don*, 263.

34. Sholokhov, *Quiet Flows the Don*, 206–7.

35. Sholokhov, *Quiet Flows the Don*, 267–68.

36. Sholokhov, *Quiet Flows the Don*, 361.

37. D. Maznin, "Kakova ideia–Tikhogo Dona," RAPP 1 (Moscow, 1931), 167, quoted in Richard Hallett, "Soviet Criticism of Tikhiy Don 1928–1940," *Slavonic and East European Review* 46, no. 106 (January 1968): 66.

38. Remarque, *All Quiet on the Western Front*, 216.

39. Remarque, *All Quiet on the Western Front*, 223.

40. Remarque, *All Quiet on the Western Front*, 226.

41. Sholokhov, *Quiet Flows the Don*, 247.

42. Sholokhov, *Quiet Flows the Don*, 271.

43. Sholokhov, *Quiet Flows the Don*, 351.

44. Sholokhov, *Quiet Flows the Don*, 352. This scene of fraternizing with the working-class enemy was removed from the novel between 1941 and 1953. See Murphy, Butt, and Ermolaev, *Sholokhov's Tikhii Don*, 70–72.

45. Sholokhov, *Quiet Flows the Don*, 810; Ermolaev, *Sholokov and His Art*, 96–97.

Suggested Readings

Audoin-Rouzeau, Stéphane, and Annette Becker. *14–18: Understanding the Great War*. New York: Hill and Wang, 2003.

Barker, Christine R., and R. W. Last. *Erich Maria Remarque*. London: Oswald Wolff, 1979.

Berghahn, Volker R., and Martin Kitchen, eds. *Germany in the Age of Total War*. Totawa, NJ: Barnes & Noble, 1981.

Chickering, Roger. *Imperial Germany and the Great War, 1914–1918*. Cambridge: Cambridge University Press, 2004.

Eksteins, Modris. *Rites of Spring*. New York: Anchor Books, 1990.

Ermolaev, Herman. *Sholokhov and His Art*. Princeton, NJ: Princeton University Press, 1982.

Gatrell, Peter. *Russia's First World War: A Social and Economic History*. Harlow, UK: Pearson, 2005.

Fussell, Paul. *The Great War in Modern Memory*. London: Oxford University Press, 1975.

Holquist, Peter. *Making War, Forging Revolution: Russia's Continuum of Crisis, 1914–1921*. Cambridge, MA: Harvard University Press, 2002.

Jahn, Hubertus F. *Patriotic Culture in Russia during World War I*. Ithaca, NY: Cornell University Press, 1995.

Keegan, John. *The First World War*. New York: Vintage, 2000.

Sanborn, Joshua A. *Drafting the Russian Nation: Military Conscription, Total War, and Mass Politics, 1905–1925*. Dekalb: Northern Illinois University Press, 2003.

Stockdale, Melissa. "My Death for the Motherland is Happiness: Women, Patriotism, and Soldiering in Russia's Great War, 1914–1917." *American Historical Review* 109, no. 1 (2004).

Stone, Norman. *The Eastern Front, 1914–1917*. New York: Charles Scribner's Sons, 1975.

Welch, David. *Germany, Propaganda, and Total War, 1914–1918*. New Brunswick, NJ: Rutgers University Press, 2000.

Wildman, Allan K. *The End of the Russian Imperial Army*. Vols. 1 and 2. Princeton, NJ: Princeton University Press 1980, 1987.

Winter, Denis. *Death's Men: Soldiers of the Great War*. New York: Penguin, 1975.

Winter, Jay. *Sites of Memory, Sites of Mourning*. Cambridge: Cambridge University Press, 1998.

CHAPTER EIGHT

~

"Ask the Doctor!"

Peasants and Medical-Sexual Advice in Riazan Province, 1925–1928

STEPHEN P. FRANK

Beleaguered by the Great War, Russia in 1917 experienced a radical set of revolutions whose aftershocks transformed the twentieth-century world. With millions of peasant conscripts dying on the front, and the wartime economy buckling, popular unrest came to a head. In March (February of the Julian calendar used by Russia), crowds of hungry women took to the streets of Petrograd (now known as St. Petersburg) demanding bread. Other protesters soon joined. When Tsar Nicholas II ordered his troops to shoot at the crowds, soldiers instead joined the demonstrators. In the face of the "February Revolution," Nicholas II abdicated, and a provisional government attempted to establish a liberal constitutional democracy.

Revolution continued to spread throughout the country. The Bolsheviks, the radical wing of the Socialist Party, became increasingly powerful. Soviets, or councils of workers and soldiers, competed with the Provisional Government for power. Peasants spontaneously seized estates in the countryside, and soldiers deserted from the front. The Provisional Government enacted some liberal reforms, but it did not address key popular demands: land reform and an end to Russian involvement in the war. With Bolshevik leader Vladimir Ilyich Lenin's popular slogan, "Peace, Land, and Bread," armed workers and soldiers toppled the Provisional Government on the night of November 9 (October 25) in what became known as the October Revolution. Bolsheviks were now in power and began the process of consolidating communism in Russia. The country fell into a civil war that lasted until 1920, in which the Bolshevik Red Army fought against the anti-Bolshevik White armies and military forces sent by Britain, the United States, France, and other anticommunist nations. The grassroots, self-governing style of the soviets gave way to a centralized, autocratic party that saw itself as the "vanguard," a Leninist idea that stressed the role of a revolutionary elite to lead the people toward class consciousness and communism.

After the Civil War, the Bolsheviks embarked on the task of radically restructuring Russian society in order to create new, enlightened Soviet men and women. Their goal was not just to revolutionize the Russian economy, but also to transform traditional views of ordinary citizens on such topics as science, technology, family, gender, and sex. In this chapter, Stephen Frank analyzes one such effort to educate and uplift peasant societies in the 1920s. The bulk of Russia in this period remained agrarian with masses of impoverished peasants. Focusing on the time of the New Economic Policy (a period when Bolsheviks allowed peasants some autonomy and private ownership), Frank discusses Dr. V. N. Voskresenskii and his efforts to pass medical knowledge on to the countryside. However, as Frank demonstrates, provincial efforts such as the doctor's did not always conform to new Soviet ideals about women's liberation and family. His advice reinforced traditional, prerevolutionary values, and the peasants themselves were often more sophisticated than the doctor expected.

Writing from the provincial capital of Riazan in 1928,[1] local doctor V. N. Voskresenskii produced a lengthy official report about state-sponsored rural newspapers and their role in the important task of bringing hygienic and medical knowledge to the peasant population during the anxious period of the NEP (1921–1928).[2] Voskresenskii's report focused on a medical advice column that appeared in the largest rural news organ in the province, *Derevenskaia gazeta* (*Village news*), and on the hundreds of letters received from peasant readers who had responded to the frequently published advertisement: "Readers! What do you wish to know from the doctor? Send him your questions—he will answer."[3] Given the Soviet government's concern in these years with raising the cultural level of the countryside and especially with improving public health, Voskresenskii played a critical role not only as editor of the newspaper's advice column but also, more important, as the sole respondent to peasant inquiries and the "official" interpreter of their significance and meaning. His report and the letters on which it was largely based therefore provide insight into medical and official views about sex, as well as about the rural population in general, during the mid- to late 1920s. At the same time these sources allow us a glimpse—albeit a very fragmentary one—into the everyday concerns of Russian peasants over issues of family and private life that historians have not previously examined.

In addition to their better-known economic and social impact on the peasantry, the catastrophic events through which Russia had recently passed—World War I, the 1917 February and October revolutions, civil war, and famine—devastated medical care primarily by stripping the countryside of trained physicians and paramedics (feldshers) and of funding for local medical stations and provincial hospitals. Although rural health care witnessed modest improvements during the last decades of the tsarist regime, it nevertheless remained grossly insufficient, and extremely primitive or nonexistent in many areas. In 1913 only about 7,000 physicians were employed in rural practice throughout the entire Russian Empire, serving a population of over 100 million. Some 35 percent of all Russian towns had no hospital beds in 1913, and only 21 percent of existing hospitals had more than twenty beds. Even when peasants did turn to professional medical practitioners, therefore, they usually saw either a feldsher or midwife rather than a doctor.

By contemporary estimates, one-half or more of the prerevolutionary peasantry continued to rely on traditional folk healers (*znakhari*), either because they mistrusted medical professionals as being outsiders or did not have ready access to modern medical assistance. With the decimation of the ranks of rural feldshers and especially physicians during World War I and the Civil War, even the slow progress of the late imperial era was dramatically reversed. The 1920s saw a number of successes in efforts to reestablish an improved public health network, but despite the government's "Face to the Countryside" policy, by 1928 medical care for the peasantry remained far less available and of poorer quality than was the case for town dwellers. Over 40 percent of rural areas had no hospital beds in 1925, for example. In 1926 the entire countryside counted slightly fewer than 6,500 physicians—a figure that grew to only 8,937 by 1929. As a result, the Soviet government would ultimately be forced to rely, like its predecessor, on feldshers and midwives in rural medical practice, and the continued poor state of rural health care and lack of access to modern medical advice or treatment can best be seen during this period in the widespread revival of folk healers as the principal medical practitioners to whom peasants might turn for aid or advice.[4]

Forged from the Bolsheviks' firm faith in science, materialism, and "enlightenment" (understood primarily as education), early Soviet health policy focused on the science of "social hygiene," the practitioners of which, as historian Susan Solomon explains, "were to examine the social conditions within which disease occurred and spread and to propose social measures which would contribute to the . . . goal of preventing disease."[5] Preventive medicine, however, proved extraordinarily difficult to implement in the impoverished countryside, where it collided with limited state resources, the pressing need for immediate treatment, and the extreme reluctance of medical professionals and semiprofessionals to devote precious time to propaganda and educational campaigns against such problems as alcoholism. Still, this policy certainly influenced Dr. Voskresenskii's selection of peasant letters for his advice column, allowing him to discuss prevention above all else (the choice of questions about venereal disease stands out most prominently here). It also helped to shape the type of advice that he gave on matters of abortion or sex, although in this important area other elements came into play as well. Chief among these was a widespread and long-standing elite view of the rural population that saw peasants not simply as ignorant and backward but also innocent and nonsexual, still existing in a more "natural" state than members of other classes.[6] Only the continued strength of such views can fully explain how medical professionals such as Voskresenskii might ignore direct evidence to the contrary as it was presented regularly in his correspondents' own words (and in numerous contemporary studies of village life). Instead, as we shall see, he used peasant letters to reinforce prevailing opinions about sex and about the peasantry itself, often ignoring entirely the content of their requests for advice—requests that reflected the continued plight of rural health care, which left a substantial proportion of country people with no local, confidential recourse to trustworthy medical advice.

The newspaper *Nasha derevnia* (*Our countryside*), which served as an official organ of the Riazan Provincial Committee and the Provincial Executive Committee of the Russian Communist Party, began as a weekly in 1925 with a publication of just over 3,000 copies per issue. Renamed *Derevenskaia gazeta* at the end of that year, the paper's circulation grew to 12,800 in 1926, 17,400 in 1927, and reached 23,000 in 1928.[7] Unfortunately, the majority of questions sent by peasants to the paper's advice column was not published, and many of the original letters have not survived, making it impossible to provide a precise breakdown of the questions. Voskresenskii explained that most inquiries were answered by mail, with only a small portion printed in the newspaper. Nearly all of the questions demanded earnest attention, he stressed, with the exception of those that were "absurd, empty, or not serious."[8] In his opinion, the fact that peasants flooded the newspaper's advice column with questions was a clear indication of their "extreme need for medical advice" (and, by extension, the shortage of such advice). Indeed, it was the lack of sufficient medical assistance, especially in the many localities that did not have ready access to medical stations, that was abetting the universal revival and growth of folk medicine (*znakharstvo*).

Despite Voskresenskii's use of their questions as evidence of widespread ignorance, the peasants' letters often demonstrate at least a basic understanding of disease—a fact that would often contradict contemporary commentary on rural medical knowledge. Voskresenskii voiced his disappointment, however, over the fact that the letters expressed very little interest in matters of public or social hygiene. Rather, Riazan villagers appeared far more concerned with personal health and disease prevention. Not a few inquired about the possible effects of tobacco and alcohol: "Does tobacco act harmfully on the organism?" "What is the danger of vodka and tobacco?" "How does alcoholism affect children?" "Can mothers drink liquor?" for example.[9] "Is it possible to contract cancer from smoking and drunkenness?" asked one correspondent. "How does one recognize the beginning of cancer?" another wished to know. Yet most inquiries addressed the contagious diseases that remained widespread throughout rural areas during the 1920s. Some hoped to learn whether it was possible to prevent measles, and, if so, how. Many requested information about tuberculosis, including its symptoms, whether it was contagious or hereditary, how one contracted the disease if it was not passed on by one's parents, and if one could marry a woman whose husband had died of tuberculosis. Echoing long-standing beliefs that the communal shepherd was often a source of contagion, at least one peasant asked *Derevenskaia gazeta* which specific illnesses might shepherds transmit to others in the community. Individual peasants or groups of villagers sought out advice on matters of personal hygiene, including how to maintain healthy teeth and how to bathe properly. Others were interested in whether sports were good, whether fasting was useful (a clear reference to the frequent fast days in the Orthodox calendar that still influenced rural life), or "what can happen as a result of difficult work?" Finally, we might note certain questions that involved issues traceable to health concerns expressed by medical professionals as far back as the mid-nineteenth century, such as whether it was unhealthy or dangerous to keep livestock in peasants' cottages, or how to dry out the land upon which one's cottage stood.[10]

Dr. Voskresenskii left questions touching upon sexual life to the final pages of his report, although he admitted that they were the subject of many letters. Interest in questions about sex was growing rapidly, he noted, a fact evidently explained solely by the peasants' "complete ignorance and lack of education" about the most basic matters. This evident concern over sex did not rest simply upon assumptions of "ignorance," however, but drew from widespread worries during the 1920s over what many people perceived as a weakening of traditional sexual mores among the rural population, and especially the "freer forms" that "mutual relations between the sexes" had taken among village youths.[11] Perhaps as a direct result of such fears about "innocent" peasants sinking into what some social hygienists termed "disorderly sexuality," the thrust of Voskresenskii's replies to their letters was clearly intended to urge his village readers back on the path to "normalcy"—that is, to a more traditional and "natural" type of sexuality. His frequent emphasis as to what constituted "normal" and "abnormal" sex, like his advice concerning the fundamental purpose of sexual relations, repeatedly if only implicitly raised the distinction, held by many in the medical profession, between urban and rural sex. As one sexologist explained this difference based on a 1929 study of the sexual lives of Ukrainian village women, "rural sexual life was not characterized by the same 'lust' as in the city; it was more natural."[12]

Letter writers asked a broad array of questions on topics ranging from birth control and pregnancy to anomalies of the sex organs, prostitution, and sexually transmitted diseases. Although we cannot know the actual range for certain, among letters published in *Derevenskaia gazeta* and those discussed in Voskresenskii's report the most frequent subjects of peasant inquiry were birth control, masturbation, and venereal disease (specifically, syphilis and gonorrhea), each of which will be discussed below. As for other questions, some peasants requested information that we might have expected to be readily available in the village. Women sent in a number of letters about menstruation, for example: "When do 'the monthlies' happen?" "What is the right way to deal with menstruation?" or "If menstruation does not occur for several months in a row, is this harmful to a woman's health?" One Firsova, from the large commercial village of Beloomut, wrote in 1928 asking simply "about menstruation." In addition to telling Firsova when menstruation began among most Russian women and pointing out its temporary cessation during pregnancy and breast-feeding, Voskresenskii also stressed that sexual relations during menstruation could be dangerous for women.[13] Other letter writers, inquiring as to the age at which puberty or sexual maturity began, received surprisingly inconsistent answers. Among men, one correspondent was told in 1927, puberty usually began at age 19–20, "and therefore this will be the very youngest age at which normal impregnation is possible." Several months later, however, a reply to the same question stated that male sexual maturity began at about fifteen to sixteen years of age, while for women the onset of puberty "begins at 13–15 years of age, and is completely developed after age 15."[14] Some peasants even wrote to learn the best age to get married.

"Nocturnal emission" (spermatorrhea, or *polliutsiia* in Russian) concerned at least several peasants sufficiently to send letters to the advice column. Some merely asked what it was, while others sought treatment. To one such question in 1927, *Derevenskaia gazeta* explained that if nocturnal emission occurred rarely (only once or twice per month), then it was unnecessary to take any specific measures. But if it happened frequently, leading to weakness or other symptoms, the doctor recommended taking a half-hour walk before sleeping, washing or bathing in cold water, and not eating at night. One should sleep in a cool room, not covered too warmly, and it was best not to sleep with one's face to the pillow but instead on the side or back. Finally, and perhaps more difficult, "it is necessary to eliminate everything that might bring on sexual arousal."[15]

I. Makarov and M. Kriuchkov of Kamenets village wrote to *Derevenskaia gazeta* in September 1927 asking whether sexual intercourse affected one's intelligence; they were told that, for the most part, it did not, but only "when one does not have excessive, inordinate sexual relations." The doctor advised them to limit themselves to a "normal" amount of sexual intercourse—"up to two times per week." Here, peasant writers likely thought that they had not received direct or complete answers to their questions. Surely the female correspondent who asked, in 1926, "how often does [a man] need to have relations with a woman," could not have been fully satisfied with Voskresenskii's response, for he altered the question to focus solely on the "goal of impregnation," which could occur with a single act of copulation. Once pregnant, he added, returning readers to the regular theme of "normal" sex, "the woman's sexual attraction to the man disappears"; moreover, "sexual relations during pregnancy are abnormal and, for the woman, unpleasant." As long as a woman continued to breast-feed her child, sexual relations remained similarly "abnormal."[16] In short, peasants were being told repeatedly that conception was the fundamental, if not sole, purpose of intercourse.

It would appear that questions about sexual relations were much less likely to be published or to receive a direct answer. Among those not published, for example, were letters asking how one could know for certain whether a maiden was no longer a virgin, what was the danger in having sexual relations while standing, and "why is it that when a young man is close to the female sex organ, he gets an erection?"[17] Questions that could be interpreted in different ways were given the briefest of replies that ignored other possible meanings of what was being asked.

R. V. Rogachev, for instance, wrote in early 1928 to ask: "Can a man be made into a woman?" Voskresenskii answered with a few terse sentences concerning various scientific experiments that had been conducted on transplanting sex glands from animal to animal, human to human, and animal to human, but explained that it was "impossible to completely change the sex of a person." In a reply to a question from I. S. Baron of Kiselevo village, the doctor explained: "Venereal diseases of humans cannot be passed on to livestock, and, likewise, people cannot contract sexual diseases from livestock or horses."[18]

Although few of their questions were published, peasants sought explanations and possible cures for impotence or other sexual afflictions which they obviously believed could not be discussed openly among themselves, or even within the family: "I read in *Derevenskaia gazeta* that they give doctors' advice about all illnesses," wrote "the Suffering One." "I have been afflicted for about two months with impotence and I therefore ask you to give me an answer about whether this can be cured and how it can be cured. Answer in *Derevenskaia gazeta* because I subscribe to it, and if you send a letter by mail it would lead to unpleasantness in the family." Among the more peculiar (and unpublished) questions asked—the reply to which is not known—was the following: "When I got married I had normal sexual relations, but after awhile things changed completely so that now during sex I have no desire at all, which I conclude is because of a curvature of my sexual organ which worries me a lot; and therefore I beg the editors to tell me how to cure this and why it happened, because my sexual organ does not fit into the vagina."[19]

Not surprisingly, a substantial portion of letters directed to *Derevenskaia gazeta* from women asked for information on how to prevent pregnancy. Here we find a particularly revealing exchange between peasants seeking knowledge and the often contradictory positions taken by medical officials on birth control. Doctors such as Voskresenskii were greatly concerned by a dramatic increase in the number of abortions during the early 1920s—a method that, for many rural women, served as the only available means of birth control. Most replies in the advice column therefore usually began with stern warnings about the danger of abortion, stressing the health risks that could result especially when the procedure was done by "nonspecialists" such as traditional healers or midwives. Voskresenskii also informed his readers, including a woman who wrote in 1926 to ask whether abortions were now performed in hospitals, about the laws pertaining to abortion. These procedures were to be carried out only in hospitals and only by doctors, he explained, underscoring the fact that it was illegal to perform abortions outside of hospitals. Among women who turned to a midwife or healer, he noted, more than one-half ended up as invalids unable to work, and many died from blood infections. In short, "you must go to your hospital to request an abortion."[20]

Still, rural women throughout Riazan province continued to "ask the doctor," sending letters (often signed by several villagers) throughout the years 1925–1929 that repeated over and over (and with growing frequency) the same request for advice on birth control "without having to turn to abortion." Primarily with the aim of fighting abortion, then, Voskresenskii advised correspondents of several birth-control options that might be tried, although he emphasized that, at the present time, there was no sure means of preventing pregnancy. Incorrectly, women were told to avoid sexual relations during the first week after menstruation. They might also use a douche solution of water and two tablespoons of pyroligneous acid (wood vinegar). Among "artificial" methods, the doctor noted that while protective coverings (usually metal) existed that fit over the cervix, these often caused irritation inside the vagina. By far the most "trustworthy" means of preventing pregnancy was to use a condom (commonly mispronounced "gondon" in the countryside) before copulation. Although already available for several decades in Russia, peasants still had limited or no access to condoms or else remained concerned about the possible harm that might result from their use, for at least one person wrote to ask whether it was dangerous for either the man or the woman to have sexual relations using a gondon.

Judging by the number of questions regarding its possible health effects, many Riazan peasants practiced "the withdrawal method" (coitus interruptus) but obviously were apprehensive about it. One peasant wrote: "When having sexual relations with my wife and being concerned with not making her pregnant, . . . I withdraw my sexual organ from my wife and everything that's there comes out onto the bedding, and I have used this method for two years and my wife hasn't gotten pregnant, but I am worried that [our] health might suffer from this so I beg you to reply." "Is it harmful to the health," another asked in 1925, "if, during copulation, the husband artificially ejects semen not into the sexual organs, but externally?"[21] Voskresenskii's replies could not have put his correspondents' minds at ease, for while he admitted that coitus interruptus was one possible means of preventing conception, it could have a serious impact on the health of both men and women. In one reply from late 1925 the doctor noted that medical opinion differed on the question of "such abnormal copulation": some specialists considered it not at all unhealthy, while others viewed it as harmful, "especially for the man or, in general, for people with weak nerves." In later replies, however, Voskresenskii spoke only in negative terms. Coitus interruptus, he told I. A. Naumov in 1928, could result in various maladies of the female sex organs and cause disorders of the nervous system among men.

In another letter that same year he informed a group of peasants who had written for advice on birth control that the withdrawal method had a serious impact on women: "Not having received complete sexual satisfaction, nervous disorders can develop among women, and sometimes an inflammation of the internal sexual organs."[22] In other words, he told them, a woman could be fully satisfied only when a man did not withdraw before ejaculating inside her, and thereby completed intercourse in a "normal" manner (potentially leading to pregnancy).

One last, particularly revealing commentary recited to peasant women who asked about birth control emphasized their duty to bear children. The question of preventing pregnancy, after all, was no simple matter but a very grave issue, Voskresenskii wrote in 1926 when replying to "Citizen" (*grazhdanka*): "A woman should remember that her calling is to bear children," and for not wanting to do so "she will often pay in the future with a series of illnesses, especially in those cases when an abortion is carried out." Here, unlike in other replies, Voskresenskii did not even bother to answer the woman's question as to "how one protects oneself against pregnancy," but instead advised her to purchase the book by Dr. M. F. Levi entitled *The Prevention of Pregnancy as a Means of Fighting Abortion*, which was sold in Moscow for 20 kopecks.[23]

According to Voskresenskii, the subject of masturbation (onanism) appeared "completely unexpectedly" in a great many letters. As a "secret vice," the doctor explained, masturbation was not a matter of open discussion for the masses. But the guarantee of secrecy offered by his advice column had elicited this question, thereby leading outsiders like himself to speculate on the extent of masturbation among the peasantry. These letters, he stressed, were written without circumlocution and were clear requests for help and a cure from "this difficult misfortune." Given the symptoms about which correspondents wrote, moreover, it would appear that nearly all writers whose questions appeared in print were male. Certainly, letters published in *Derevenskaia gazeta* and those discussed in Voskresenskii's report all speak of the harmful effects of masturbation on men rather than on both sexes. The only exception was a single query, written by a woman, asking whether female masturbators can bear children and whether male masturbators are capable of impregnating a woman.

Selectivity definitely played a major role in the nature of the questions published, for without exception all asked whether masturbation was harmful, how it affected penis size, and whether and how it could be cured. There was, then, a convenient match between the letters chosen for inclusion in the newspaper's advice column and prevailing official, medical, and traditional views on this topic.[24] In one of the most detailed (and thus unpublished) questions, a peasant signing himself "Interested" asked: "Is it possible to cure masturbation, which began at age 18 but hasn't been practiced too frequently, but which in my opinion has anyway affected the growth of my member (*chlen*) and my health [because] I have become very anemic and sluggish. In this condition can I have a wife and am I able to make her pregnant? I beg you to reply whether it is possible to hope for a cure of impotence and for the growth of [one's] member." The same worries were expressed in another letter, whose author wanted to know whether the results of masturbation could be cured without regard to one's age. Specifically, this peasant voiced particular concern about impotence and nervous disorders, which he attributed to masturbation, and also asked if it were possible to increase the size of his penis.[25]

In all replies to letters of this sort, Dr. Voskresenskii sought to emphasize the "unnatural" or "abnormal" nature of masturbation when compared to "natural sexual relations." To those peasants (including "Masturbator") who asked whether masturbation was harmful, the doctor told them that many men suffered from this "secret vice" and ruined their health in the process: "The onanist excites himself, forcing his imagination to paint a voluptuous picture. This is a great strain on the nervous system and the heart. The consequences of masturbation are extremely serious and often lead to impotence—that is, the inability to have normal sexual relations."[26] Commenting on another letter in 1928, Voskresenskii explained to K. M. Durov that "the artificial ejaculation of semen" (evidently his own definition of masturbation) was harmful, for it could result in a dramatic, negative impact on the organism. In the lengthiest response, given by the doctor to a question from N. Morgunov, he wrote that masturbation (also called, literally, "fornication by the hand," or *ruko-bludie*) was a disease that damaged a person's health: "Sexual stimulation during intercourse with women concludes more quickly than during masturbation. Masturbation is dangerous . . . causing a series of disorders of the nervous system, the appearance of irritability, depression, loss of weight, and significant changes in sexual ability during intercourse. In the childhood years, masturbation influences growth and leads to obtuseness and the poor mastering of science."[27] We might underline here Voskresenskii's telling comment on the more rapid achievement of ejaculation during "intercourse with women," and the imbedded counterpoint suggesting the abnormality of lengthy self-stimulation. Once again, peasants read that "normal" sex was brief and that its implicit outcome was conception.

Rather than fulfilling its stated goal to provide "ignorant" peasants with an enlightened source of information on questions that concerned them the most, Voskresenskii's advice column served, above all, to disseminate traditional views (which remained strong during and after NEP) about sex, gender, and the very nature of the peasantry itself. These views could be seen most sharply in his writings on syphilis, for here he—as well as much of the Soviet health profession—continued to perpetuate the opinion, which originated in the prerevolutionary era, that the transmission of syphilis among peasants was primarily nonsexual. "Infection with syphilis," he explained in a 1925 reply, "takes place through both sexual and nonsexual means. In the countryside, nonsexual syphilis is most widespread." He stressed the same causation in 1927, writing that "common syphilis" had become prevalent in villages of Riazan province "not through sexual means." Instead, "crowded conditions, congestion, and lack of culture lead to mass infection. Syphilis is brought to the countryside by soldiers, and by peasants who go off to work in crafts and factories." The struggle against rural syphilis, he argued, should be fought by "increasing culture and literacy in the villages, by improving daily life and living conditions" as well as personal hygiene. In other articles, too, he emphasized strict observance of good hygiene as the main way to avoid infection by syphilis. Peasants were therefore advised to stop the dangerous custom of kissing as a common greeting ("conscious citizens should cease kissing people they do not know"), to not share cigarettes with others or drink vodka with "unknown people," to not use another's razor or towels, and to thoroughly wash the benches at the bathhouse. Only in 1928 did Voskresenskii begin telling his correspondents on a more regular basis that transmission of syphilis and gonorrhea also occurred during sexual relations, and that a man should therefore never have relations with unknown women, "especially when intoxicated."[28] But even when acknowledging infection through sexual intercourse, Voskresenskii continued to include lengthy information about nonvenereal sources of transmission.

As they had done before the 1917 revolutions, during the 1920s peasants sought beneficial knowledge and solutions to serious problems wherever they might find them. Given the poor state of rural health care and a lack of ready access to medical advice in the countryside, it is easy to understand why so many of them composed letters to *Derevenskaia gazeta*, sending their questions about disease or sex to the professionals in the provincial capital and waiting for knowledge to reach them either through the mail or in the "Ask the Doctor" column. The peasantry's willingness or eagerness to write to outsiders in the case of inquiries about more "delicate" or embarrassing matters of a sexual nature is especially evident, since these problems were not easily discussed at home or in the wider rural community.

What may appear remarkable at first glance, however, is the strikingly conservative tone of the replies, particularly in light of the radical views that pervaded early Soviet ideology on subjects such as social and personal life, or even sexuality. We might attribute this apparent contradiction between pronouncements and practice to the simple fact that so much of the historical study of the 1920s has focused on ideology and ideological struggles within the Bolshevik/Communist Party. Such works have emphasized the conflict of early Bolshevik utopianism or radicalism with the practical problem of reconstruction and ruling, a conflict that culminated in the Great Retreat to more conservative policies and approaches at the end of the decade. Yet, as Dr. Voskresenskii's advice column attests, and as more recent investigations of problems at the lower levels of administration have shown, in a vast range of areas of early Soviet life the utopianism of small segments of the social or political elite was not necessarily shared throughout the party apparatus, state administration, or especially society. The prerevolutionary cultural construction of the Russian peasants' "nature" and "sexuality"(or lack thereof), much of which carried over into the 1920s and was highly visible in *Derevenskaia gazeta*'s advice column, did not always correspond comfortably with theoretical or policy-oriented discussions of either village life or sex, since relatively conservative and paternalistic views of peasantry remained, to a great extent, dominant throughout and far beyond the era of NEP.

Notes

1. Among the poorest and most agricultural areas in central Russia, Riazan province is directly to the southeast of Moscow.

2. The report, "Krestianskie gazety i sanitarnoe prosveshchenie," is located in the manuscript division of the Riazanskii Istoriko-Arkhitekturnyi Muzei-Zapovednik in Riazan (hereafter cited as RIAMZ), III/828, No. 315.

3. *Derevenskaia gazeta*, no. 9, February 1, 1926.

4. This information is drawn from Mark G. Field, *Soviet Socialized Medicine: An Introduction* (New York: Free Press, 1967), 27; Samuel C. Ramer, "Traditional Healers and Peasant Culture in Russia, 1861–1917," in *Peasant Economy, Culture, and Politics of European Russia, 1800–1921*, ed. Esther Kingston-Mann and Timothy Mixter (Princeton, 1991), 207–32; Samuel C. Ramer, "Feldshers and Rural Health Care in the Early Soviet Period," and Neil B. Weissman, "Origins of Soviet Health Administration: Narkomzdrav, 1918–1928," both in *Health and Society in Revolutionary Russia*, ed. Susan Gross Solomon and John F. Hutchinson (Bloomington: Indiana University Press, 1990),121–45, 97–120.

5. Susan Gross Solomon, "Social Hygiene and Soviet Public Health, 1921–1930," in *Health and Society*, 175.

6. Susan Gross Solomon, "Innocence and Sexuality in Soviet Medical Discourse," in *Women in Russia and Ukraine*, ed. Rosalind Marsh (Cambridge: Cambridge University Press, 1996), 121–30, discusses this view of the peasantry. For its origins in the prerevolutionary period see Laura Engelstein, *The Keys to Happiness: Sex and the Search for Modernity in Fin-de-Siècle Russia* (Ithaca, NY: Cornell University Press, 1992), 165–211.

7. RIAMZ, III/828, No. 315, 28. A brief history of the rural press in Riazan province is provided on pp. 28–36.

8. Ibid., 7.

9. Ibid., 32.

10. Ibid., 33.

11. For one of many such commentaries see V. A. Murin, *Byt i nravy derevenskoi molodezhi* [Life and morals of rural youth] (Moscow, 1926), 95–96.

12. Solomon, "Innocence and Sexuality," 124.

13. Ibid., 39–40; *Derevenskaia gazeta*, no. 23, March 25, 1928.

14. *Derevenskaia gazeta*, no. 18, March 9, 1927; ibid., no. 65, September 4, 1927.

15. Ibid., no. 4, January 16, 1927.

16. Ibid., no. 63, August 22, 1926.

17. RIAMZ, III/828, No. 315, 39.

18. *Derevenskaia gazeta*, no. 7, January 26, 1928; ibid., no. 7, January 24, 1929.

19. RIAMZ, III/828, No. 315, 38–39.

20. *Derevenskaia gazeta*, no. 96, December 23, 1926.

21. RIAMZ, III/828, No. 315, 37; *Derevenskaia gazeta*, no. 46, December 12, 1925.

22. *Derevenskaia gazeta*, no. 46, December 12, 1925; ibid., no. 19, March 11, 1928; ibid., no. 23, March 25, 1928.

23. *Derevenskaia gazeta*, no. 27, April 10, 1926.

24. For a brief discussion of Soviet medical views on masturbation see Eric Naiman, *Sex in Public: The Incarnation of Early Soviet Ideology* (Princeton, NJ: Princeton University Press, 1997), 120–23.

25. Compare prerevolutionary opinions in Engelstein, *Keys to Happiness*, 226–28, 234–37, 244–48; RIAMZ, III/828, No. 315, 38.

26. *Derevenskaia gazeta*, no. 25, April 3, 1926.

27. Ibid., no. 75, October 8, 1927.

28. Ibid., no. 45, December 9, 1925; ibid., no. 24, April 2, 1927; ibid., no. 87, November 24, 1927.

Suggested Readings

Bernstein, Frances Lee. *The Dictatorship of Sex: Lifestyle Advice for the Soviet Masses.* DeKalb: Northern Illinois University Press, 2007.

Engel, Barbara Alpern. "Peasant Morality and Pre-Marital Relations in Late 19th Century Russia," *Journal of Social History* 23 (1990): 695–714.

Engelstein, Laura. *The Keys to Happiness: Sex and the Search for Modernity in Fin-de-Siècle Russia.* Ithaca, NY: Cornell University Press, 1992.

Field, Mark G. *Soviet Socialized Medicine: An Introduction.* New York: Free Press, 1967.

Fitzpatrick, Sheila. "Sex and Revolution." In *The Cultural Front: Power and Culture in Revolutionary Russia,* 65–90. Ithaca, NY: Cornell University Press, 1992.

Frank, Stephen P. "'Simple Folk, Savage Customs?' Youth, Sociability, and the Dynamics of Culture in Rural Russia, 1856–1914," *Journal of Social History* 25 (1992): 711–36.

Kenez, Peter. *The Birth of the Propaganda State: Soviet Methods of Mass Mobilization, 1917–1929.* Cambridge: Cambridge University Press, 1985.

Kozlov, V. A. *Kulturnaia revoliutsiia i krestianstvo, 1921–1927.* (Po materialam Evropeiskoi chasti RSFSR) [Cultural revolution and the peasantry, 1921–1927. Based on materials from the European part of the RSFSR]. Moscow, 1983.

Naiman, Eric. *Sex in Public: The Incarnation of Early Soviet Ideology.* Princeton, NJ: Princeton University Press, 1997.

Solomon, Susan Gross. "Innocence and Sexuality in Soviet Medical Discourse." In *Women in Russia and Ukraine,* edited by Rosalind Marsh, 121–30. Cambridge: Cambridge University Press, 1996.

Solomon, Susan Gross, and John F. Hutchinson, eds. *Health and Society in Revolutionary Russia.* Bloomington: Indiana University Press, 1990.

Worobec, Christine D. *Peasant Russia: Family and Community in the Post-Emancipation Period.* Princeton, NJ: Princeton University Press, 1991.

~

CHAPTER NINE

In the Name of an Italian Widow

Nationalism, Patriotism, and Gender in Mussolini's Fascist Italy

MAURA E. HAMETZ

Throughout Europe, World War I left an indelible imprint on postwar politics, culture, and society. The searing experience of four years of unimaginable trench warfare, death, and destruction radically changed the political landscape across Europe; economies were in shambles, millions of soldiers had died or were wounded, and the veterans and civilians who survived searched for order and sought direction in places where instability reigned. Leaders and parties espousing ideologies at the extreme ends of the political spectrum captured the imagination of the disenfranchised and disappointed across the continent. Italy, having unified in the 1860s, had entered the war with hopes of securing territorial gains and greater recognition by the major European powers. Its hopes were dashed, however, during the peace negotiations following the war.

Attempting to capitalize on the Italian government's failures to secure significant gains and Italian disappointment with the postwar settlement, a former socialist and populist journalist, Benito Mussolini, founded the Fasci di Combattimento (Combat Groups), a far-right political movement. Conforming to the practices of other far-right paramilitary movements in interwar Europe, the movement took aim at the Socialist Party, which was reemerging as the major political opposition to the postwar liberal order. Between 1920 and 1922, Mussolini's Fascists, as they became known, drew support from the lower middle classes and played on the sympathies of the upper classes and conservatives, who distrusted the working classes and Socialist supporters, to become a major and violent force in Italian politics. In

1922, Mussolini entered the formal government, invited by the king to become prime minister after a threatened coup. From there, Mussolini embarked on a program to remake Italy through coercion, violence, and intimidation of political enemies. By 1925 Mussolini, known by then as Il Duce (the Leader), was firmly in control as dictator. His Fascist government sought to enshrine what it considered to be masculine virtues—bravery, comradeship, honor, and force—at the heart of national politics and to remake the state in this image.

In this chapter, Maura Hametz plumbs the case of a widow who dared challenge the authoritarian dictates of the Fascist state. She argues that Signora Petrovich successfully drew on notions of Italian womanhood, nationalism, and family honor to prevent the Italianization of her Slavic-sounding name. To this end, Hametz explores the values and goals of Mussolini's Fascists in their efforts to remake Italy and shows how seemingly ordinary citizens found ways to counter the totalizing efforts of the Fascist government.

In January 1931, Fascist officials informed Signora Petrovich that she was henceforth to be known as Signora Petri.[1] The official decree announced the "restoration" of her "deformed" married surname to its original Italian form. At the age of seventy-four, the widow did not want, nor think she needed, an Italianized surname. So, taking advantage of a rarely used provision of the name restoration legislation, she petitioned authorities asking them to rescind the decree.

An elderly widow of comfortable means, Signora Petrovich was indistinguishable from many women living fairly contentedly under Mussolini's Fascist government in the early 1930s. Yet, she took a step that was extraordinary and seemingly somewhat dangerous. She protested a decree issued by authorities in Italy, a state under Fascist governance since 1922. While Mussolini's rule was not totalitarian, his dictatorship showed little tolerance for political opposition. The murder in the summer of 1924 of Giacomo Matteotti, a representative of the Italian Chamber of Deputies who spoke against Fascist election law machinations, made clear the Fascists' aims. Waves of violence that struck the Fascist opposition in response to the crisis provoked by Matteotti's death signaled the rule of dictatorship in 1925. Until Mussolini's fall from power in 1943, Italy remained under Fascist governance.[2]

Centralization and the promotion of nationalism remained core aims of the Fascists who sought to revolutionize, modernize, and strengthen Italy. By the early 1930s, the Fascist government had enforced its nationalizing will on the population through intimidation, coercion, and, if necessary, violence. Protests like the Signora's against nationalizing measures could be construed as disloyal and antithetical to the state's interests. The guide to name corrections published in 1929 in the Signora's home city of Trieste, a port on Italy's northeastern border at the head of the Adriatic Sea, painted appeals as ridiculous, selfish, and unlikely to succeed.[3] Appeals were not considered by jury in a public trial. Rather, Fascist authorities handled them. First, they were referred for reconsideration to officials who had ordered the correction. Then, petitioners could appeal further to a panel of judges in Rome appointed by the state or could petition the king, who maintained titular power throughout the years of Mussolini's rule.

Signora Petrovich did not believe that she needed to acquiesce in accepting the new name to affirm her patriotism, loyalty to Fascism and its goals, or her Italianness. Her petition to retain her married surname was considered and rejected by local officials in Trieste. The prefect of Trieste painted her as a malcontent, noting that "of the many thousands whose names had been restored," the Signora was only the fourth to file an appeal. Yet she persisted. Risking official ire, the Signora took her appeal to the Court of Cassation in Rome.

Several elements combine to explain the Signora's temerity. Economic privilege and elevated social status enabled her to pursue the bold course of action. Fascism came to power in the wake of World War I with the support of the propertied classes that believed in the system's potential to combat Socialist threats and to help restore social order and economic stability. The Signora, while not extremely wealthy or privileged, was able and willing to bear the substantial costs of litigation. She possessed sufficient capital and social status to engage a lawyer to define and defend her interests.

The seventy-four-year-old woman could hardly be considered a dangerous troublemaker or potential political threat. She was an elderly widow who could reasonably claim to be an Italian patriot, or at least the wife and mother of a loyal and patriotic Italian family. Her protest was bothersome to officials in Trieste and took the time of authorities in Rome, but it did not cause undue concern for the regime nor did it incur the wrath of Fascist officials. In fact, in January 1932, the high court ruled in the Signora's favor. Fascist officials in Rome annulled the name restoration decree, allowing Signora Petrovich to keep her married surname. In addition, they awarded her compensation for legal expenses related to her case.

Fascism and Nationalism

Name restoration legislation formed one aspect of nationalist policy promoted by Benito Mussolini's regime. Prior to World War I, nationalist rhetoric promoted Italian grandeur and the proud heritage of Italy based on its links with ancient Rome. After World War I, Mussolini's emphasis on Italian nationalist ideals helped the Fascists to gain power. Nationalists and Fascists took aim at communist and socialist elements seen as foreign influences threatening and infiltrating Italian life after the triumph of the Bolsheviks in Russia and with the reemergence of socialist power through Europe after World War I. Mussolini won adherents among disaffected soldiers, unemployed after the war, who were called on to fill the ranks of the Fascist, or "Blackshirt," squads. Just as the Germans were angered by the terms of the Treaty of Versailles, so too were the Italians upset by the terms of the post–World War I treaties. Unlike Germany, Italy had been on the winning side, but Italian nationalist aims had been frustrated, and many felt that in the Paris peace negotiations Italy had been "stabbed in the back" by her allies. Mussolini capitalized on Italian disappointment and frustrated desires to gain *irredenta* ("unredeemed" lands claimed as Italian) and colonies.

Nationalizing measures initiated after the Fascists took power in 1922 demonstrated the Italian state's strength to repudiate what some perceived to be the laxity and weakness of Italy's prior liberal government. Although Fascist policies superficially resembled later Nazi measures in their emphasis on coercion to promote national superiority, the ideological roots and fundamental intents of Italian fascism differed significantly from those of German Nazism. Particularly in the 1920s and early 1930s, and prior to Italy's alignment with Germany, Fascist nationalist ideology was inclusionary, promoting Italianness and membership in the Italian nation, rather than exclusionary in the vein of the Nazi model. Political allegiance, not racial background or bloodline, formed the basis for nationalist determination. Opponents of the Fascist state were denied membership in the Italian nation, but supporters, even Jews, were welcomed as citizens of Fascist Italy until the mid-1930s.

By January 1924, Mussolini's government had managed to gain some disputed territory along the northeastern border, including parts of Istria and the port city of Fiume. This sated Italian nationalist appetites but presented a challenge to the post–World War I international order advocated by Woodrow Wilson that emphasized national self-determination. Extension of Italy's border to the east meant the inclusion of Slavic, particularly Croat and Slovene, populations into the Italian state in addition to those Germans and Slavs included under the terms of the Paris Peace Conference in the Treaty of Saint-Germain.

Throughout Italy, fragmented political, economic, and social structures inherited from the Unification period in the 1860s and 1870s and the liberal government period stymied Fascist attempts to centralize Italian state power. Regional cultural differences contributed to a sense of fragmentation. Localism in the borderlands presented a particular problem. Italianization plans and policies for the New Provinces (territories joined to Italy after World War I in the wake of Italian victory and the collapse of the Austro-Hungarian Empire) and the lands added in 1924 emphasized patriotism and nationalism in border territories where claims of Italianness might be challenged.

Fascist officials' confusion with regard to the Signora's national loyalty, and that of other inhabitants of the northeastern borderland, could be traced to the history of the territory and the alignments of the provincial capital, Trieste. The lingua franca (or language of trade and common public usage) in the city historically was Italian, but the population living at the crossroads of the Italian, German (Habsburg Austrian), and Slavic (Slovene and Croatian) worlds was of mixed origins. The city enjoyed Habsburg patronage for more than five hundred years prior to annexation to Italy. Surname measures initiated in 1926 and 1927 followed closely on the heels of measures that, under the guise of administrative changes, altered toponyms (place names) to Italianize border territories.

The decree that rectified Signora Petrovich's surname was issued under legislation that charged Italian officials to "restore" surnames changed by foreign officials who allegedly had conspired to erase evidence of Italian identity prior to World War I. The legislation purported to correct the "bastardization" of Italian culture, to restore to border populations their rightful inheritance. It provided for two types of corrections. "Automatic corrections" were made on the basis of the inclusion of a name on the official list of surnames to be corrected. "Corrections by petition" were made on official review of an individual's request to conform to the nationalist spirit of the legislation and modify a name that did not appear on the list. Between 1927 and 1943, Fascist functionaries in Trieste Italianized, or according to them "re-Italianized," the names of as many as 100,000 people in the population of approximately 450,000. The vast majority accepted "restoration" or "correction" without complaint, demonstrating the far-reaching powers of the interwar Italian state bent on shaping a new society on the Fascist model.[4]

The Signora's married surname was restored to the form of "Petri" based on the decision of a Fascist committee of experts (linguists, other academics, and local officials) to list Petrovich, a name sounding Slavic, as one of the "deformed" Italian surnames. Emphasis on the "correction" (rather than change) of the name, the manner of execution of the legislation, and local officials' arguments in favor of their decree reveal much about the coercive relationship between the Italian population and the Fascist state. At the same time, the Signora's ability to appeal, officials' response, and the outcome of the case demonstrate the limitations of the state's ability to enforce its will over individuals living in the Fascist society. The Signora worked within the framework of the legislation and, in a broader sense, within the strictures of Fascist society and with a clear respect for Italian Fascist expectations to make a viable case for her position.

The brief that the Signora's lawyer filed in Rome on her behalf played on Fascist officials' traditionalist assumptions and inevitable sympathy for an elderly widow. The lawyer's challenges to the validity and utility of the decree fell into three categories. First, taking advantage of the Fascist view that a woman's primary responsibility lay in her role as the protector of her family, the lawyer sought to demonstrate that the name alteration undermined Signora Petrovich's contributions as a revered wife and as the mother of an Italian family. Second, he presented evidence of the family's Italian heritage and actions on behalf of the modern Italian state, appealing to authorities' duty to promote nationalism, patriotism, and Italian sentiment. Third, he raised legalistic objections to the specifications of the decree and the manner of its execution, challenging Fascist officials to uphold claims that the regime functioned as a modern state on the basis of respect for law and order. Objections in all three categories seemed to bolster the Signora's case. They also laid bare inconsistencies in Fascist ideology and policy, ambiguities of political purpose, and shifting priorities that undermined the "totalitarian" nature and repressive power of Italian fascism.

Fascism and the Family

The Fascist government's promotion of the archetype of devoted *madre e moglie* (mother and wife) as a romantic ideal for women and as the aim of their ambitions resonated deeply in a country that traditionally revered mothers and motherhood.[5] It was also consistent with the demographic aims of the regime. Fascist policies, like later Nazi policies, sought to encourage women to leave the workforce and return to the home to rear children to invigorate the state. In 1925, the Fascists created ONMI, the National Agency for Maternity and Infancy. With his Ascension Day speech of May 1927, Mussolini initiated the official demographic campaign of the Fascist state to promote the health and fertility of Italians to increase their numbers to support state initiatives.[6] OMNI, staffed largely by "bourgeois" women of means (similar in station to the Signora), who had been active volunteers in social welfare initiatives prior to and during World War I, took on an aspect of maternal beneficence in its attempt to assist poor and disadvantaged women. Ostensibly, the organization harnessed women's political energies in support of the regime. In effect, it relegated women to work only with policies related to the family. The women of OMNI administered aid to the less fortunate by helping them with state maternity benefits, nutritional assistance, and medical care designed to inspire confidence in and support for the regime.

Women's virtue and role in the family were linked to Catholic virtue, faith, and adherence and obedience to the church and state. Early on, Catholic parties had constituted the strongest opposition to the rise of the Fascists' power. However, after 1922, Mussolini pursued a conciliatory stance, and by 1929, he concluded the Lateran Pacts with the Vatican. Ostensibly, the agreement reconciled the modern Italian state and the Catholic Church, which had been at odds over the secular nature of Italian Unification since the nineteenth century, and it resolved the "Catholic question" that had been plaguing Italian politics.

Officials in Rome understood the Signora's objections to the name restoration in the context of broader Italian reverence for the "trinity of Woman-Country-Family."[7] The Signora's lawyer ennobled her as a virtuous and feminine figure, a superior female citizen. She stood as a defender of the moral way of life propounded by the regime. The widowed mother of an Italian family, a proponent of patriotic pronatalism, she had exercised well her duties as a member of the "body politic." Her wish to keep the name Petrovich was attributed to the desire to venerate her dead husband and honor his memory. Modifying the surname, the Signora's lawyer argued, could be viewed as dishonorable and disrespectful. The lawyer gave the impression that the Signora had launched her protest to protect, literally, the name of her family and to safeguard herself and her children against a domineering state interfering without cause in the private (or woman's) sphere.

Changing the surname to Petri negated the sacrifices that the Signora's husband and the entire family had made for the good of Italy. This idea of sacrifice in the name of Italy resonated with Fascist expectations that women should demonstrate their support for the regime through selfless acts, particularly those related to support of the family and child rearing.[8] Cast in this light, the Signora's appeal to keep the name Petrovich appeared as a defensive rather than an offensive act. Family members bearing the name Petrovich had a proud, patriotic Italian heritage. Despite its Slavic sonance, the name provided the family's "indissoluble link" to Italian honor throughout the ages.

The protest was launched in the public judicial realm, but the Signora remained in the background. She acted for the private good of her family through the public actions of a male lawyer. In essence, the Signora appropriated official agendas of the misogynist regime to gain personal ends using the Fascist archetype of the "wife and mother" to shield her from censure.

The success of her protest demonstrated how women successfully negotiated their positions under fascism, acting as "mothers of invention" within the framework of traditionalist assumptions of the Fascist society.[9]

Fascism, Nationalism, and Patriotism

The Signora's protest also pointed out that enforcement of the surname legislation set two central concepts of fascism in opposition. The measures forced a choice between loyalty for family by maintaining a family name and support for country by Italianizing it. Fascist nationalization of the borderlands was consistent with a broad shift in Italian state policies to a more aggressive international stance. The 1926 resignation of Salvatore Contarini, secretary-general of the Italian Ministry of Foreign Affairs, signaled the change in orientation of Italian policy. Contarini left his post ostensibly over a disagreement on policies for the Brenner Pass, an area including German populations in the northern territory of the New Provinces, but his downfall also related to a simmering feud over policy for the Adriatic (including areas near Trieste) and the Balkans. Mussolini wished to take a more militant stance than did the experienced diplomat who had begun his career under the liberal government.

An important aim of Fascist leadership, particularly in the phase of consolidation of power after 1925, was to encourage support for the regime. While coercion and intimidation could be effective, Fascist officials generally sought to inspire support through rhetoric and promises designed to appeal to the desires and needs of the masses. Formation of the national community required the participation of the population. From the perspective of Fascist officials, this included demonstrating the willingness of border populations, including citizens whose names were Slavic, German, or associated with another ethnic group, to be cleansed of an imposed identity—evidenced by their foreign surnames—and to be incorporated into the Italian national community. The state's representative argued in building his case against the Signora: "All good Italians must consider the restitution of Slavic surnames to the Italian tongue a dutiful gift from the Fatherland."

Rather than welcoming the correction as a "gift," and contrary to officials' expectations, the Signora found the decree insulting. She resented its implication that her husband's foreign-sounding surname linked him and the family to a foreign nationalist association. Association of a foreign-sounding surname with a particular allegiance was particularly problematic in Trieste. The Italian national movement had deep roots in the city. Prior to World War I in Habsburg Trieste, Italian nationalists occupied positions of power in local government and exercised their influence in the port's economic networks. After the war, the city's population was one of the earliest in Italy to show its support for the Fascists and their nationalist platform.

According to court documents, the Signora's family's commitment to Italy was beyond question. Her husband had "fought in the battle against Austria and for the defense of *italianità* until his death." Her sons had been irredentists (supporters of Italy's claims to Trieste and other "Italian" territories) from 1905 to 1915. Austrian officials had imprisoned them during World War I for their pro-Italian stance. The Signora herself had an unimpeachable record. In the eastern borderland, an additional responsibility was added to women's nurturing role. The state expected them to promote Italianness and a combative brand of border fascism to fend off challenges to Italian society and culture emanating from outside Italy's borders. The Signora had inculcated Italian loyalty and love of country in her family and had suffered at the hands of Austrian officials in the name of Italy.

Aside from the nationalist offense, the Signora likely took affront at what she perceived to be officials' slight of her family and their failure to recognize her status and position. The names of the most privileged members of Triestine society did not appear on the list for automatic restoration. Such shipping magnates as the Cosuliches maintained their foreign-sounding name. Fulvio Suvich, a native Triestine, continued to bear his name while serving in a variety of national posts including Mussolini's financial representative to the League of Nations from 1931 to 1932 and undersecretary for foreign affairs from 1932 to 1936. The Signora's protest was likely meant to call local officials' attention to what she saw as her family's elevated position and to demonstrate officials' error in assuming that her family was simply one in the masses and without influence. In essence, it was a call to officials to respect her family, its heritage, and its status.

Fascism and the Modern Italian State

Not only did the enforcement of the legislation potentially set loyalty to family against loyalty to country, it had the unintended effect of accentuating regional differences rather than unifying the nation. It set a standard for the New Provinces that differed from that for pre-1918 Italy and highlighted differences in nationalist understandings between the center in Rome and periphery in Trieste. Officials in Trieste enforced the surname legislation with an eye toward assimilating loyal Italians. Those in Rome understood the legislation in a different light. Despite rhetoric that harped on the Italianness of border populations, Fascist officials in Rome harbored suspicions that the inhabitants of recently annexed territories were, in some way, insufficiently Italian.

The Signora's lawyer, well ensconced in Rome but with strong family ties to Trieste, played to national officials' prejudices, raising technical arguments that made Triestine officials appear to be somewhat alien, bumbling provincials. The legislation required that officials prove that a surname had an Italian or Latin root or had been altered or translated from an Italian form. The lawyer contended that the name Petrovich was of Slavic origin—it had no Italian root. Emphasis on Slavic origin was a particularly risky strategy. Slavs were often suspected to be Yugoslav agents or anti-Fascist communists or socialists. In the climate of increased foreign policy attention to Italian interests in the Balkans, Slavic attachments or association with Slavic causes was sufficient to brand an individual an enemy of the state. Enemies of the state risked being tried by Mussolini's Special Tribunal for the Defense of the State, which imposed harsh punishments for disloyalty, among them imprisonment, hard labor, exile, or even death. The Signora's lawyer's insistence that Petrovich was of Slavic origin suggested that he believed Fascist judicial authorities' commitment to upholding Italian law would outweigh aspirations to promote nationalist agendas and Italianization.

In fact, the lawyer had crafted his argument carefully to prove remote origins of the name Petrovich while at the same time affirming the family's long-standing loyalty to Italy. According to the affidavit, the Petrovich family hailed from Zara (today, Zadar, Croatia), a city nicknamed, according to the lawyer, "the rock of the Italianness of Dalmatia," an area of the Adriatic coast, much of which was in Yugoslav hands in the early 1930s but remained contested by Italy. Copies of birth and marriage records showed that the family's name had been Petrovich at least as far back as the eighteenth century. The lawyer argued that any contention that the name had been altered to a Slavic form earlier, prior to the eighteenth century, was "absurd and illogical" because Zara had been under the control of Italian Venice from AD 1200.[10] The lawyer further argued that the suffix "ich," as opposed to "ic," testified to a tradition of fealty to Venice. "Common knowledge held" that Venetian officials added an "h" to signal sympathies for the Republic. By implication, then, the family had taken part in maintaining Zara's Italianness. Separating the origins of the surname from the actions of the individuals and family involved, the lawyer divorced national loyalty from association with an inherited surname, effectively calling into question the bases of the legislation.

The lawyer's other arguments of a technical nature painted Triestine officials as careless in their work and possessing little knowledge or understanding of the subtleties of Italian law. The lawyer undermined the credibility of

Triestine officials by asserting that the Signora to whom the decree referred "did not exist": Signora Petrovich was born in June 1856, not May 1854. He argued that the decree failed to identify his client as the "widow Petri," a requirement for any woman who wished to use her deceased husband's surname. The lawyer also noted that changing the widow's married surname was proscribed because Italian law prohibited changing the name of a dead man. Such arguments made the lawyer, and the Signora by extension, appear to be protectors of the honor of Italian law and of the state.

Fascist Priorities

In January 1932, the Judicial Branch of Central Council of State directed Triestine officials to rescind the name restoration decree and to pay the Signora's court costs. They ruled that officials in Trieste had failed to prove that the name Petrovich was originally a name of Italian origin that had been altered over the course of history. Therefore, Triestine functionaries had exceeded their authority and falsely applied the law.

Despite the superior court's decision, officials in Trieste continued to "restore" surnames in much the same manner as they had prior to the trial. They still referred to the list to initiate automatic corrections, and they even added more names to it. Authorities in Rome took no action to impede the continued flow of restoration decrees nor did they step in to oversee the name restoration process despite their rebuke of Triestine officials. A handful of surname correction cases were subsequently referred to Rome for adjudication, and in each case, representatives of the higher court simply scolded the Triestines once again for excessive zeal and referred to the Signora's case as the legal precedent. Central authorities' disregard suggests that despite fascism's rhetorical emphasis on nationalism, nationalization of the border populations was a peripheral concern.

The gulf between aims and policies set in Rome and understandings of Rome's intent in the peripheries was evident in Triestine officials' response to other issues raised in the Signora's case but ignored by the Court of Cassation in reaching its verdict. Officers of the Rome court said that the lawyer's additional arguments, those made on the basis of nationalist orientation, gender roles, and the validity of the decree (outside of proof of the name's origin), were not considered in light of the abuse of authority. But Triestine officials heeded the lawyer's admonishment regarding the prohibition on alteration of a dead man's name. After the adjudication of the Signora's case, they discontinued the correction of widows' married surnames and refused to grant alterations to widows who requested them. The case's effect on

Fascist policy reflected the regime's adherence to traditional gendered views that affirmed a wife's tie to her husband (even after his death), as well as its intention to uphold the male's legal rights and status. These gender-based notions that actually preceded fascism continued to have an impact under Mussolini's government and, in such cases as the Signora's, even outweighed what appeared to be specifically Fascist priorities.

Conclusion

Local zeal to promote nationalization brought Signora Petrovich into conflict with authorities. Her appeal to Rome and the outcome of her case revealed the tensions within the Fascist system. Seen as highly centralized, repressive, and even violent, the Italian Fascist state suffered under the weight of tensions and misunderstandings that undermined its powers and inhibited its actions. The Signora's protest showed how resourceful citizens could choose, if they had economic means, stature, and creativity, to ignore or even challenge Fascist authorities without incurring the wrath of the state.

The Signora's case demonstrates that "agency," what some scholars term the ability of an individual to choose and follow a specific course of action, remained a viable option for many members of the population under fascism. Shrouded in the language of compliance with Fascist ideals, the Signora's protest, as presented by her lawyer, invoked the very ideals articulated by the Fascist regime for a woman in her position. The Signora's ability to act was rooted in her social and economic status as well as her family's position. The Signora made no claim to feminism nor was she an activist. The story of her triumph over Fascist dictates is, ironically, one of compliance with and acceptance of the expectations and limitations imposed on her by Fascist society.

The progress of the Signora's case also demonstrates the contradictions inherent in nationalist policies and the lack of coherence in notions of national identity. In Trieste, where officials dealt regularly with border issues and overlapping or competing identities, the threat to Italian nationalist aspirations was palpable. Zealous enforcement of the legislation had immediate and visible effects. Rome was distant in both geographic and ideological terms.

Mussolini's fall from power in 1943, while related to Italy's poor wartime performance and home-front difficulties and shortages, was facilitated by the erosion of Fascist power from within. It resulted, at least in part, from fascism's failure to deal effectively with problems and concerns that preoccupied populations around the country and outside the center of power. It was a result, too, of the Fascist reliance on the facade of consensus or promotion of compliance to demonstrate Italian support for the regime. Consensus required flexibility that compromised the regime's authority and power.

Mussolini did rely on violence and intimidation to gain and maintain power. He did establish a dictatorship. However, his Fascist society was built on traditional social divisions and relied on the maintenance of social privileges accepted throughout interwar Europe and Western society. Touted as a middle road between Western-style capitalist democracy and communism, Italian fascism gained international recognition and even approval for a time in the period between the world wars. To cast the Signora as a vindicated victim of the Fascist regime overlooks the realities of her situation and misrepresents the position of the Fascist state. Signora Petrovich enjoyed very real advantages in Fascist society. Her social status and connections enabled her to throw down the gauntlet and challenge the decree. Triestine authorities' overzealousness served as the basis for the Signora's legal triumph, but she won her case not at the expense of the regime, but in collaboration with it. The Signora recognized her role in Fascist society, and through the efforts of her lawyer, launched her appeal based on broad understandings and expectations related to traditionalist assumptions that carved her niche in Italian Fascist society and interwar Europe.

Notes

I am grateful to Alexander De Grand for his helpful comments and criticisms on a draft of this chapter. I also wish to thank participants in the conference "Women, Gender, and the Extreme Right in Europe, 1919–1945," held in Cardiff, Wales, in July 2001 for their comments on a paper recounting the Signora's experience.

1. All documentation of the Signora's case is contained in the file bearing her name in Trieste–Archivio di Stato–Prefettura della Provincia di Trieste, Divisione I: Riduzione Cognomi Trieste, No. 11419 (1926–1943). The collection includes documents and decrees related to the surname statutes of January 1926 and April 1927. Officially sealed to protect the rights of individuals, the files were consulted by special permission. Petrovich and Petri are pseudonyms assigned to protect the identity of the Signora and her family. They capture the essence of the modification.

2. From September 1943 to April 1945 Mussolini, propped up by Hitler's Third Reich, held titular power over northern Italy in the Salò Republic, a puppet state of Nazi Germany.

3. Aldo Pizzagalli, *Per l'italianità dei cognomi nella provincia di Trieste* (Trieste: Treves-Zanichelli, 1929), 87–106.

4. According to existing documentation, as many as one in four names were corrected by petition. Although initiated by the individuals concerned, these "corrections"

did not necessarily indicate zeal for nationalization. Rather, in the Fascist society, officials encouraged such petitions and they could be politically expedient or necessary, particularly for those occupying government, civil service, teaching, or other state-supported posts. Even those in private ventures might feel pressure to Italianize in order to win the regime's favor.

5. Michela De Giorgio, *Le italiane dall'unità a oggi: Modelli culturali e comportamenti sociali* (Bari: Laterza, 1993), 18.

6. On the demographic campaign, see David Horn, *Social Bodies: Science, Reproduction, and Italian Modernity* (Princeton, NJ: Princeton University Press, 1994), 44–48.

7. De Giorgio, *Le italiane*, 10–13.

8. For example, a wedding band contribution was initiated in December 1935 to allow women to demonstrate their support for Italian military efforts.

9. Robin Pickering-Iazzi, ed., *Mothers of Invention: Women, Italian Fascism, and Culture* (Minneapolis: University of Minnesota Press, 1995), offers a variety of perspectives on women's ability to navigate Fascist structures.

10. Surnames, as recognized in the modern context, would not have been used prior to the Venetian period. On the development of surnames in Europe see James C. Scott, John Tehranian, and Jeremy Mathias, "The Production of Legal Identities Proper to States: The Case of the Permanent Family Surname," *Comparative Studies in Society and History* 44, no. 1 (2002): 4–44.

Suggested Readings

Bosworth, R. J. B. *Mussolini's Italy: Life under the Dictatorship, 1915–1945*. New York: Penguin, 2006.

Cannistraro, Philip V. *Historical Dictionary of Fascist Italy*. Westport, CT: Greenwood Press, 1982.

De Felice, Renzo. *Interpretations of Fascism*. Cambridge, MA: Harvard University Press, 1977.

De Grand, Alexander. *Fascist Italy and Nazi Germany: The "Fascist" Style of Rule*. New York: Routledge, 1995.

———. *Italian Fascism: Its Origins and Development*. Lincoln: University of Nebraska Press, 1982.

De Grazia, Victoria. *How Fascism Ruled Women: Italy, 1922–1945*. Berkeley: University of California Press, 1992.

Gentile, Emilio. *The Struggle for Modernity: Nationalism, Futurism, and Fascism*. Westport, CT: Praeger, 2003.

Griffin, Roger. *Fascism*. Oxford: Oxford University Press, 1995.

Hametz, Maura. *Making Trieste Italian, 1918–1954*. London: Royal Historical Society—Boydell, 2005.

Horn, David. *Social Bodies: Science, Reproduction, and Italian Modernity*. Princeton, NJ: Princeton University Press, 1994.

Ipsen, Carl. *Dictating Demography: The Problem of Population in Fascist Italy*. Cambridge: Cambridge University Press, 1996.

Koon, Tracy. *Believe, Obey, Fight: The Political Socialization of Youth in Fascist Italy, 1922–1943*. Chapel Hill: University of North Carolina Press, 1985.

Lyttleton, Adrian. *The Seizure of Power: Fascism in Italy, 1919–1929*. New York: Scribner, 1973.

Mack Smith, Denis. *Mussolini*. New York: Alfred A. Knopf, 1982.

Pickering-Iazzi, Robin, ed. *Mothers of Invention: Women, Italian Fascism, and Culture*. Minneapolis: University of Minnesota Press, 1995.

Quine, Maria Sophia. *Italy's Social Revolution: Charity and Welfare from Liberalism to Fascism*. New York: Palgrave, 2002.

Sarti, Roland. *Fascism and the Industrial Leadership in Italy, 1919–1940: A Study of the Expansion of Private Power under Fascism*. Berkeley: University of California Press, 1971.

Schnapp, Jeffrey, Olivia Sears, and Maria Stampino. *A Primer of Italian Fascism*. Lincoln: University of Nebraska Press, 2000.

~

CHAPTER TEN

The Herbert Baum Groups

Networks of Jewish, Leftist, and Youth Resistance in the Third Reich

JOHN COX

With Germany's defeat in World War I in 1918, revolution led to the collapse of the German Empire and the establishment of Germany's first democracy, the Weimar Republic. The republic faced significant challenges, including economic hardship and popular resentment over the terms of the post–World War I settlement. The Treaty of Versailles had imposed on Germany large war payments to Britain and France and the moral guilt of the sole responsibility for the war. In the interwar period, the rising Nazi Party (National Socialist German Workers Party) under the leadership of Adolf Hitler profited from these conditions to become a mass party with increasing popular support.

When Adolf Hitler came to power in Germany on 30 January 1933, he destroyed the weak parliamentary democracy of the Weimar Republic. The Nazis then began the process of consolidating their dictatorial control over the German government and society. With the policy of Gleichschaltung (roughly translated as "coordination"), the Nazi program attempted to take over most aspects of civil society, from schools and youth groups to sports clubs and churches. Hundreds of thousands of Germans became a part of Nazi-controlled organizations, such as the Hitler Youth and the League of German Girls. Under the Nazi vision, all of German society was to be incorporated into the party's ultranationalist, racist, militaristic, and authoritarian program.

However, the Nazis' control over German society was not absolute, as this chapter demonstrates. Here, John Cox examines networks of leftist, Jewish youth *groups that organized around the leadership of a young man named Herbert Baum. Living in the midst of the Third Reich's extreme anti-Semitism, anticommunism, and oppressive dictatorial rule, these young people risked their lives as both leftists and German Jews. They arranged underground readings and music gatherings, distributed anti-Nazi leaflets, and even staged an attack against a Nazi-organized anti-Soviet exhibit. Overall, the anti-Nazi underground's efforts against the Third Reich within Germany were small, and its abilities to pose a significant challenge to the Third Reich's political power were extremely limited. The tragic fate of most members of the Baum networks illustrates the immense challenges faced by any who tried to resist. Yet in countless everyday oppositional activities, these German Jewish young people represented individuals who attempted to maintain their integrity, political principles, and sense of self in the face of dictatorship. The inability of such groups to gain wider support among the German population also reminds us of the mass popularity, or at least tolerance, of the Nazis, an attitude that ultimately helped the Holocaust to occur.*

On 8 May 1942, Soviet Paradise, an exhibition staged by Nazi propaganda minister Joseph Goebbels depicting the poverty and degradation of Russia under its supposed "Jewish-Bolshevik" regime, opened with great fanfare in the Lustgarten square in Berlin. One newspaper optimistically predicted that it would be "the most successful political exhibition yet. . . . Several million people shall visit."[1] However, not everyone was quite as enthusiastic. At approximately eight o'clock on the evening of 18 May, several explosives ignited around the periphery of Soviet Paradise. Although fire trucks responded quickly, a portion of the installation burned that evening. The German press was predictably silent, but news of the attack spread by word of mouth, and the dictatorship suffered a rare embarrassment. Had Goebbels and his immediate superior, Adolf Hitler, known the identity of the saboteurs at the time, they would undoubtedly have been even more enraged: this bold action was perpetrated by young Jews—moreover, they were German Jews who belonged to leftist organizations.

The Gestapo was too efficient and methodical to allow such an act to go unpunished. Within days, the police had rounded up, tortured, and sentenced to death most of the members of two underground groups led by Herbert Baum, who had organized the attack. While the spectacular assault on Soviet Paradise increased the outside world's knowledge of the internal leftist opposition, the Baum groups had already earned a reputation within the German underground resistance. Herbert Baum had begun building his network of dissident groups and circles in the first days of the dictatorship, and it would become the largest organization of German-Jewish resisters. The story of the Baum groups is also significant because it is only one example of a broader history of anti-Nazi activism among young Jews living under Hitler's reign of terror.

Herbert Baum was born in February 1912 in Prussia. His political activity commenced at an early age, which was not unusual at that time. Baum belonged to the Social Democratic youth movement, the Red Falcons, from 1925 to 1928. From 1928 on he was a member of the German-Jewish Youth Society (DJJG), where he met his future wife, Marianne Cohn. Around the time that the DJJG broke up, in 1931, Baum joined the Communist Party youth organization, the KJVD. In each of these groups he quickly assumed a leading role.

Baum was a gifted organizer, melding personal charisma with political passion. An acquaintance of Baum's from the 1920s recalled, "In his calm style he always pleaded for justice. . . . [He spoke] in such a persuasive and simple manner, that everyone not only understood him, but also agreed with him. He had everything that a natural-born leader" should possess. Another old friend from the Jewish youth movement attested to these qualities, adding, "We all tried to outdo ourselves when 'Hebbi' [Baum's nickname] participated."[2] These traits were augmented by a "combative nature," according to another former comrade, who explained that Baum declined to flee Germany in the late 1930s because "he saw himself as head of a group with special responsibilities and believed in the imminent defeat of fascism."[3]

Baum's principal allegiance was to the German Communist Party (KPD), the world's largest such party outside the Soviet Union in the 1920s and early 1930s. Larger yet was the German Social Democratic Party (SPD). Along with smaller radical groups, the KPD and the SPD grew substantially during the turbulent years of Germany's Weimar Republic (1919–1933), and together the two parties enjoyed the support of millions of workers and more than one-third of the electorate. But the left was not the only political force to gain sustenance from Germany's deepening economic and political turmoil. Initially a minor grouping in the spectrum of nationalist and racist organizations, the National Socialist German Workers Party (NSDAP, or Nazi Party) drew German nationalists, anti-Semites, and other right-wingers under its banner during the Weimar years. Founded as the German Workers Party in early 1918, the party adopted its full name in early 1920, a few months after a thirty-year-old demobilized army veteran from Austria, Adolf Hitler, found his way into its ranks.

In the early 1920s the Nazis were based in Munich, the site of their ill-fated 1923 Beerhall Putsch, which led to the deaths of a few members and Hitler's conviction and imprisonment. A sympathetic criminal-justice system ensured that Hitler served less than one year of his five-year sentence. The NSDAP languished in the political wilderness for several more years following Hitler's release from prison, but gained greater support as well as converts at the end of the 1920s. The Nazi Party quadrupled its membership in the second half of the decade, from 25,000 to 100,000, although this was still not a large number on the landscape of German politics.

The Nazis combined radical-sounding populism with ultranationalism and extreme anticommunism and anti-Semitism. Their paramilitary squads and penchant for street battles with leftists appealed to wayward youths, and they benefited from an upsurge in nationalist sentiment. While most of the Nazis' vote, as well as membership, came from lower-middle-class Germans, by the early 1930s they received significant support from workers as well.

The worldwide economic depression brought about the collapse of Weimar's governing coalition. The centrist parties were pushed to the sidelines by the Far Right and Far Left, whose parties made significant electoral gains in the early 1930s, and in July 1932 the NSDAP gained the largest share in federal elections. These elections mirrored the severe polarization of German politics, which was now embodied in the spectacle of 100 uniformed KPD deputies and 196 brown-shirted Nazi deputies sitting in the parliament (Reichstag). By this point a growing number of Germany's landowning and industrial elites had come to see the Nazis, whose hooliganism and overheated rhetoric they had earlier disdained, as their best defense against the far more frightening specter of revolution from the Left. In January 1933 President Paul von Hindenburg and other ruling conservatives appointed Adolf Hitler chancellor, believing they could thereby rein in the Nazis. They would be grossly mistaken, as Hitler and his movement consolidated their rule over the next year and a half.

Baum had one foot firmly planted in the thriving subculture of the German-Jewish youth movements, and the other foot in the Communist milieu, when disaster struck in 1933. Hitler's victory would violently shatter each of those social and political worlds. The German Left and labor movements were the regime's first victims: By the end of Hitler's first year in power tens of thousands of KPD members were under arrest, many of them doomed to that feature of Nazism that would come to define its rule throughout Europe—the concentration camp. Approximately half the KPD's 1933 membership was subjected to Hitler's extensive, ghastly jail and camp system, and some 20,000 Communists perished under the Third Reich.

Meanwhile, life for Germany's Jews grew steadily more intolerable as Hitler consolidated his regime. The 1 April 1933 anti-Jewish boycott proclaimed by the government is often considered the beginning of the institutionalized offensive against German Jewry; in the weeks preceding the boycott, however, Jews were victimized by Nazi militants in cities throughout the country, including Berlin, where storm troopers seized several dozen east European Jews to be shipped off to concentration camps. Thus began the process that would ultimately lead to the death camps, although in those first days of the Hitler regime neither the perpetrators nor the victims imagined the "final solution."

New Forms of Resistance

From the first days of the Third Reich, Baum coordinated a network of small groups comprising young radicals, most of them Jewish. While Baum tried his best to follow the political lead of the KPD, his groups accommodated a variety of political viewpoints. Unable to wage an open struggle against the Nazi state, resisters in the Baum groups engaged in covert forms of resistance, surreptitiously dropping leaflets around Berlin, scrawling anti-Hitler graffiti on walls, and seeking allies among the forced laborers in the factories where they worked. Baum's groups coordinated political discussions and carried out some clandestine leafleting. The leaflets would usually contain brief slogans or exhortations ("Be a good citizen—think for yourself," "Love your country, think for yourself. A good German is not afraid to say 'no'").[4] Some of these actions were rather bold and imaginative given the conditions of life under the police state. One former member described an action led by Baum in July 1934: "Explosives with detonators were contrived by the anti-fascist underground and placed in tin cans. A metal plate covered the explosive material and on top of the plate leaflets were stuffed. These cans were placed on rooftops. An hour later they blew up and scattered the leaflets onto the streets."[5]

But the main activities of the Baum groups were semi-informal evenings—usually called by the members *Heimabende*, literally "home evenings" or study groups—that revolved around discussions of novels, political texts, and music. Some veterans of the Baum groups later emphasized that they would have liked to have threatened and confronted the Nazi state more directly. Yet the evening meetings clearly served a purpose beyond their educational and social value. They imparted cohesiveness, helped the participants maintain morale, and attracted new members to Baum's resistance network. While such gatherings were not the monopoly of German-Jewish youth organizations, their centrality for the Baum groups clearly suggests a debt to the backgrounds of many of their members in the once-vibrant German-Jewish youth organizations. Gerhard Bry, a Jewish

youth activist during the Weimar Republic and later a member of a dissident communist group, remembered that he and his fellow youth activists
"talked about everything that existed between heaven and earth."[6] Other
veterans of the German-Jewish youth movements have similar recollections. The centrality of the Heimabende within the Baum network was also
a function of the youthfulness of the Baum groups' members—anyone
whose teenage or college years included impassioned, late-night rumina-
tions on theory, philosophy, and life can identify with the youths attracted
to Baum's niche within Berlin's dissident subcultures.

The Heimabende were characterized by youthful enthusiasm and an almost limitless intellectual curiosity. Rita Zocher hosted meetings in her
apartment, where she and her comrades read Heinrich Heine and more contemporary authors, while also discussing such orthodox Marxist literature as
The Communist Manifesto and Engels's *Origin of the Family, Private Property,
and the State*. The group included several musicians, and they listened to and
discussed works by various composers, including Beethoven and
Tchaikovsky. Zocher and her colleagues chafed under the restrictions that
prevented them from enjoying "theater or concerts, good music and literature."[7] She recalled that one of the group's favorite plays was Goethe's
Egmont. Goethe's tragedy—which was considered a radical, democratic statement in its time—is set in the early years of the sixteenth-century Dutch revolt against Spanish rule. The hero perishes knowing that his cause will not
prevail until after his death. Count Egmont sees the future in a dream vision
shortly before his execution: "She [the vision of Liberty] bids him be of good
cheer, and, as she signifies to him that his death will achieve the liberation
of the provinces, she hails him as victor."

Two momentous events altered the political and social landscape for
Baum's groups in 1938 and 1939. The first of these was the Kristallnacht
pogrom of November 1938, a night of anti-Semitic terror unleashed by
Goebbels and other Nazi leaders, which heralded a drastic escalation of the
Nazis' anti-Jewish persecutions. The second, Germany's invasion of Poland
the following September, marked the start of World War II. Over the next
two months the Nazi government implemented numerous laws and policy
initiatives that harshly aggravated the plight of German Jewry: among the
more egregious sanctions in the wake of Kristallnacht were that all Jewish
business activity would be banned as of the end of the year, and Jews would
have to "sell their enterprises, as well as any land, stocks, jewels, and art
works"; they would be "forbidden public entertainments"; and Jewish children were expelled from German schools.[8]

When the war began, the anti-Jewish offensive proceeded on several fronts. Curfews became more restrictive; food rations were cut and the list of foods forbidden to Jews grew ever longer; and the Nazis began evicting many Jews from their homes on short notice, continually forcing them from place to place, reducing them to a status of "refugees within their own country."[9] And for all Jews—but especially for those engaged in anything that could be deemed "subversive"—the danger of arrest and incarceration loomed ominously. This debilitating fear was also exacerbated by the events of 1938 and 1939: a month after Germany's invasion of Poland, Heinrich Himmler "ordered the immediate arrest and incarceration in a concentration camp of any Jew who failed to comply immediately with any instruction or who demonstrated antistate behavior in any other way."[10]

The start of the war held additional ramifications for the Baum groups and other leftist resisters. One week before invading Poland, the Nazi government signed the Nonaggression Pact with the Soviet Union, leading immediately to a reversal of policy by Communist parties throughout Europe. No longer was Hitler the chief "enemy of peace" in Communist propaganda and oratory, but simply one in a list of "imperialist warmongers." KPD rhetoric and literature, as well as action, adapted accordingly, and the Communist underground resistance was virtually suspended inside Germany for the next twenty-two months.

New Opportunities, New Dangers

Although many historians have categorized the Baum network as Communist, it operated independently of any dictates from Moscow or the exiled German Communist leadership. And over time the groups became increasingly heterogeneous in their politics, incorporating elements of varied traditions that always included a strong influence from the pre-1933 German-Jewish youth movements. Some surviving members later recalled heated debates within the groups about the Nonaggression Pact and its implications, as Baum and a few others attempted to defend the new line from Moscow, while others rejected the notion that anti-Nazi resistance should be subordinated to Soviet diplomacy. At any rate, while the tempo of their activity slowed after the pact, the Baum groups maintained their operations and undertook new forms of resistance.

From 1940 Herbert Baum, along with several of his closest comrades, was a forced laborer at the Elmo-Werke. Baum was elected representative of the Jewish workers, and he coordinated a small circle of resisters within the plant and had some success in planning resistance activities—such as sabotaging production at the factory—in conjunction with Dutch and French slave laborers. Baum also had indirect contact with the Robert Uhrig organization, a large Communist-led resistance network that was based in Berlin's factories. In the autumn of 1940, Baum learned that Rudi Arndt, a Jewish Communist and leader of the underground resistance at Buchenwald, had been murdered there. Arndt, who was one of the first prisoners at the notorious camp, "encouraged his fellow prisoners to write poems and songs," according to one source, "and made the greatest efforts to combat the degradation of humanity" that characterized existence in the camp. He was permitted to assemble a string quartet, which performed works by Mozart, Haydn, and Beethoven. Arndt was also acknowledged by the Buchenwald authorities as a spokesperson for the prisoners, and was derisively termed the "king of the Jews."[11]

Baum and his colleagues, who by this time—a year into the restraint of the nonaggression period—were impatient for action, decided to hold a memorial gathering for Arndt in Berlin's large Jewish cemetery, the Weißensee. This was a particularly risky venture, as it involved a congregation of approximately fifty people at a time when any sort of a crowd would arouse police suspicion. The memorial was held successfully, and this bold action bolstered the spirits of the participants and whetted the appetites of many for further action.

Baum's group met in various apartments in Berlin during this time, including that of Charlotte Paech. Paech was born in 1909, and thus was, like the Baums, older than many other members of the groups. She had briefly met Herbert as a member of the DJJG in the early 1930s, and was reacquainted with him in 1939 when he checked into the Jewish hospital where she worked as a nurse.[12] Her future husband, Richard Holzer—who, along with Charlotte, escaped the Gestapo roundup and survived the war—was also part of Baum's closest circle, which met weekly and discussed various literary and political texts. Like several others who had drifted into Baum's orbit over the previous decade, Holzer had once been a member of an anarchist group called the *Schwarzer Haufen*.

Furthermore, under Baum's loose supervision, Martin and Sala Kochmann, who were also relatively old—they were both born in 1912—organized a group out of their apartment near the old Jewish synagogue in the center of Berlin. Martin had been a member of the DJJG in his teenage years and during the first year of the dictatorship had spent a few months in jail for his participation in a "leaflet action."[13] The couple (they married in 1938) had known Baum since the early 1930s. Sala played a leading role in this circle, making it one of the very few to be led or co-led by a woman.

It was also during this period that Baum began collaborating with the Joachim Group, which was organized by Heinz Joachim and included about a dozen young Jewish men and women, split almost evenly between the sexes. Born in 1919, Joachim played several instruments and studied clarinet at a private music school in Berlin. In 1941 he was pressed into forced labor at the Siemens Elmo-Werke, where he organized an underground group independent of Baum's network in 1940 and early 1941. Joachim initiated contact with Baum in 1941, and from that time on they collaborated. Joachim held weekly meetings in his apartment in the Berlin neighborhood of Prenzlauer Berg for a circle that included his wife, Marianne, who was nearly three years younger than he, and about ten other young Jewish intellectuals and activists.

Like her husband, Marianne Prager was a talented musician and an intellectually adventurous youth. The couple, like most of the young adults in Baum's network in its final incarnation, were too young to have had more than a year or two of experience in the pre-1933 Jewish youth subculture, although Marianne had joined a Jewish youth group in 1935. She was raised in a musical family, and played the piano; a voracious reader, she was particularly fond of Thomas Mann and Leo Tolstoy. "Marianne was so attached to literature and music," according to one account, "that she told the family shortly after Kristallnacht: 'If they ever come for my books or my piano, they will have to take me first!'"[14]

Baum worked closely with two other groups after the invasion of the Soviet Union: the Hans Fruck group, a small band of Communist youths, and a group led by Joachim Franke and Werner Steinbrinck. These two groups would be instrumental in initiating and carrying out the arson of Soviet Paradise. Franke had been a member of the Communist Party in the late 1920s but, according to his testimony under interrogation, left the party in 1928 due to "my oppositional attitude."[15] Steinbrinck was a "committed Marxist," as he would defiantly state to Gestapo interrogators, and had been a member of the KJVD since 1933, when he was fifteen years old. Steinbrinck had participated in numerous underground KJVD cells and informal dissident circles. Through his employment as a chemical technician at the Kaiser Wilhelm Institute he would obtain the materials for the firebombing of Goebbels's exhibition.[16]

"We Have Gone on the Offensive"

In the early morning of 22 June 1941, three million German soldiers, supported by 600,000 motorized vehicles, thousands of tanks, and 2,740 airplanes, stormed across the Soviet Union's western border. With the Soviet Union now drawn into the war, Communist-related resistance groups throughout Europe, including Baum's, reenergized their efforts to combat Nazism by whatever means were at their disposal. Within the first few months following the invasion, the Baum groups' activities became more bold and open, and the members gained a confidence that at times bordered on the reckless. This audacity was inspired by more than simply an implicit duty to defend the Soviet Union; it was also spawned by a combination of hope and misplaced optimism. Early in 1942, Baum wrote a letter to Communist officials in exile in which he expressed his view that a "mass movement," which the underground was ostensibly on the verge of creating, could "transform" the imperialist war into a "civil war."[17] He added, "We have gone on the offensive." If this perspective seems unrealistic in retrospect, there were some tangible causes for optimism: the slowing of the German offensive by the Soviets' successful defense of Moscow in December 1941, aided by an unusually early and bitter winter; Hitler's ill-advised 11 December declaration of war on the United States; and growing discontent on the home front.

The increased assertiveness of the Baum-coordinated underground stemmed not only from this optimism, but also from a desperation fueled by the increasing tempo of deportations of German Jews to the east. The German government had begun deporting Jews from Berlin in October 1941, sending 1,000 Jews to the Lodz ghetto. By January 1942, about ten thousand Jews had been forcibly transported from Berlin to ghettos in eastern Europe. Many of those deported were friends and relatives of the Baum groups' members.

While exuding confidence, members of the Baum's circles were not immune to the deepening gloom and anxiety that gripped Berlin's dwindling Jewish population. Unknown to Berlin's Jews, if perhaps dimly perceived by a few like Baum who had access to outside reports, the destruction of European Jewry was well under way. And even if it was impossible to imagine the intent and scale of the unfolding genocide, Berlin's Jews were undergoing their own personal miseries. "The year 1942 was a particularly fertile one for the creative bureaucrats of persecution," historian Christopher Browning later observed. "Perhaps precisely because their victims were fast disappearing into death camps in the east and their years of accumulated expertise in Jewish affairs would soon be professionally irrelevant, they hastened to construct legislative monuments to their own zeal."[18] "Not a day without a new decree against Jews," wrote an aging Jewish academic in his diary in mid-March.[19] Time was running out on the Baum groups.

Soviet Paradise

"Words and pictures are not enough to make the tragedy of Bolshevist reality believable to Europeans," began the exhibition's accompanying pamphlet, so Goebbels's team assembled a collection of dilapidated shacks and other ramshackle buildings to illustrate the "misery and hopelessness of the lives of the farmers and workers." Rita Zocher, a friend of Herbert Baum's since childhood, recalled that Soviet Paradise was replete with "a great big pile of dung . . . old apartments, old farmers' huts," depicting a society in which "nothing [was] newly built" and "the people were all robbers and criminals."[20] The catalog accompanying Soviet Paradise was explicit in its anti-Semitism and in its identification of Judaism with bolshevism.

Werner Steinbrinck had been working as a lab technician for about two years at the Kaiser Wilhelm Institute in Berlin. He was able to purloin a kilogram of explosive black powder, as well as a flammable solution, carbon disulfide.[21] He also went to a library, by coincidence only a couple of hundred meters west of the Lustgarten, and borrowed a book on fireworks. On Sunday, 17 May, Steinbrinck brought the materials he had procured from his workplace to Joachim Franke's apartment, and the two worked for several hours constructing a few rudimentary explosive devices, while Franke's wife, Erika, attended to the couple's eight-year-old son.

Beginning at seven o'clock the next evening, eleven members of the Baum and Franke groups made their way to Soviet Paradise in groups of one or two. Marianne Baum and Hilde Jadamowitz arrived first, mingling with a crowd that grew to number approximately two thousand visitors. Steinbrinck made his way to the Lustgarten and handed Baum one of the explosive devices. Franke was to deposit another one in a cupboard in the so-called Speisehaus, or meal room, of the ersatz Soviet village. The conspirators were compelled to look for another location, however, upon finding that the Speisehaus was closed that day.[22] Steinbrinck joined Franke, and they threw one of the explosives into a shack that was part of the exhibit, and then fled the scene when another device, held by Steinbrinck in a briefcase, began to emit smoke. They tossed it into a sewer drain a few blocks away. When Herbert Baum's small firebomb also malfunctioned and began incinerating the bag that contained it, Baum fled the exhibit, as did the other members at about the same time, approximately an hour and a half after most of them had arrived.

Despite these difficulties, Baum and his compatriots had succeeded in placing one firebomb, which burned the shack and a small part of the exhibit before firefighters arrived and a large police contingent cordoned off the area. Although the Baum and Steinbrinck-Franke groups had damaged a minor part of Soviet Paradise, the exhibit opened as usual the next day. The German press dutifully neglected to report the incident, but the Gestapo set to work immediately, forming a special investigating committee. Heinrich Himmler, in his capacity as chief of the Gestapo and of all the German police, received a telex that afternoon informing him of the "sabotage attack on the anti-Bolshevik exhibition, the 'Soviet Paradise.'"[23]

Arrests and Reprisals

Steinbrinck had planned to meet Baum five days later, on Saturday, 23 May, but that meeting never took place. At noon on 22 May, Herbert and Marianne Baum, Gerhard Meyer, and Heinz Rotholz were arrested at their workplace, the Elmo-Werke. Joachim Franke, Werner Steinbrinck, and all the members of their group were arrested the same day. Another four dozen people—some of whom were only tangentially linked to the Baum groups—were arrested in June and July.

The courage and spirit of defiance of many of the young resisters is evident from the transcripts. Heinz Rotholz stated, "I wish to add that I knew about the preparations of the sabotage action against the 'Soviet Paradise.' Had the comrades not excluded me from the act because of my Jewish appearance, I would have gone on Monday to the exhibit and taken part in the act." Lotte Rotholz told her inquisitors, "One must utilize every opportunity to fight against the present regime. . . . But one thing was clear to me: as a Jew I must not lag behind . . . my ties were and remain with Baum."[24] Herbert Budzislawski stated that he was compelled as a Jew to fight "injustice in Germany"—the only way, as he saw it, to find a way to "live in Germany as a human being."[25]

The police dragged Baum back into the Elmo-Werke plant, hoping that he might reveal some of his collaborators or that some of this friends would inadvertently expose themselves when they saw their badly beaten comrade. This effort failed.[26] On 11 June the Gestapo informed the state prosecutor that Herbert Baum had been declared a suicide, although it is likely that he had been tortured to death in the three weeks after his arrest—in either case, a victim of state terror.[27] The Gestapo kept no interrogation records on the case, and simply noted, without providing a coroner's report or other evidence, that Baum had "hanged himself."[28] At least three other members of Baum's groups died in police custody, either murdered or by their own hand. All told, thirty-two members and supporters of Baum's groups were executed or otherwise murdered by the German authorities over the next year and a half. Sixteen of those executed were no more than twenty-three years old. Most were charged with "high treason" and tried before the Nazis' "special courts," which prosecuted political crimes.

Others far beyond the periphery of the Baum groups would feel the wrath of the Nazi state in the aftermath of the Soviet Paradise attack. On 29 May 1942 the Gestapo rounded up Leo Baeck and a number of other prominent Jews, including officials of the National Association of Jews in Germany—established in 1939 and chaired by Baeck—in order to inform them of the attack, and the fact that 250 Jews had just been shot in response. Another 250 Jewish Berliners were arrested and sent to a nearby concentration camp, where they were killed soon thereafter.[29] It took little time for the Nazi authorities to realize the fears of some of Baum's fellow conspirators: that their actions would be used to destroy other Jews.

A small number of Baum's colleagues eluded the police dragnet. Charlotte Paech dodged the Gestapo for several months until her arrest in October 1942. Paech's fate seemed to be sealed when she was informed in June 1943 that she had been sentenced to death, and was thrown into a cell with three non-Jewish Polish women who were also awaiting their deaths. As they were each "taken away, I remained and waited for my execution." But shortly thereafter she was transferred to another prison in central Berlin. Paech used her medical training to help victims of typhus there, and, strengthened by the camaraderie of some of her fellow inmates and a slightly less brutal regimen, decided to escape if and when the opportunity arose. "To my help came a bombing raid. . . . I used the confusion to flee."[30] She survived the last year of Nazi Germany hiding out in the homes of various people whose addresses fellow inmates had given her. She eventually reunited with another survivor of the Baum groups, Richard Holzer, who was at one point deported to Ukraine and ended up in a Soviet camp for POWs. They married and, with a few other veterans of the Baum groups—mostly people who had left Germany in the 1930s, long before the Soviet Paradise attack—the Holzers organized memorial meetings in postwar East Germany to keep alive the memory of Berlin's Jewish left-wing resistance.

Legacies

German Jews learned quickly that there was no place for them in Hitler's Germany. Anti-Semitic actions and persecutions commenced in the first days of the regime, both in an organized manner—the April 1933 boycott, for example—and through violent actions by Nazi mobs. The shock was greatest for older Jews, who were more likely than their children and grandchildren to believe that they could preserve the social advances they had acquired over the course of previous decades. The younger generations of German Jews, far less inculcated with German patriotism than their elders, held few such hopes. Jewish youths tried to maintain some sense of community and contact with friends and acquaintances from their youth groups, which had played such a vital role in their lives. They also struggled to maintain or expand the narrow space they had for social and political life, which by necessity was only among fellow Jews. But the more radical of them sought a means to realize their desire to resist the assault on their rights and dignity.

Were the Baum groups successful? The success or failure of any form of resistance cannot be measured in an empirical, immediate sense. There was never any chance that the Baum groups would threaten the existence of the Third Reich. But seemingly humble and nonthreatening actions—cultural activities and self-education, for example—thwarted the Nazis' ambition to dehumanize and crush their victims. Collections for families of political prisoners, food distribution operations, working in a Jewish hospital as Charlotte Paech did—such acts could not topple the Third Reich, but they prevented the dictatorship from corrupting its victims morally and spiritually. Leaflet and graffiti actions, and the rare spectacular act, alerted portions of the public that not everyone had submitted, that it was possible to resist. And perhaps most important, these acts of resistance and refusal have a lasting, residual effect. If the history of world civilization is replete with war and tyranny, it also shows that decent, honorable impulses and the instinct for human solidarity can never be fully suppressed.

Notes

1. Quoted in Kurt Schilde, *Jugendorganisationen und Jugendopposition in Berlin-Kreuzberg 1933–45: Eine Dokumentation* (Berlin: Elefanten Verlag, 1983), 114.

2. Eric Brothers, "Wer war Herbert Baum?" in *Juden im Widerstand: Drei Gruppen zwischen Überlebenskampf und politischer Aktion*, ed. Wilfried Löhken and Werner Vathke (Berlin: Edition Hentrich, 1993), 85.

3. Hans-Rainer Sandvoß, *Widerstand in Mitte und Tiergarten* (Berlin: Gedenkstätte deutscher Widerstand, 1999), 169.

4. Bundesarchiv-Lichterfelde, Berlin (BA), NJ 1403; Centre de documentation juive contemporaine (CDJC), Paris, CCCLXXXI-35.

5. Eric Brothers, "On the Anti-Fascist Resistance of German Jews," *Leo Baeck Institute Yearbook* 32 (1987): 372.

6. Gerhard Bry, *Resistance: Recollections from the Nazi Years* (West Orange, NJ: published by author, 1979), 18–19.

7. Yad Vashem Archives (YVA), 03/4134, "Testimony of Rita Zocher," dictated by Zocher in 1979 in Tel Aviv.

8. Saul Friedländer, *Nazi Germany and the Jews: The Years of Persecution, 1933–1939* (New York: HarperCollins, 1997), 181–82.

9. Marion Kaplan, *Between Dignity and Despair: Jewish Life in Nazi Germany* (Oxford: Oxford University Press, 1998), 152–53.

10. Christopher Browning, *The Origins of the Final Solution: The Evolution of Nazi Jewish Policy, September 1939 to March 1942* (Lincoln: University of Nebraska Press, 2004), 174.

11. Stephan Hermlin, *Die Erste Reihe* (Dortmund: Weltkreis-Verlag, 1975), 37–43, and Lucien Steinberg, *Not as a Lamb: The Jews Against Hitler* (Glasgow: University Press, 1970), 30–31.

12. YVA, 03/3096, "Testimony of Charlotte Holzer," February 1964.

13. Bundesarchiv Zwischenarchiv Dahlwitz-Hoppegarten, Berlin (BA Zw), NJ 648. 11 September 1934 indictment against Kochmann and others.

14. Eric Brothers, "Profile of a German-Jewish Resistance Fighter," *Jewish Quarterly* 34 (1987): 33.

15. BA, NJ 1400. 22 May 1942 Joachim Franke interrogation record.

16. BA Zw, Z-C 12460. 26 May 1942 Werner Steinbrinck interrogation record.

17. Michael Kreutzer, lecture at opening of Juden im Widerstand exhibition (Halle, Germany, 4 March 2000).

18. Browning, *Origins*, 175.

19. Victor Klemperer, *I Will Bear Witness: A Diary of the Nazi Years 1942–1945* (New York: Random House, 1999), 29. The Nazis had just enacted "a ban on Jews buying flowers," Klemperer reported.

20. YVA 03/4134, "Testimony of Rita Zocher," dictated by Zocher in 1979 in Tel Aviv.

21. BA Zw, Z-C 12460, folder 5. 22 May 1942 Werner Steinbrinck interrogation record.

22. BA Zw, Z-C 12460. 26 May 1942 Werner Steinbrinck interrogation record.

23. Regina Scheer, *Im Schatten der Sterne: Eine jüdische Widerstandsgruppe* (Berlin: Aufbau-Verlag, 2004), 272.

24. Konrad Kwiet and Helmut Eschwege, *Selbstbehauptung und Widerstand: Deutsche Juden im Kampf um Existenz und Menschenwürde 1933–1945* (Hamburg: Hans Christians Verlag, 1984), 131.

25. BA Zw, Z-C 10905. 13 November 1942 Herbert Budzislawski interrogation record.

26. Helmut Eschwege, "Resistance of German Jews against the Nazi Regime," *Leo Baeck Institute Yearbook* 15 (1970): 176.

27. Bernard Mark reported that other inmates had witnessed his murder. Mark, "The Herbert Baum Group: Jewish Resistance in Germany in the Years 1937–1942," in *They Fought Back: The Story of Jewish Resistance in Nazi Europe*, ed. Yuri Suhl (New York: Schocken Books, 1967), 66.

28. Scheer, *Im Schatten*, 306.

29. Kwiet and Eschwege, *Selbstbehauptung und Widerstand*, 128.

30. YVA, 03/3096, "Testimony of Charlotte Holzer," February 1964.

Suggested Readings

Bauer, Yehuda. "Jewish Resistance and Passivity in the Face of the Holocaust." In *Unanswered Questions: Nazi Germany and the Genocide of the Jews*, edited by François Furet, 235–51. New York: Schocken Books, 1989.

Benz, Wolfgang, and Walter H. Pehle, eds. *Encyclopedia of German Resistance to the Nazi Movement*. New York: Continuum, 1996.

Brothers, Eric. "On the Anti-Fascist Resistance of German Jews." *Leo Baeck Institute Yearbook* 32 (1987): 369–82.

Eschwege, Helmut. "Resistance of German Jews against the Nazi Regime." *Leo Baeck Institute Yearbook* 15 (1970): 143–80.

Kaplan, Marion. *Between Dignity and Despair: Jewish Life in Nazi Germany*. Oxford: Oxford University Press, 1998.

Löhken, Wilfried, and Werner Vathke, eds. *Juden im Widerstand: Drei Gruppen zwischen Überlebenskampf und politischer Aktion*. Berlin: Edition Hentrich, 1993.

Peukert, Detlev J. K. *Inside Nazi Germany: Conformity, Opposition, and Racism in Everyday Life*. New Haven, CT: Yale University Press, 1987.

Scheer, Regina. *Im Schatten der Sterne: Eine jüdische Widerstandsgruppe*. Berlin: Aufbau-Verlag, 2004.

Suhl, Yuri, ed. *They Fought Back*. New York: Crown, 1967.

Tec, Nechama. *Resilience and Courage: Women, Men, and the Holocaust*. New Haven, CT: Yale University Press, 2003.

~

CHAPTER ELEVEN

Imperialists without an Empire

Cercles Coloniaux *and* Colonial Culture in Belgium after 1960

MATTHEW G. STANARD

The end of World War II brought a significant development that profoundly shaped Europe's postwar history: the collapse of European colonial rule in Africa and Asia. This process signified the decline of western European powers on the global stage. Within the two decades following World War II, most of the African and Asian colonies that had been dominated by European powers since the late nineteenth century achieved their independence. Independence movements that had developed during and after World War I intensified after World War II. World War II devastated European economies and reduced the ability of colonial powers such as Britain, France, Belgium, and the Netherlands to retain hold of their overseas possessions. The Cold War divide between the communist Soviet Union and the capitalist United States also intensified the process of decolonization and made it more violent. When Vietnamese communists led a popular campaign for independence against France, the United States responded by militarily intervening in what became a protracted war. Some former colonies achieved their independence without fighting a war against their colonial ruler, as was the case in India's independence from Britain in 1947. Others had to fight long bloody wars of independence, as in the Algerian National Liberation Front's efforts from 1954 to 1962 to win freedom from French rule.

Even after former colonies achieved independence, however, cultural, social, and political legacies of imperialism continued to have an impact on both the newly independent states and Europe. European settlers who had previously lived in the colonies migrated to Europe, often bringing with them nostalgic memories of the "glory days" of empire. Hoping to take part in Europe's postwar economic recovery, former colonial subjects immigrated to Europe from Pakistan, India, and North Africa, adding to the religious and ethnic diversity of European societies. In this chapter, Matthew G. Stanard examines the continued impact of colonialism on Belgian culture after the decolonization of the Belgian Congo in 1960. Imperialism in the Congo had been particularly brutal. As Stanard shows, pro-imperial "colonial clubs" remained active in Belgium even after 1960, praising European "heroes" of imperialism and ignoring the violent and racist character of Belgian colonial rule. The activities of such clubs help us gauge the level of popular support for colonialism both during and after the days of Belgian rule. As this chapter tells us, colonial culture continued to shape Europe long after the end of colonial rule.

On the afternoon of 5 July 2000, a dozen people walked through the Parc du Cinquantenaire in Brussels, a park only a short walk from European Union headquarters buildings. As they proceeded toward their destination that Wednesday afternoon, they would have passed through the shade of the trees lining the park's pathways. Some, if not all of them, were retracing steps they had taken in the past. It is doubtful the gathering was festive, for they had come together to commemorate the dead, that is, fellow Belgians who had died conquering central Africa a century earlier. Not only were they celebrating the dead, the very *idea* that underlay the commemoration—imperialism—was itself dead.

The group came to a halt in front of their objective, the simply named Colonial Monument. Gazing at the memorial the group would have seen in its foreground a young African lying down, representing the Congo River. On the left, a European soldier could be seen combating the "Arab" slave trade while figures to the right represented another colonial soldier tending to a wounded comrade. The large central panel depicted the African continent, "henceforth open to civilization," and a group of soldiers surrounding their king, Leopold II. Atop the monument the group would have seen a young woman representing the country of Belgium, "welcoming the black race."[1] Two members of the group advanced solemnly toward the memorial and, kneeling, placed wreaths down to consecrate the memory of Belgium's colonial pioneers.[2]

Who were these people and what were they doing at a monument to imperialism in the middle of Brussels—perhaps, in the center of Europe—in 2000? The people represented a number of groups that were successor organizations to various pro-empire *cercles coloniaux*, or "colonial clubs," dating back to the colonial period.[3] The object of their commemoration, the Colonial Monument, was built between 1911 and 1921 in the Parc du Cinquantenaire to honor Belgian colonial pioneers who had died during the conquest of the Congo. The Congo is an enormous territory—eighty times the size of Belgium—that from 1885 to 1908 was King Leopold II's *personal* colony, called the Congo Free State. From 1908 until independence in 1960 it was a Belgian colony called the Belgian Congo. Like many colonial memorials in Belgium, the Colonial Monument commemorates Belgians who died during the period of Leopoldian rule from 1885 to 1908. According to a present-day explanatory plaque, the monument is indicative of the colonial spirit at the time it was built (1911–1921), which historical developments and research since have brought into question. During the colonial period the monument was a site of annual commemorations that promoted imperialism. As such, in 2000 the group enacted a ceremony performed many times in the past. But why commemorate the conquest of Africa as late as 2000, decades after Belgian imperialism had ended? If, as the 2000 event shows, colonial monuments have continued to be sites of commemoration in the decades since Congolese independence in 1960, does this mean colonialism became in some sense an enduring part of Belgian—and perhaps European—culture? We know that imperialism significantly impacted peoples and cultures outside Europe. But what impact did imperialism have on Europe itself?

This chapter introduces the issue of European "colonial culture" by looking at such culture in Belgium. Specifically, the chapter examines cercles coloniaux and the fate of these groups after Congolese independence in 1960.[4] Cercles coloniaux members were mainly male and middle class, and included pro-empire enthusiasts, colonial veterans, businessmen, and Belgians who had lived and worked in the Congo and relocated back to Europe. Although the membership in and number of cercles coloniaux declined after 1960, the clubs have remained active for decades. While the extent to which these groups have produced a deep colonial culture in Belgium is open to debate, it is clear that by commemorating the colonial past and advocating a positive view of imperialism, they have at least helped shape Belgians' knowledge of the Congo and Africa.

To understand colonial culture and how cercles coloniaux may have contributed to such a culture, one must first know what imperialism was. Accordingly, the chapter begins with an introduction to nineteenth- and twentieth-century European overseas imperialism, followed by a discussion of the specific contours of Belgian colonialism in Africa. Having summarized imperialism and the Belgian case, the chapter then examines Belgian cercles coloniaux during the colonial and postcolonial periods. Finally, the chapter will consider the issue of colonial culture by looking at the impact that cercles coloniaux may have had on such culture in Belgium.

New Imperialism

Colonial culture, to the extent it has existed, resulted from a new era of imperialism that originated in the late nineteenth century. Beginning around 1870, a number of European nations expanded overseas, mainly into Africa and Southeast Asia. Historians often refer to this wave of conquest as "New Imperialism" to distinguish it from the period of exploration and conquest beginning in the 1400s that led to European expansion into the Americas and other areas of the globe. The New Imperialism was most remarkable in Africa: between 1870 and 1914 Europeans conquered virtually the entire continent, an area three times the size of the continental United States. European rule brought benefits such as improved medicine, literacy in European languages, and technologies like steam power. Yet the costs were tremendous because Europeans brutally suppressed resistance, colonial boundaries divided communities, and businesses exploited African labor. Perhaps worst of all, imperialism was premised on European notions of African inferiority, and colonial regimes based on systems of inequality, which remained in place for decades, only reinforced these ideas of African inferiority.

Surprising about this new wave of conquest is that in the late 1800s Europe supposedly represented the pinnacle of civilization. So why would Europeans subjugate foreign peoples, impose repressive regimes, and maintain those regimes into the latter half of the twentieth century? Historians point to several explanatory factors. First, much of Europe in the late 1800s was undergoing intense industrialization, leading to competition for raw materials and overseas markets in which to sell manufactured goods. Second, growing nationalism drove states to expand overseas to boost national prestige, such as when France accelerated its overseas expansion after suffering a humiliating defeat at the hands of Prussia in 1870–1871. Two additional factors provoking European expansion were an increase in scientific exploration and a revival of missionary activity. Moreover, when explorers or missionaries got into trouble in distant corners of the globe, governments felt pressured to intervene, often by means of military action. Finally, new conceptions of race and society justified to Europeans the conquest of peoples who did not look like them. Scientific racism, or the idea that the world was divided into a racial hierarchy, explained "superior" Europeans' control over so-called inferior races. Furthermore, social Darwinists such as Herbert Spencer conceived of a world order based on competition among races, making conflict not only possible but desirable.

Belgian Imperialism

While colonial conquests shared common motivations, Belgian imperialism was distinct in important ways. For example, Belgian industrialists and merchants thrived on intra-European trade and had little desire to control overseas markets or raw materials. As citizens of a small, neutral, and formerly subject nation—independent only in 1830—Belgians had few imperial aspirations and generally were indifferent to colonial objectives. Similarly, church leaders displayed little enthusiasm for proselytization abroad. Rather, the driving force of Belgian imperialism was the king, Leopold II (ruled 1865–1909), who felt trapped in a smallish nation encircled by great powers, and therefore channeled much of his energy elsewhere. After numerous failed plans to secure a colony (including one to purchase the Philippines), he secured the Congo at the time of the 1885 Berlin Conference on Africa. Leopold II had employed the explorer Henry Morton Stanley to stake claims along the Congo River, and parlayed those claims into control of the Congo by asserting to other European leaders that he could act as a disinterested neutral party. It was a sign of the times that those assembled in Berlin did not consult any Africans on their decisions.

But Leopold II was not disinterested, and he quickly transformed the Congo into his *personal* colony, called (inaccurately) the Congo Free State. From Europe he directed the exploration, conquest, and administration of the Congo using European officers and African troops recruited from various regions. After depleting his private savings, Leopold turned to the exploitation of natural rubber, ivory, and African labor in order to finance his colony, leading to a brutal regime of forced work. While scholars disagree on the figures, and exact numbers are unknowable, it is undisputed that Leopold's reign led to several million African deaths from overwork, abuse, hunger, killings, or disease. This suffering provoked a reform movement led by the Briton E. D. Morel, and after years of domestic and foreign pressure Leopold finally ceded control of the Congo to the other country he ruled, Belgium, in 1908.[5]

After the Congo Free State became a Belgian colony in 1908 it was called the Belgian Congo, which it remained until its independence in 1960. While some abuses continued, Belgium did invest in Congo's economy and population, especially after World War II. With Leopold II gone, support for the colony came from three "pillars": the Catholic Church, colonial businesses, and the administration. But what about the population as a whole? Did support for the colonial venture change from 1885 to 1960, and what happened after 1960?

Cercles Coloniaux in Belgium, 1885–1960

Colonial groups across Europe urged their governments to expand overseas during the New Imperialism and generated domestic support for such expansion. In the decades after 1870, the Comité de l'Afrique Française (Committee of French Africa), the Gesellschaft für deutsche Kolonisation (Society for German Colonization), and the British Empire League, among many others, promoted imperialism in France, Germany, and Britain respectively. Historians have drawn contradictory conclusions from the existence of such groups. Some have argued that these groups reflected an ardent interest in empire, perhaps even a culture of imperialism. Others, however, have maintained that the fact that such groups were needed to drum up imperialist sentiment is evidence that pro-colonialist feelings in Europe were weak. Which of these two conclusions is correct? The chapter will return to this question after considering the case of Belgian pro-colonial clubs.

As in other imperialist European states, a number of pro-empire groups came into being in Belgium. Yet virtually all of these groups arose after the fact—*after* Leopold II had acquired the Congo in 1885—thus reflecting Belgians' indifference to imperialism. One of the first to organize was the Cercle Royal Africain, founded in 1889 by collaborators of Leopold's Congo Free State endeavor. Up to 1908, and then beyond, numerous other imperialist groups appeared around the country, from Antwerp in Belgium's Flemish-speaking northern half to Arlon in the country's southern, French-speaking region, and even in small towns such as Vielsalm, Spa, and Linkebeek. Members were predominantly middle class—lawyers, bankers, managers, government administrators, military officers, engineers, doctors, industrialists—and overwhelmingly male: in 1935, only one of the Cercle Africain de Châtelet-Châtelineau's 108 members was female.[6] Members included people living in the Congo, those who had been to the colony and returned home, imperial enthusiasts, and businessmen with colonial commerce. Group size varied but was modest, with membership numbered in the dozens or hundreds rather than the thousands. The Cercle Africain de Charleroi-Thuin, for example, boasted 128 members by 1935, and the distinguished Cercle Royal Africain grew from an initial membership of 72 in 1889 to 307 by 1920 to 800 by 1948.[7]

While membership size varied, cercles coloniaux generally had three goals: networking, commemoration, and education. The first of these, networking, was straightforward: cercles aimed to foster good relations and business contacts among Belgians who had connections with the colony. Club publications included "notices" sections in which members could read about events in other members' lives such as marriages, births, deaths, departures for the colony, and arrivals back home. Cercles held business meetings and social events such as banquets, and some groups acted as mutual associations to help members in times of need. All of this served to keep Belgians with colonial interests connected with others of similar backgrounds.

The second goal cercles coloniaux shared was commemoration. Cercles memorialized heroes, local sons, and other notables who had helped establish the African empire, especially those who had fought and died serving Leopold II before 1908. This goal was self-serving to the extent that club members memorialized local sons and associates, sometimes even friends or family. Commemorations also legitimized Belgian imperialism by using the Leopoldian period to invent a heritage of overseas expansion where none existed, and by directing attention away from the abuses of that period by celebrating positive accomplishments. Commemorations generally took two forms. First, cercles organized festivities such as annual *journées coloniales* (colonial days) during which members participated in parades, masses, and other events to celebrate the colony. Second, these groups built—or helped build—colonial memorials, in particular monuments to Leopold II, helping transform him during the post-1908 era into the heroic founder of the Belgian empire. One example is the monument the Cercle Colonial Arlonais erected in 1951 featuring a statue of the king accompanied by a flattering quotation attributed to him: "I undertook the work of the Congo in the interest of civilization and for the good of Belgium."[8] From left to right, the memorial's two wings constitute "before and after" depictions of Belgian rule: a panel on the left shows cowering, half-clothed Africans enslaved by Arabs in turbans with whips, whereas the right panel depicts clothed Africans as carpenters, scientists, blacksmiths, miners, and students; one wears a cross, symbolizing Christianity.[9] The Arlon monument and others like it served to legitimize Belgian colonialism.

The third goal of cercles coloniaux overlapped with the second: the groups provided colonial education in order to foster support for imperialism and to prepare future colonials to settle in the colony. Some cercles founded colonial libraries or museums. In 1912, for example, a colonial club in Namur created a colonial museum, only to see a bombardment destroy it during World War I. While a reconstituted museum struggled during the interwar years, the impulse to educate persisted, and in 1951 the Cercle Colonial Namurois created yet another museum, which became the Musée Africain de Namur that still exists today. Clubs also hosted talks at their locales and in surrounding areas—often inviting expert speakers—and held movie nights to show colonial films: again in Namur, the Cercle Colonial Namurois in the first half of 1954 held a dozen screenings for schoolchildren and other groups

The Cercle Colonial Arlonais monument to Leopold II in 2003. (Photograph by Matthew G. Stanard.)

in and around the city.[10] To test and reward schoolchildren's knowledge of the colony, clubs held annual *concours colonials* (colonial competitions) such as the one held by the Cercle Africain Borain in 1936–1937 that attracted more than ten thousand schoolchildren and teachers.[11] Clubs arranged exhibits, participated in national expositions, and organized outings to the colonial section of Belgium's several World's Fairs as well as the country's main colonial museum, the Musée Royal de l'Afrique Centrale.

To pursue their networking, commemorative, and educational objectives, cercles coloniaux often collaborated with other groups. Several clubs received budgetary or special subsidies from the Ministry of Colonies, which by the mid-1950s was allocating 200,000 francs annually to various colonial groups.[12] City and regional governments also provided subsidies, and local cercles teamed up with national counterparts to advance their goals.[13]

Imperialism after 1960, or Colonial Culture in Europe

While Belgian cercles coloniaux and their equivalents in France, Britain, and elsewhere sought to strengthen European imperialism, they could not counteract the growing anticolonial forces at work in the years after World War II or the nationalists propelling decolonization throughout the colonial world. The 1949 Communist victory in China, the 1955 Bandung Conference of independent African and Asian states held in Indonesia, and the 1956 Suez Crisis in Egypt signaled to many the end of European global dominance and a new epoch of African and Asian self-determination. By the late 1950s, much of European empire was in turmoil as forces of decolonization developed apace.

Nevertheless, decolonization in the Congo arrived unexpectedly because, amid turmoil the world over, the Belgian colony appeared to be an oasis of tranquility. Heavy post–World War II investment in the colony seemed to be paying off through growing productivity and wealth.[14] Moreover, the Congo was deep within sub-Saharan Africa, insulated by South Africa's apartheid regime, strong white settler presences in British east Africa, and Portugal's retrograde rule in Mozambique and Angola. When riots broke out in January 1959 in Leopoldville, the Congo's capital, and pressure from Congolese nationalists followed, the government agreed to talks and hastily set independence for 30 June 1960. Many scholars have pointed out how Belgian colonialism did not prepare the Congolese for self-rule; for example, in 1960 there was only a handful of university graduates among a population of around fifteen million. But Belgian rule likewise did not prepare the *Belgian* population for Congolese self-rule, and independence came as a shock, particularly among colonials and enthusiasts such as members of colonial clubs. Awaking the morning of 1 July 1960, cercles coloniaux members suddenly found themselves to be imperialists without an empire.

Yet cercles coloniaux did not disappear overnight. Rather, these clubs continued to function, albeit with altered methods and objectives. Local cercles coloniaux continued to act as networks keeping former colonials connected, an activity made perhaps more important after 1960 as many returned to Europe from the former colony. Some club publications ceased, but others persevered or merged.[15] In the 1980s, one still could find at least a dozen active colonial clubs and more than a dozen other associations of former colonial soldiers, professionals, or students, altogether producing two dozen publications.[16] Furthermore, cercles continued to hold meetings and organize social functions to keep members connected.

Cercles coloniaux also continued to educate, now with refashioned goals. With the colony now gone there was no need to drum up support for the empire or to prepare future colonials. After 1960, as the Congo first endured civil war, then Mobutu Sese Seko's dictatorship, and finally became a "failed state," there was a great deal of public silence in Belgium regarding the colonial past.[17] Outside Europe, colonial studies scholars were highly critical of European imperialism; Belgian scholars, on the other hand, became discouraged and teaching about the Congo and colonialism dropped off the radar.[18]

Nonetheless, cercles coloniaux continued to engage in public discourse, now to "set the record straight" regarding Belgium's colonial past in a postcolonial world generally indifferent or hostile to imperialism. For example, an umbrella organization for former cercles and other colonial groups, the Union Royale Belge pour les Pays d'Outre-Mer (Royal Belgian Union for Overseas Countries), has published numerous documents to assert the positive legacy of Belgian colonialism and to refute negative accounts.[19] Former colonials in and around Namur continue to maintain the aforementioned Musée Africain de Namur dedicated to the memory of the colonial past.[20] In all of this, cercles and their successor organizations have maintained the narrative they asserted during the colonial period, namely that Leopold II was a hero, pioneers of the 1885–1908 period of conquest should be honored, and Belgian rule in central Africa was not only legitimate, but civilizing and beneficial as well.

Cercles coloniaux further advanced their positive colonial narrative after 1960 by continuing to commemorate those who had played a role in the creation of the empire, in particular Leopold II. The start of this chapter described one such recent commemoration, but it is important to stress that the Colonial Monument ceremony of 2000 was no isolated case. In every year since 1960 cercles coloniaux and their members have commemorated their imperial past at memorials across the country.[21] Although the number of attendees has dropped, the enormous number of such commemorations since 1960 precludes any attempt to list them here, let alone address them thoroughly.

To historians of European imperialism, the work of cercles coloniaux during and after the colonial period is intriguing for two reasons. First, these efforts by a large number of people and groups contradict the accepted view that Belgians were largely uninterested in overseas empire. As noted earlier, historians dispute whether the existence of imperialist interest groups demonstrates that the German, British, French, and other peoples were excited about empire. Yet most historians would agree that Belgians were disinterested in the Congo and that it was first Leopold II and then after 1908 the church, the administration, and businesses that sustained the empire. Yet the proliferation of cercles coloniaux indicates that there was not only a serious attempt to mobilize the masses in support of colonialism, but considerable grassroots enthusiasm as well. A second reason colonial clubs' activity is intriguing is that it raises the question of how these groups affected culture in Belgium. Did cercles coloniaux create a colonial culture in Belgium? What impact did the New Imperialism have in general on European culture? These questions have gained increased attention as scholars have renewed their focus on the persistence of imperialist ideas and ideology in Europe in the postcolonial era.[22]

On the one hand, it is at best debatable that cercles coloniaux had a significant impact on European culture. While grassroots support for Belgian imperialism might appear surprising, generally it is true that in Belgium, as elsewhere, people were not viscerally interested in colonial affairs. One official wrote at the end of the colonial period that because of the lack of interest in the colony, the administration "was for years in a state of isolation; it was obliged to act alone."[23] Resignation among Belgians in the face of the decision to decolonize also indicates apathy toward colonial affairs.[24]

On the other hand, there is strong evidence that although Belgians might not have been deeply interested in maintaining their overseas empire, cercles coloniaux and other vectors of pro-imperialism such as the Ministry of Colonies did have a significant impact in terms of developing a colonial culture. Knowledge of and attitudes toward the Congo and Belgium's colonial past changed over time. A poll taken toward the end of the colonial period indicates that despite Leopold II's duplicitous diplomacy to acquire the Congo and subsequent abuses under his and Belgian rule, by the 1950s Belgians generally believed that their presence in central Africa was justified and beneficial.[25] Furthermore, the shock with which Belgians greeted Congolese independence in 1960 suggests they felt self-assured of a lasting colonial future.

The significance of cercles coloniaux and similar groups elsewhere in Europe also can be seen in European attitudes toward colonialism, namely the lack of a general and profound repudiation of imperialism in the postcolonial period. It is interesting to compare post-1960 European views of imperialism with attitudes toward and memories of other discredited twentieth-century ideologies. After World War II, Europeans disavowed and removed relics of German Nazism and its collaborationist governments, and for many years forgot the Holocaust. After 1989, Europeans repudiated communism—certainly its Soviet variety—and relegated communist monuments to "cemeteries."[26] Monuments to imperialism, however, were neither banished nor torn down, nor have the many streets named after notable imperialists undergone a wholesale rebaptism.[27] The fact that cercles coloniaux (or their successor organizations) in Belgium continued to publish journals, honor imperialists, refute anticolonialists, and praise Leopold II and his many collaborators shows there was not a total rejection of imperialism in Belgium after 1960. Of course many Belgians, especially younger ones, were not taught about their colonial past, or viewed it with indifference. Yet others learned from cercles coloniaux and their successors that Belgian imperialism in Africa not only was legitimate but was a benediction, only prematurely terminated by forces beyond Belgium's control.

Therefore, the most important impact of cercles coloniaux on Belgian culture was in how they helped "write" history. When members of cercles coloniaux commemorated colonialism they honored *Europeans* who died in Africa, not Africans; they celebrated the achievements rather than the costs of Leopold II's brutal regime. Dozens upon dozens of memorials to Leopold II and colonial heroes—many built by cercles coloniaux—still dot the Belgian landscape today. Yet there is no monument to the millions of dead Africans. In *King Leopold's Ghost*, Adam Hochschild writes of a "Great Forgetting" by which Belgians conveniently forgot the atrocities of their colonial past.[28] It is not that Belgians totally forgot their colonial past, but rather that cercles coloniaux and others instilled a version of that history with which Hochschild does not agree.

Belgians are not alone in maintaining a largely positive, Eurocentric view of their imperial past. When in 2002 the French government finally built a memorial to the 1954–1962 French-Algerian War, it was one dedicated only to the *French* soldiers who died during the conflict.[29] In Germany, visitors to the Friedhof Columbiadamm (cemetery at Columbiadamm) in Berlin can visit the Hererostein, a memorial to German soldiers who died during the 1904–1907 suppression of a Herero uprising in German Southwest Africa (present-day Namibia).[30] No mention is made of the tens of thousands of deaths the Germans caused that led to the near extinction of the Herero and Nama peoples. Only in 2004 did a German minister travel to Namibia to participate in commemorative ceremonies and express German responsibility for the killings.[31]

Colonial memories and culture in Europe continue to be relevant. Britain's colonial past continues to shape its foreign and domestic affairs. Immigrants from former colonies comprise large segments of Britain's total immigration, and Britain's historically equivocal stance toward European unity derives in no small part from its relations with the Commonwealth (and with another erstwhile possession, the United States). France maintains close ties with former colonies, particularly in Africa, and Islam has become France's second religion due in no small part to former colonials and immigrants from North Africa. A 2005 law stipulating that French schools teach a positive version of colonialism unleashed a debate not only about the government's role in the teaching of history, but also about the nature of France's imperial past. The Matonge neighborhood in Brussels is a thriving testament to Congolese culture in Belgium and the two countries' mutual bonds. More significantly, Belgium has intervened in central African affairs repeatedly since 1960, and the country continues to have numerous special connections with the Democratic Republic of the Congo. Immigration has become a major issue in Belgium, as it has elsewhere in Europe, and past experience continues to shape attitudes toward foreigners. As such, knowledge of the colonial past, the impact of cercles coloniaux, and the extent of colonial culture in Belgium and elsewhere in Europe are areas where additional research needs to be done.

Notes

A Belgian American Educational Foundation fellowship made much of the research for this chapter possible, as did funding from the Graduate School and the History Department at Indiana University, Bloomington.

1. Explanatory plaque at monument.

2. Cercle Royal des Anciens Officiers des Campagnes d'Afrique, *Bulletin Trimestriel*, no. 3 (September 2000): 7.

3. While French, Flemish, and German are spoken in Belgium, proper names of Belgian particulars are presented here only in French (with English translations) for considerations of clarity and space.

4. These were popular colonial clubs, as opposed to narrow commercial groups (e.g., Union des Producteurs de Café du Congo Belge), scientific or academic groups (e.g., Institut Royal Colonial Belge), business groups (e.g., Association des Intérêts Coloniaux Belges), and religious organizations.

5. On Leopold II's Congo administration see: Adam Hochschild, *King Leopold's Ghost: A Story of Greed, Terror, and Heroism in Colonial Africa* (Boston: Houghton Mifflin, 1998); Daniel Vangroenweghe, *Du sang sur les lianes: Léopold II et son Congo* (Brussels: Didier Hatier, 1986); and E. D. Morel, *Red Rubber: The Story of the Rubber Slave Trade Flourishing on the Congo in the Year of Grace 1906* (London: T. Fisher Unwin, 1907).

6. See, for example, "Liste des Membres du Cercle Royal Africain des Ardennes" in *Rapport d'Activité du C.R.A.A. au cours de l'année 1959*, portefeuille 62 Infopresse, Archives Africaines, Ministère des Affaires Étrangères, Brussels. The Archives Africaines at the Ministère des Affaires Étrangères is hereafter abbreviated AA. On male membership: Ville de Charleroi, *L'Étoile. Organe de la Fédération Provinciale des Cercles Coloniaux du Hainaut. Numéro spécial des Journées Coloniales organisées par les Cercles Africains de Charleroi-Thuin et du Châtelet-Châtelineau* (June 1935): 37–43, 51, 53, 55.

7. Ville de Charleroi, *L'Étoile*, 37–43; *Le Cercle Royal Africain: Cinquante années d'existence, 1889–1939* (Brussels: R. Louis, [1939]), 34; *Le Cercle Royal Africain: Soixante années d'existence* [Brussels, 1949], 9.

8. "Érection d'un monument au Roi Léopold II à Arlon," *Revue Congolaise Illustrée*, no. 2 (February 1950): 40.

9. Author's visit, March 2003.

10. Untitled note, portefeuille 62 Infopresse, AA.

11. A. Briand, M. Jorion, E. Lerat, A. Pierrot, G. Pohl, Garcy, and Labeau, "Comité Scolaire: Rapport sur le concours Colonial organisé par le Cercle, pendant les années 1936–1937," in copy of *Bulletin Mensuel*, no. 7 (June 1937). Located at liasse *205.812.22 Expos et foires diverses organisées en Belgique, Exposition de Cuesmes 24 et 25 juillet 1937*, portefeuille 445 Office Colonial, AA.

12. R. Lavendhomme, "Note pour Monsieur le Ministre," 15 April 1955, no. 303/Inf., liasse *29A. Subsides 1955. Généralités*, portefeuille 59 Infopresse, AA.

13. When in the interwar years the group the Ligue du Souvenir Congolais attempted to place a plaque in each applicable municipality to commemorate every Belgian who had died in Africa serving Leopold II's Congo Free State, in some communities it took the lead while in others it worked alongside the local cercle colonial.

14. See one Africanist's impressions in the 1950s: Basil Davidson, *The African Awakening* (London: Jonathan Cape, 1955).

15. Some publications ceased or merged with others before decolonization, and therefore the termination or merging of publications after 1960 might not be viewed as resulting solely from the end of colonialism.

16. José Clément, "Les Associations d'Anciens d'Afrique et Leurs Bulletins de Liaison," *Bulletin de liaison des Anciens du Congo et du Ruanda-Urundi/Schakelblad van de "Anciens" van Kongo en Ruanda-Urundi*, no. 75 (January 1986): 3–6.

17. On the Congo (Zaire) as a failed state, see Crawford Young, "Zaire: the anatomy of a failed state," in *History of Central Africa: The Contemporary Years since 1960*, ed. David Birmingham and Phyllis M. Martin (London: Longman, 1998), 97–129.

18. On colonial studies in Belgium after 1960, see Jean Stengers, "Belgian Historiography since 1945," trans. Frank Perlin, in *Reappraisals in Overseas History*, ed. P. C. Emmer and H. L. Wesseling (The Hague: Leiden University Press, 1979), 161–81. The lack of education in terms of colonial history continues today, and young Belgians know surprisingly little about their imperial past. When a leading expert on central Africa recently retired from the Université Catholique de Louvain, one of Belgium's preeminent universities, no attempt was made to hire an Africanist of his caliber to replace him.

19. Union Royale Belge pour les Pays d'Outre-Mer, at www.urome.be/ (accessed 15 May 2006).

20. Musée Africain de Namur, at www.museeafricainnamur.be/ (accessed 16 May 2006).

21. One recent example was the June 2003 Cérémonie nationale d'hommage au drapeau de Tabora to celebrate a victory against German colonial troops in Africa during World War I that began at Namur's Leopold II monument. See www.ville .namur.be/agenda/manifestation /06.html (accessed 16 March 2003).

22. John M. MacKenzie launched studies of imperialism and popular culture with his *Propaganda and Empire: The Manipulation of British Public Opinion, 1880–1960* (Manchester: Manchester University Press, 1984) and the edited volume *Imperialism and Popular Culture* (Manchester: Manchester University Press, 1986). On French

empire and popular culture see Edward Berenson, "Making a Colonial Culture? Empire and the French Public, 1880–1940," *French Politics, Culture & Society* 22, no. 2 (Summer 2004): 127–49, and Eric T. Jennings, "Visions and Representations of French Empire," *Journal of Modern History* 77, no. 3 (September 2005): 701–21.

23. Georges Brausch, *Belgian Administration in the Congo* (London: Oxford University Press, 1961), 66.

24. Belgians were opposed to military action to retain the colony. Jean Stengers, "Precipitous Decolonization: The Case of the Belgian Congo," in *The Transfer of Power in Africa: Decolonization 1940–1960*, ed. Prosser Gifford and Wm. Roger Louis (New Haven, CT: Yale University Press, 1982), 305–35.

25. G. Jacquemyns, "Le Congo belge devant l'opinion publique," *Institut Universitaire d'Information Sociale et Économique «INSOC»*, nos. 2–3 (Brussels: Parc Léopold, 1956).

26. Beverly James, "Fencing in the Past: Budapest's Statue Park Museum," *Media, Culture & Society* 21 (1999): 291–311.

27. Since 1960 some memorials have been removed or destroyed in the course of reconstruction and development; others have been relocated, indicating an abiding importance. On street names in France, see Robert Aldrich's essay in *Promoting the Colonial Idea: Propaganda and Visions of Empire in France*, ed. Tony Chafer and Amanda Sackur (Basingstoke, UK: Palgrave, 2001).

28. Hochschild, *King Leopold's Ghost*.

29. Including their North African auxiliaries, the *harkis*, who fought alongside the French against Algerian independence fighters.

30. Kriegerdenkmäler in Berlin, at www.kriegerdenkmal.com/deutschland/Berlin/neuk/Garnisonsfriedhof_Columbiadamm/35.jpg (accessed 21 May 2006).

31. Susanne Sporrer, "Hundert Jahre nach Völkermord an Hereros in Namibia—Wieczorek-Zeul bat um Vergebung," *Welt am Sonntag*, 15 August 2004.

Suggested Readings

Aldrich, Robert. *Vestiges of the Colonial Empire in France: Monuments, Museums and Colonial Memories*. New York: Palgrave Macmillan, 2005.

Chafer, Tony, and Amanda Sackur, eds. *Promoting the Colonial Idea: Propaganda and Visions of Empire in France*. Basingstoke, UK: Palgrave, 2001.

Cooper, Nicola. *France in Indochina: Colonial Encounters*. Oxford: Berg, 2001.

Hochschild, Adam. *King Leopold's Ghost: A Story of Greed, Terror, and Heroism in Colonial Africa*. Boston: Houghton Mifflin, 1998.

MacKenzie, John M., ed. *Imperialism and Popular Culture*. Manchester: Manchester University Press, 1986.

Young, Crawford. "Zaire: The Anatomy of a Failed State." In *History of Central Africa: The Contemporary Years since 1960*, edited by David Birmingham and Phyllis M. Martin. London: Longman, 1998.

Adriano Olivetti. (Courtesy of the Archivio Storico Olivetti, Ivrea.)

~

CHAPTER TWELVE

Adriano Olivetti

Agent of Italian-American Exchange in the Postwar Years

PAOLO SCRIVANO

The United States has never had as much power over the world as it had in 1945. It stood as the only major power undamaged by the war, and its economy towered over all others. In 1947, the U.S. government announced two foreign policy programs that would define U.S.-European relations during the Cold War: the Truman Doctrine and the Marshall Plan. With the Truman Doctrine, named after President Harry Truman, the United States announced in March 1947 that it would send political, economic, or military support to any country that might become communist. In June of the same year, U.S. Secretary of State George Marshall proclaimed a massive aid program to assist European recovery after World War II. In effect, the Marshall Plan (the European Recovery Program) served as an economic corollary to the Truman Doctrine. From 1948 until the end of 1951, the United States provided approximately $13 billion worth of aid to European countries in an effort to prevent the further spread of communism. The European Recovery Program intended to restructure European economies, everything from farming to heavy industries to consumer products, along U.S. models. According to Marshall Plan thinking, if European economies could become more productive, these nations would become more stable economic and political partners for the United States. American officials also hoped that Europeans without economic worries would no longer find communism appealing.

Europeans greeted the announcement of the Marshall Plan in a variety of ways. When some Eastern European states expressed interest in the plan, the Soviet

Union, fearing U.S. influence in the Soviet-dominated Eastern bloc, forced them to refuse American aid. In many Western European states, some leftists viewed the Marshall Plan with suspicion as an arm of American imperialism. Many others embraced it and sought to work closely with U.S. officials to restructure their economies.

The Marshall Plan was part of a broader postwar trend that some scholars have termed "Americanization." The United States had a significant influence on many aspects of Western European life, from manufacturing models and architectural styles to soft drinks and blue jeans. While many Europeans, especially youth, embraced American culture as modern, others feared the loss of distinct European national and local identities. Would a German still be a German if he drank Coca-Cola rather than beer? Scholars stress that while the United States' impact on Europe was profound, Europeans also adapted American culture to their own local needs. Paolo Scrivano illustrates this process with his examination of Adriano Olivetti, one of Italy's leading industrialists. While Olivetti embraced some American ideals about economic and physical planning, he also modified those ideals to fit his vision for postwar Italian society.

"Adriano Olivetti looks like an intellectual, mild Mr. Pickwick, with an exceptional high-domed forehead, curly blond hair and a somewhat rueful expression. Plump and comfortably sloppy looking, Signor Olivetti wears a bright blue suit, white shirt and white linen necktie as we lounge in modernistic leather chairs and sip pre-prandial cocktails."[1] These were the words with which the *New York Times* portrayed in 1954 one of Italy's leading industrialists, a man who was at the helm of a company internationally renowned for the quality of its products as well as for its advanced social policies. The interest of the *New York Times* in Olivetti was well justified. At the time of the article's publication, in fact, the Italian entrepreneur had not only achieved a worldwide reputation as a businessman but was also regarded in his home country as a respected publicist, publisher, and politician.

Born in 1901 into a wealthy family of inventors and entrepreneurs, Olivetti inherited a well-established business.[2] In 1908, his father, Camillo, had founded a company that manufactured electrical instruments and that later specialized in the production of typewriters. After graduating in 1924 from the Politecnico di Torino with an engineering degree, Adriano Olivetti started a career in the family company, becoming its managing director in 1933. In this capacity, he launched a vast program of social services for the company's employees, which included the construction of housing, schools, infirmaries, and cultural centers, all designed by renowned architects. These initiatives were part of a larger political project that Olivetti began to elaborate on during the 1930s but fully developed in the late 1940s and during the 1950s.

Olivetti expounded his views in *L'ordine politico delle comunità* (The Political Order of Communities), a book he wrote between 1944 and 1945 during his exile in Switzerland.[3] In *L'ordine politico delle comunità*—and in the other books and articles that followed—Olivetti proposed a democratic model for society based on achieving a balance between centralized power and local autonomy. In his idea of community, democratic representation was of a twofold nature, with representatives elected by universal suffrage working with members of trade unions and cultural groups. Upon his return to Italy at the end of World War II, Olivetti worked to put in practice his sociopolitical ideals, founding the Movimento di Comunità, a movement that gained wide popularity in the area around Ivrea, the northwest Italian city where the activities of the Olivetti company were located.

Despite this remarkable record of achievements, however, the Americans' curiosity was inspired by rather different motivations. In fact, while the *New York Times* article praised Olivetti for his social commitments by comparing him to the nineteenth-century British reformer Robert Owen, it also placed him side by side with five other supposedly emblematic Italian characters who were chosen to exemplify the wide spectrum of the country's opposition to communism: a priest from Romagna, a peasant from Calabria, a Florentine woman who had formerly been a member of the parliament for a moderate party, the Christian Democratic mayor of Florence Giorgio La Pira, and the archbishop of Bologna, Cardinal Lercaro. Written less than one year after the end of the Korean War, amid the tensions of the Cold War, the article clearly aimed at sensitizing public awareness of the need for anticommunist action in postwar Italy.

It is not surprising to see Olivetti used by the U.S. media for such an explicit ideological goal. In the eyes of the Americans, Olivetti appeared as a potential agent of the transatlantic exchange, a prospective reference for the implementation of Washington's geopolitical strategies.[4] In reality, the goals of the Italian entrepreneur were somewhat different from those of the Department of State. Olivetti, in fact, tried to adopt aspects of America's reconstruction programs, not in pursuit of official U.S. goals, but in terms of his own agenda for social and cultural change. In his in-between position, he often found himself in the uncomfortable situation of trying to reconcile American needs and wills with Italian cultural and political peculiarities. It is worth noting what Olivetti declared to the *New York Times* reporter: "The Italian worker is fundamentally a Socialist. The problem is to make him a democratic Socialist and not a Communist."[5] One can only guess if this statement corresponded to the actual expectations of the American government.

Recently, a growing number of studies have disclosed the role played during the Cold War years by several U.S. agencies in the attempt to steer Europe's cultural debate toward pro-American goals.[6] The CIA, for instance, clandestinely supported the activities of the so-called Congress for Cultural Freedom, an international organization that tried to promote progressive yet not Communist intellectuals and that counted among its members the Italian writer Ignazio Silone, a close collaborator on the Olivetti-funded periodical *Comunità*. There is no evidence of Olivetti's involvement in any covert plan supported by the Americans. It is certainly clear, however, that Olivetti perfectly embodied the model of a balance between the opposite extremes of fascism and communism: a "third force" that, at least until the mid-1950s, represented for the United States the ideal interlocutor in Europe.

Olivetti's espousal of American culture was more than "an experiment in labor-management relations . . . attracting international attention as a challenge to communism," as another *New York Times* article of the time put it.[7] Italian sociologist Franco Ferrarotti, one of Olivetti's closest associates during the 1950s, has asserted that the Italian entrepreneur was rather wary of organization models imported from the United States, such as Taylorism or the theory of productivity, as well as of the same Marshall Plan.[8] While it is difficult to completely concur with Ferrarotti's claim, it is certainly true that Olivetti maintained a critical position toward American intervention in Italy. For instance, in an open letter sent to the American-based review *World*, Olivetti warned about the inefficacy of U.S. assistance programs in fighting communism in Europe.[9] More than an appraisal of the way the United States was acting, in fact, Olivetti's article sounded like a critique of his own country. Olivetti denounced the fact that American funds were appropriated by "the very monopoly and bureaucracy that had created or accepted fascism" and cautioned that aid to heavy industry undermined the foundations of Italian democracy. The "marriage" between capitalism and government—argued Olivetti—had sidestepped competition with relevant consequences on the country's social equilibrium. To be sure, Olivetti's remarks on Italy's postwar political situation never matched the anticommunist rhetoric of some of his American counterparts.

Olivetti's first encounter with American culture took place in 1925, when he embarked on his first trip to the United States. During a six-month stay, he visited New York, Providence, and Boston, with stops in Hartford, Ilion, and Groton, hometowns of, respectively, Underwood, Remington, and Corona, all competitors of the Olivetti Company in the field of typewriter manufacturing.[10] A key moment of Olivetti's American experience occurred on the Detroit leg of the trip, when he visited Ford's Highland Park and River Rouge plants and the Lincoln factory. Although Olivetti's trips to the United States were devoted primarily to the investigation of American industrial organization, after the very first one Olivetti began to turn his attention to urban and regional planning and to the relationship between planning and economic development. His sponsorship during the 1930s of agencies such as the Ente Nazionale per l'Organizzazione Scientifica del Lavoro (ENIOS—National Body for the Scientific Organization of Work), which had been founded in 1926, or the support of publications such as *Tecnica e Organizzazione*, reflected Olivetti's interest in the close interconnections between economic and physical planning, an attention that unquestionably originated from his American journeys.[11]

Olivetti's initial engagement in planning consisted of the sponsorship of the 1936 plan for the Aosta Valley, a project he personally supervised and coordinated. For the design of the plan Olivetti called on a handful of established and promising Italian architects such as Piero Bottoni, the BBPR group, Luigi Figini, and Gino Pollini, all of whom were well connected to the international design milieu of the time. Although he himself was neither an architect nor a planner, Olivetti became one of the key brokers in the Italian architectural scene, in particular during the postwar years. His primary contribution was to initiate the reorganization of the INU (National Institute of Town Planning), an institution that had been active since the 1930s.

But if there is no doubt that the prewar journeys to the United States kindled Olivetti's interest in the potential relationship between planning and social change, it was actually after the war when the Italian entrepreneur fully developed the belief that American culture could be, if filtered, adapted to the needs of Italian society of the time. For instance, no evidence exists that before the end of World War II Olivetti was fully aware of the American debate over urban and regional planning, but the surfacing of this subject in his discourse right after the conflict might indicate the gradual evolution in his awareness. Evidence of this is the postwar publication of the Italian translation of Lewis Mumford's book *The Culture of Cities*, a work that illustrates the impact of American culture on Olivetti's thought and actions.

The Italian version of *The Culture of Cities* was published in 1953 by Olivetti's publishing house, Edizioni di Comunità, fifteen years after the original American version.[12] The text had actually been circulating in Italy since the end of the war within intellectual milieus particularly interested in its contents:[13] despite multiple attempts to establish contacts with Harcourt, Brace, Mumford's American publisher, no initiative had been taken to translate the book into Italian. Apparently, another Italian publisher, Bompiani, had initially acquired the rights to the translation of *The Culture of Cities*, as well as of other books by Mumford.[14] Negotiations for the transfer of the rights to Edizioni di Comunità were not held until 1951 and involved, besides the Italian and the American publishers, the office of the United States Information Service (USIS) in Rome.[15]

It is important to emphasize that the arrival of *The Culture of Cities* to Edizioni di Comunità was far from accidental. Olivetti had surely known Mumford's work at least since the 1940s, although probably indirectly. In 1942, in fact, in a note to his secretary regarding book purchases, Olivetti made reference to the volume "The mesure [*sic*] of cities" by "L. Mumford."[16] This is a particularly interesting error as it suggests that Olivetti was familiar with the name of the author but not necessarily his writings. It is therefore difficult to assess how deep Olivetti's knowledge of Mumford's work was at that time and, in general, how strong was his familiarity with imported American ideas about planning. However, it is possible to hypothesize that the circles of Italian political expatriates in the United States and in Switzerland—with whom Olivetti was surely in contact—were well acquainted with Mumford's name. In the United States, for instance, Mumford corresponded with Italian historian and politician Gaetano Salvemini, who involved the American author in a campaign aimed at drawing the American public's attention to the antifascist cause.[17]

Connections to the network of members of the Italian political diaspora definitely allowed Olivetti to strengthen his acquaintance with American culture. Olivetti, in fact, spent several months in exile in Switzerland, mostly in Lausanne at the so-called Campo Universitario Italiano (Italian University Campus), where lectures and courses were offered by and to the gathering community of fugitive Italian intellectuals. Among these expatriates, for example, were some of the future leaders in the Italian reconstruction, such as architect Ernesto Nathan Rogers, one of the dominant figures of Italy's postwar architectural debate, and scientist Gustavo Colonnetti, who in 1944 would become president of Italy's National Research Council.[18] The participants in the campus activities often debated American authors and texts.

The years between 1943 and 1948 marked a crucial period in terms of Olivetti's cultivation of American connections. For instance, upon his release from the Rome penitentiary Regina Coeli, where he had been imprisoned for antifascist activity in 1943, Olivetti fled to Switzerland, most likely thanks to the intervention of the OSS (Office of Strategic Services, the CIA's forerunner), whose director, Allen Dulles, was the brother of John Foster Dulles, who served as secretary of state during the Eisenhower administration. According to Franco Ferrarotti, Dulles was probably also instrumental in inducing the Allies not to bomb the Olivetti factories in Ivrea.[19] It is thanks to these early American contacts that Olivetti came to occupy a prominent position in the Italian reconstruction during the postwar years.

An example of Olivetti's engagement in the construction of an important link between American and Italian planning and architectural cultures can be seen in his role in UNRRA-CASAS, a binational agency whose mission was to make use of funds from the European Recovery Program (ERP).[20] UNRRA-CASAS was formed in 1946 and organized as two committees: one to implement building plans and the other to handle financial tasks.[21] The UNRRA-CASAS housing office operated from 1947 to 1963 (when it became ISES, Istituto per lo Sviluppo dell'Edilizia Sociale [Institute for the Development of Social Housing]) and was responsible for the construction of more than a thousand villages all over Italy. As a member of the housing committee from 1951 and vice president of the agency from 1959, Olivetti steered UNRRA-CASAS to try new policies for social redistribution.

Olivetti's aspiration to widespread reform eventually clashed with the committee's official policy, which favored a response limited to needs determined by war damage and, later, by natural disasters.[22] The agency focused mainly on the construction of villages formed by standard units arranged in small groups. Nevertheless, thanks to Olivetti's efforts, the study center of the UNRRA-CASAS housing committee developed characteristic settlement schemes that were based on the model of the communitarian aggregation and designed by renowned architects who worked outside the agency's technical staff.

For instance, the well-known village of La Martella, near Matera, in the southern region of Basilicata—a city that gained public attention in the postwar period for its profound state of poverty and underdevelopment—was the work of a group of architects directed by Ludovico Quaroni, one of the foremost Italian postwar architects. With its two-family dwellings grouped along the roads that converged toward the town center, La Martella fully represented the ideal new community. Perhaps more importantly, this type of settlement involved redefining customary land organization, something that UNRRA-CASAS did not do in most of the other villages it built.

Olivetti invested much of his energies in the UNRRA-CASAS project. He contributed to the definition of the guidelines in important plans such as the one for La Martella, urging the application of principles that would become the reference point for building programs throughout the entire country and that would initiate land reform. For instance, at the end of 1950, Olivetti established contact with UNRRA-CASAS officials in order to start discussions with American authorities on housing plans in Italy.[23] Contact was resumed in 1951 and 1952 when Olivetti traveled to Washington, D.C., to discuss housing issues and to promote a funding campaign to support housing initiatives for southern Italy. Through his encounters with his American counterparts, Olivetti endorsed plans for interventions that he personally supervised. An example of this is a series of proposals architect Nello Mazzocchi Alemanni developed under Olivetti's guidance. Early in 1950, in fact, Mazzocchi Alemanni sent to UNRRA-CASAS officials a plan for a *demanio lucano* (a state property in the Lucania region).[24] The project's "fundamental concept," wrote Mazzocchi Alemanni in the letter accompanying the study, was that of a *borgo residenziale*, a residential neighborhood. Interestingly, this proposal matched the idea of La Martella and its mix of residential units and a civic center.

The experiments carried out within the UNRRA-CASAS program point to Olivetti's attempts to cooperate with U.S. authorities while at the same time negotiating American cultural influence. In other cases, the Italian industrialist acted outside the umbrella of official U.S. initiatives, still embracing ideas imported from the other side of the Atlantic Ocean. An interesting example is the activity of the Ufficio Consulenza Case Dipendenti (Employees' Housing Consultancy Office), part of the vast array of services offered by Olivetti's company to its workforce. Active in and around Ivrea, the office aimed at assisting employees in repairing or transforming existing dwellings, or in building new ones. Financing came from loans issued at a low interest rate (4 percent), to cover up to 60 percent of total expenses, and design and building execution were offered for free.[25] The initiative's scope and success were remarkable. Even though it acted in only a limited area, between 1951 and 1959 the office issued loans totaling 517 million lire, a significant amount of money at the time. The program assumed a particular significance in that it wedded social politics to the attempt to modernize the architectural "taste" of the people living in the area it served.

Under the direction of its chief designer, architect Emilio Aventino Tarpino, the office built more than six hundred dwellings for Olivetti employees. Moreover, in 1957 the Olivetti company contacted leading avant-garde Italian architects—Luigi Figini and Gino Pollini, Franco Albini and Franca Helg, and Mario Fiorentino—to develop typological schemes to be used in the office's design activity.[26] Conceived by Adriano Olivetti, this undertaking aimed to draw up a "catalogue composed of a select number of projects for standardized and typified houses" from which employees could choose their own home design.[27]

The objective of this plan was to disseminate "high" architectural quality while building technically sound housing. More importantly, the proposed prototypes took on ideas popularized by the American media, including fully equipped kitchens, separate rooms for dining and entertaining, and a covered space in which to park the car; the project by Albini and Helg, for example, featured the garage on one side of the single-story, single-family building.[28] The program ultimately revealed Olivetti's role in facilitating the reception (and adaptation) of ideals imported from the United States. From this perspective, it was not insignificant that Olivetti's workforce, comprised of an unusually high ratio of white- to blue-collar workers, proffered a model for consumption still uncommon in Italy.

It lies beyond the scope of this chapter to fully describe Olivetti's attempts at integrating American influence into Italian postwar culture, specifically in the fields of architecture and planning. Many examples could be cited. For instance, the reorganization of the INU (of which Olivetti became president in 1950) or the reestablishment of its official mouthpiece, the influential review *Urbanistica*, were instrumental in advancing the circulation in Italy of ideas and models of American origin. With a luxurious (and expensive) polychromatic graphic layout and funded for the most part by Olivetti, *Urbanistica* became a key reference for Italian planners and architects in the late 1940s and early 1950s. Similarly to *Urbanistica*, the architectural magazine *Metron* paid particular attention to the American scene. Between 1945 and 1948, *Metron* published a total of twenty-four articles about American architecture or planning, or whose authors were active in the United States. Needless to say, *Metron* was also largely financed by Olivetti.

In the postwar years, circulation and adoption of American culture was a complex phenomenon, contingent on regional contexts and characterized by the interaction of a variety of factors: a phenomenon where acceptance, rejection, and hybridization often coexisted. Adriano Olivetti played an essential role of mediator, acting alternately as a principal reference for U.S. officers in charge of reconstruction programs, a fervent advocate of political and economic ideals imported from the United States, and an unrelenting supporter of American texts and authors, but also as a strong defender of local interests and needs.

For all these reasons, Olivetti occupies an important place in the history of postwar Italy and, in particular, in the history of its architecture and planning. His figure, in fact, defies any narrative based on a presumptive triumph of global modernism, defined by style rather than process, and forces historians to focus primarily on how knowledge is transmitted and hybridized. As agent of the Italian-American exchange, Olivetti surely provides an invaluable paradigm for the exploration of the history of the relations between Europe and the United States.

Notes

1. C. L. Sulzberger, "Six Vignettes That Tell Italy's Story," *New York Times*, 16 May 1954, 16.

2. Bruno Caizzi, *Gli Olivetti* (Turin: UTET, 1962), 129–65; Valerio Ochetto, *Adriano Olivetti* (Milan: Mondadori, 1985), 23–24.

3. Adriano Olivetti, *L'ordine politico delle comunità* (Ivrea: Nuove Edizioni Ivrea, 1945).

4. Paolo Scrivano, "Lo scambio inter-atlantico e i suoi attori. Il rapporto tra Stati Uniti e Italia in architettura e urbanistica e il ruolo di Adriano Olivetti," *Mélanges de l'École française de Rome. Italie et Méditerranée 2*, no. 115 (2003): 451–73.

5. Sulzberger, "Six Vignettes That Tell Italy's Story".

6. Frances Stonor Saunders, *Who Paid the Piper? The CIA and the Cultural Cold War* (London: Granta Books, 1999).

7. Paul Hofmann, "Olivetti Plan," *New York Times*, 19 June 1955, SM 28.

8. Franco Ferrarotti, *Un imprenditore di idee. Una testimonianza su Adriano Olivetti. A cura di Giuliana Gemelli* (Turin: Edizioni di Comunità, 2001), 16.

9. Adriano Olivetti, "How US Aid Boomeranged in Italy," *World. America's Magazine of World Events 1* (November 1953): 60–62.

10. Caizzi, *Gli Olivetti*, 129–65; Ochetto, *Adriano Olivetti*, 23–24; Patrizia Bonifazio and Paolo Scrivano, *Olivetti Builds: Modern Architecture in Ivrea* (Milan: Skira, 2001), 11–21.

11. Patrizia Bonifazio, *La rivista "Comunità": Il territorio e i suoi confini intellettuali*, in *Costruire la città dell'uomo. Adriano Olivetti e l'urbanistica*, ed. Carlo Olmo (Turin: Edizioni di Comunità, 2001), 114–43.

12. Lewis Mumford, *La cultura delle città* (Turin: Edizioni di Comunità, 1953).

13. Carlo Doglio, *La storia culturale di Adriano Olivetti*, in *La comunità concreta: progetto ed immagine. Il pensiero e le iniziative di Adriano Olivetti nella formazione della cultura urbanistica ed architettonica italiana*, ed. Marcello Fabbri and Antonella Greco (Rome: Quaderni della Fondazione Adriano Olivetti, 1988), 36–47.

14. Letter from Catherine McCarthy (of Harcourt, Brace and Company) to Lewis Mumford, Lewis Mumford Papers, Van Pelt Dietrich Library, University of Pennsylvania, Philadelphia (hereafter cited as LMP) b. 25, f. 2051, 5 March 1951; letter from Mario Labò to Giorgio Soavi, Archivio Storico Olivetti, Ivrea (hereafter cited as ASO) 22.623, 23 December 1948; see also letter from Labò to Soavi, ASO, 29 October 1949.

15. Letter from (Parri) to Adriano Olivetti, ASO 22.623, 17 May 1951; letter by unidentified author to Robert Crowell, ASO, 15 June 1951 (Crowell represented the USIS); letter from McCarthy to Mumford, LMP b. 25, f. 2051, 2 October 1951. See also letter from McCarthy to Mumford, LMP, 24 April 1952.

16. Letter from Adriano Olivetti to Enriques (Olivetti's collaborator), ASO 22.580, 19 January 1942.

17. Letter from Gaetano Salvemini to Lewis Mumford, LMP b. 58, f. 4283, 7 November 1938; letter from Salvemini to Mumford, LMP, 28 August 1940; letter from Salvemini to Mumford, LMP, 25 March 1946.

18. Renata Broggini, *Terra d'asilo. I rifugiati italiani in Svizzera, 1943–1945* (Bologna: Il Mulino, 1993).

19. Ferrarotti, *Un imprenditore di idee*, 61–64.

20. The acronym translates as: "United Nations Relief and Rehabilitation Administration-Comitato Amministrativo Soccorsi ai Senzatetto" (Administrative Committee for the Assistance to the Homeless).

21. Bernardo Marotta, *Unrra-Casas. Dalla ricostruzione post-bellica alla creazione dei borghi*, in *Esperienze urbanistiche in Italia* (Rome: Istituto Nazionale di Urbanistica, 1952), 110–27; R. M. (Riccardo Musatti), "I borghi residenziali Unrra-Casas," *Comunità* 13 (1952): 44–48; Modesto Fascio, *Unrra-Casas. L'attività dell'Unrra-Casas*, in *Nuove esperienze urbanistiche in Italia* (Rome: Istituto Nazionale di Urbanistica, 1956), 258–61; Ludovico Quaroni, "L'abitazione per le famiglie a basso reddito in Italia. Relazione di Ludovico Quaroni," *Urbanistica* 31 (1960): 106–13.

22. Marida Talamona, *Dieci anni di politica dell'Unrra-Casas: Dalle case ai senzatetto ai borghi rurali nel Mezzogiorno d'Italia (1945–1955). Il ruolo di Adriano Olivetti*, in Olmo, *Costruire la città dell'uomo*, 173–204; Bonifazio and Scrivano, *Olivetti Builds*, 103–25.

23. Letter from Ignazio Weiss to Guido Nadzo, National Archives and Records Administration, College Park, MD (hereafter cited as NARA), RG 469, Records of U.S. Foreign Assistance Agencies, 1948–1961. Mission to Italy. Production and Technical Assistance Division Records Relating to Housing 1948–55, b. 2, 26 November 1950.

24. Letter from Guido Mazzocchi Alemanni to Guido Nadzo, NARA RG 469, Records of U.S. Foreign Assistance Agencies, 1948–1961. Mission to Italy. Production and Technical Assistance Division Records Relating to Housing 1948–55, b. 5, 3 January 1950.

25. Roberto Olivetti, "La società Olivetti nel Canavese," *Urbanistica* 33 (1961): 77.

26. Paolo Scrivano, *La comunità e la sua difficile realizzazione. Adriano Olivetti e l'urbanistica a Ivrea e nel Canavese*, in Olmo, *Costruire la città dell'uomo*, 83–112; Bonifazio and Scrivano, *Olivetti Builds*, 149–73.

27. Letter from the Uffici della Presidenza Olivetti to Emilio Aventino Tarpino, Archivio Emilio Aventino Tarpino, Ivrea (hereafter cited as AET), 1 April 1957.

28. "Casette per dipendenti Olivetti," AET, 5 August 1958.

Suggested Readings

Bender, Thomas, ed. *Rethinking American History in a Global Age*. Berkeley: University of California Press, 2002.

Bonifazio, Patrizia, and Paolo Scrivano. *Olivetti Builds: Modern Architecture in Ivrea*. Milan: Skira, 2001.

Caizzi, Bruno. *Gli Olivetti*. Turin: UTET, 1962.

Duggan, Christopher, and Christopher Wagstaff, eds. *Italy in the Cold War: Politics, Culture and Society 1948–58*. Oxford: Berg, 1995.

Ginsborg, Paul. *A History of Contemporary Italy: Society and Politics 1943–1988*. London: Penguin, 1990.

Ochetto, Valerio. *Adriano Olivetti*. Milan: Mondadori, 1985.

Olmo, Carlo, ed. *Costruire la città dell'uomo. Adriano Olivetti e l'urbanistica*. Turin: Edizioni di Comunità, 2001.

Saunders, Frances Stonor. *Who Paid the Piper? The CIA and the Cultural Cold War*. London: Granta Books, 1999.

Scrivano, Paolo. "Signs of Americanization in Italian Domestic Life: Italy's Postwar Conversion to Consumerism." *Journal of Contemporary History* 40, no. 2 (April 2005): 317–40.

~

CHAPTER THIRTEEN

Ab-Normalization

The Plastic People of the Universe
and the Soviet Invasion of Czechoslovakia

MICHAEL KILBURN

The late 1960s was a period of popular revolt around the world. In Western Europe, a loose network of young people, in particular students, mobilized to seek social and political change. In Eastern Europe, most notably in Czechoslovakia, youths as well as reformers within the Communist Party sought alternatives to Stalinist dictatorship. These movements came to a head in 1968, when mass popular protests took place globally in cities such as Paris, West Berlin, Rome, Amsterdam, Prague, Berkeley, and Mexico City. The 1968 revolts assumed many common features. Protest movements in Italy, Germany, and France initially coalesced around university students who criticized campus overcrowding and sought a greater voice in university governance. More broadly, protesters expressed their alienation with the values of their parents' generation. They challenged rigid established social hierarchies, entrenched party politics, and excess materialism. Revolting against what they considered to be the conformist norms of the 1950s, they embraced new popular culture and sexual freedoms. In France, workers joined students to demand greater participation in management decisions and better labor conditions, circumstances that culminated in a massive general strike in May. In Germany, young people called their parents' generation to task for its silence on Nazi atrocities.

Czechoslovakia also saw a youth revolt, although it took place under a much less tolerant Soviet-bloc system. Yet a period of open criticism began in 1956 when Soviet leader Nikita Khrushchev made an internal denunciation of Stalinism in a secret speech to a Communist Party congress. This led Communists in Soviet satellite states to seek ways to reform communism as well. Disaffected young people in Czechoslovakia, inspired by dissident and underground movements in both East and West, began their own protest movement. A brutal police crackdown on students in November 1967 delegitimized the communist establishment. The ascent to power of reformer Alexander Dubček in late 1967 led Communist officials to initiate a series of reforms in the first half of 1968 that became known as the "Prague Spring." Reformers sought to create a communism with increased civil liberties and a more decentralized economy. Unfortunately, this spirit of reform was short lived. On 20 August 1968, Soviet and Warsaw Pact troops invaded Czechoslovakia to end the reforms and install more reliable conservative leaders.

Whether in Western or Eastern Europe, the 1968 protesters revolted against centralized modern bureaucracies and conservative cultural and economic institutions. In this chapter, Michael Kilburn examines the period of the Prague Spring and its aftermath through a case study of a rock band called the Plastic People of the Universe. Part of an antipolitical underground culture, these young musicians revealed the contradictions of Soviet-bloc socialism and of modern life more generally.

The year 1968 was one of challenge and transition around the world. From Berkeley and Chicago to Paris and Tokyo the postwar generation dramatically clashed with the culture, values, and structures of the establishment. Some confrontations were symbolic, and some descended into violence and threatened anarchy, but nowhere was the clash more poignant or revealing than in Czechoslovakia. The story of 1968 and its aftermath in that country is a stark allegory for the complex negotiations of progressive social change and reaction that characterized the 1970s and began the gradual denouement of Soviet communism and the Cold War. Indeed, there is even a fairy-tale quality to the story, with the imprisoned dissident Václav Havel ultimately riding a wave of peaceful, even joyous, demonstrations in the so-called Velvet Revolution to become the first post-Communist president. But the story is perhaps better told through the experiences of several simple, hapless, and ordinary young men, the rock band Plastic People of the Universe, who found themselves caught up in historical circumstances beyond their control. Their grace, humor, and integrity when faced with the hysterical might of the totalitarian regime revealed the basic contradictions of Soviet socialism and suggest the inherent contradictions of modernity itself.

Historical Context

In Czechoslovakia, 1968 was a year of giddy optimism and crushing disappointment. In January of that year, Alexander Dubček, the new secretary of the Communist Party, initiated a series of reforms in an attempt to reinvigorate and democratize socialism, a project he called "socialism with a human face." The dramatic effects of this economic and political program underwrote a social and cultural revival known as the Prague Spring, a metaphor for the signs of life after the grim, tedious winter of Stalinism that had ruled the land since shortly after World War II. Censorship was abolished, limited elections were held, the sweeping police powers of the Ministry of the Interior were checked, and basic rights and freedoms were constitutionally guaranteed.

Despite obsequious protestations of ideological solidarity, the Czechoslovak experiment was greeted with disapproval by the Soviets and alarm by other East European leaders, who feared the populist reforms might spill over into their own countries. Soviet premier Leonid Brezhnev invoked his version of the Truman Doctrine—keeping the world safe for communism—and prepared a military response to the crisis.

In the early morning hours of 21 August 1968, more than a half million Soviet and Warsaw Pact troops poured over the borders to provide "fraternal assistance" in combating the alleged forces of counter-revolution. The Dubček leadership was arrested and spirited off to Moscow for "negotiations." Their safe return four tense days later and reinstatement in office was a minor victory in itself, but the reform process was crippled by the demands of the protocols the leadership had been forced to sign in Moscow. After a series of protests, strikes, and other provocations—most tragically the self-immolation of the student Jan Palach in January 1969—Dubček was replaced by Gustav Husák, whose ruthless and autocratic style of leadership promised a more decisive resolution of the intractable contradictions between the Moscow protocols and the reformist Action Program. Husák's policy of "normalization" ultimately engineered a complete reversal of the Prague Spring reforms and an aggressively servile relationship with the Soviet Union.

Reformist elements and sympathizers were purged from all positions of responsibility in the party, the professions, the unions, and universities and schools. Censorship was reintroduced and the library system was reformed to control access to information. By the end of 1970, the numerical strength of the Communist Party had been halved and tens of thousands of people had lost their jobs. One of the earliest and most famous of these victims of occupational persecution was Dubček himself, expelled from the party and banished to clerkdom in the Slovak Forestry Ministry. Sweeping powers were returned to the Ministry of the Interior, the police, and People's Militias and were invoked to brutally suppress street demonstrations on the first anniversary of the invasion. The rehabilitation of political victims of the previous era was halted, freedoms of expression and assembly were revoked, and the liberal economic reforms that had unleashed the whole process were abandoned. After a brief and glorious spring, it seemed that winter had returned.

In the period of disillusionment following the invasion and undoing of the 1968 Prague Spring reform movement, the nation fell into a bitter, then merely cynical, lethargy. Mediocrity, conformity, and passivity were rewarded as civic virtues while talent, originality, and initiative were punished as provocation. Material well-being, bought on credit to console and pacify the population, only masked a hopeless economic, environmental, and spiritual decline. The period of so-called normalization was characterized by economic and cultural stagnation, moral ambiguity, and a social malaise of humiliating complicity as the Communist regime sought to construct a kind of negative legitimacy: a silent majority of citizens unwilling to speak out and therefore implicitly supportive, acquiescent, or at least quiescent. In this sea of dour passivity and moral compromise, this "Biafra of the spirit,"[1] an archipelago of artists, intellectuals, and freethinkers would conceive a parallel culture—a "Merry Ghetto"—within which they could "consciously and critically determine their own stance toward the world in which they lived."[2] But this theoretical position was arrived at only through bitter experience and the tedious testing of mettle. The music came first.

The Rise and Fall and Rise and Fall of the Plastic People of the Universe

Of course, politics didn't matter much to a young butcher's apprentice named Mejla Hlavsa. Like most seventeen-year-olds, the only thing that mattered to him was rock and roll, and he was particularly focused on the prospects of the band he had just assembled, the Plastic People of the Universe. Such studied indifference to political reality may seem disingenuous in the face of a military occupation, but it took some time for the neo-Stalinist bureaucrats to herd and domesticate the cultural energies that had been let loose by democratization. The Plastic People of the Universe was founded and grew to local fame in this ambivalent interzone between the Soviet-led invasion and the full imposition of normalization.

As creeping bureaucratization gradually choked the vibrant youth culture of the capital, the Plastics led by example and under duress the development of an alternative autonomous "second culture" as a refuge from the cloying politicization of life. A stubborn and later principled disaffection with politics would become characteristic of the band and the underground culture it came to represent. In the context of an aggressively ideological and politically overdetermined state, an ethic and aesthetic political indifference would prove a difficult and provocative stance to maintain. By rejecting the premise of the legitimacy and "leading role" of the ruling party and choosing to "live within the truth," the band functioned as a kind of existential threat to the regime, which targeted it accordingly. The Plastic People and their associates would endure social and economic discrimination, police surveillance, and harassment, prison, and exile for their adamantly apolitical stance. Yet the band's demonstrating the courage of its convictions had deleterious consequences for the regime as well, puncturing the suspension of disbelief, and ultimately unraveling the web of deceit that held the regime in power, and the nation in thrall.

In April 1969—the same month that Husák assumed control of the Communist Party and began the process of normalization—the group won first place in a battle of the bands called *Beat Salon*, held at one of the city's main rock clubs. It was at this show that they first met Ivan Jirous, also known as *Magor* (lunatic), a poet, art critic, and drunken provocateur who would become the band's artistic director and the principal theorist of the underground. The Plastic People, performing under a banner that read "Jim Morrison is our father,"[3] soon became the leading psychedelic band in Prague, staging elaborate shows with costumes, theatrics, pyrotechnics, and covers of American underground bands such as the Velvet Underground, Frank Zappa's Mothers of Invention,[4] and the Fugs. They were approached by Pavel Kratochvíl, the manager of the popular group Olympic, who arranged for a professional license, Western instruments, a rehearsal space, and a paying tour.

From 1970, however, the dictates of normalization began to constrict and micromanage the heretofore vibrant and expressive popular-music scene. Speaking out against the heterogeneous counterculture of the flower children, the official journal *Tribuna* declared, "We will cultivate, water and protect only one flower: the red rose of Marxism."[5] For nonconformist tendencies in all the arts normalization amounted to a death by degrees (or decrees): the withdrawal of coverage and support by the media; the restructuring of cultural organizations; the closing of rock clubs; and the banning of English names and lyrics, decadence, long hair, volume, and pessimism.

Aside from the use of police to monitor and disrupt unauthorized or unorthodox musical happenings, the main means for regulating youth culture under normalization were "requalification exams" designed to promote the cultural policies of the regime and curtail those activities that did not fit the official aesthetic. In order for a group to perform in public, it had to be licensed by the state. Licenses were granted by a panel of judges based on an audition and a set of exams that tested not only rudimentary musical knowledge but also one's political outlook and willingness to compromise. In the interest of consolidating popular culture or, as the process was euphemistically known, "improving the cultural quality," the requalification exams assumed an ideological function.

Given the choice between moral compromise and professional ruin—that is, the loss of equipment and opportunities to play publicly—most bands chose the road of accommodation: they cut their hair, turned down their amps, and modified their repertoire. In this sense, the rock scene was typical of capitulation on a wider social scale to the edicts of normalization. A stubborn principled minority, however, refused to compromise. The popular folksingers Jaroslav Hutka and Vlastimil Třesňak attempted a boycott of the exams, but were quickly isolated, charged with "illegal business activity," and eventually forced into exile. When the Plastics were offered a Faustian contract for a yearlong gig in Malaysia, their artistic director, Jirous, who also functioned as self-appointed guardian of the band's artistic and ethical integrity, refused. The band's subsequent loss of its professional license precipitated its descent into underground culture. Jirous described this realization thus:

> The *Plastic People* . . . showed that "underground" was not just an attractive label indicating a certain musical tendency, but that, above all, it involved a mental attitude towards life: *it is better not to play at all than to play music that does not flow from one's convictions. It is better not to play at all than to play what the establishment demands.*[6]

Such integrity had its costs, though. The singer, Michal Jernek, and guitarist, Jiří Štěvich, quit and the remaining members had to take jobs as foresters in order to satisfy the work requirement and to earn enough money to buy new instruments. While in the country, they borrowed and cobbled together enough equipment to play weekend concerts in the villages. Though they played under the name *Dřevorubci* (the Lumberjacks), word got out that the Plastics had resurfaced and young people began making the trip out to the country to hear them. These bored and hungry kids traipsing out to the villages to hear interesting music were the humble originators of an emergent underground community.

The Plastics returned to Prague in the fall of 1970 and acquired two new members: Paul Wilson, a Canadian teacher, on English vocals and guitar, and Jiří Kabeš on viola. In February 1971, the band performed an evening of Velvet Underground songs as a supplement to a lecture Ivan Jirous delivered on Andy Warhol and American pop art. While constrained by its amateur status, the band was beginning to rebuild its reputation, playing several concerts and developing its repertoire. But by 1972, the stultifying effects of normalization were beginning to be felt even in the amateur realm. The once-supportive press turned against the band and it was increasingly difficult to find sponsorship for shows. Then, at a concert at a workers' club in June, Jirous was arrested in a scuffle with a drunken auxiliary officer and the Plastics were banned from performing in Prague.

During a yearlong hiatus from public performance, the band significantly changed its lineup, repertoire, and direction. The addition of free-jazz saxophonist and poet Vrat'a Brabenec encouraged them toward a more experimental and all-original format. Brabenec also insisted on exclusively Czech texts, which led to Paul Wilson's gradual retirement, though he remained an active supporter and cast member. Singing exclusively in Czech was a break from rock convention and happened to coincide with the dictates of official culture, though not in ways the regime had imagined. When Jirous introduced the group to the verse of the banned poet Egon Bondy, the infrastructure was already in place for the artistic transition from psychedelia to the underground, or, in Jirous's words, from the "mythological underground" to a "genuine sociological and cultural underground."[7] Bondy's texts would dominate the band's material until 1976 and bring them international notoriety when tapes of sessions from 1973 and 1974 were smuggled to the West by Paul Wilson and released as the album *Egon Bondy's Happy Hearts Club Banned.*

The songs describe bodily excreta, substance abuse, insomnia, sex, death, and despair, with each song conveying a sense that something is not right with the world. Several of the songs mock the vapid proletarian enthusiasm of the official aesthetic, singing of tractors, world peace, and toilet paper. The song "Dvácet" (Twenty) describes the historical perspectives of those born in the fifties, the thirties, and the teens to contemporary social circumstances.

Dvácet[8]	Twenty
Když je dnes člověku dvácet	To be twenty these days
chce se mu hnusem zvracet.	Makes you want to puke your guts out in disgust
Ale těm co je čtyřicet	But those who are forty
je toho vyblít ještě více	have even more reason to spew
Jen ten komu je šedesát	Only those who are sixty,
může jít se sklerozou klidně spát	can sleep peacefully in a senile haze.

—Egon Bondy

The song suggests that the young people of the Plastics' own generation see no hope in their situation. Having come of age in the festive and open atmosphere of the sixties thaw and the Prague Spring, the closed conformity of normalization seemed to be a stale, joyless, and artificially imposed regime. Bondy's generation, on the other hand, had lived through World War II, Nazi occupation, and the Stalinist terror of the 1950s and realized the immense human suffering that lay dormant beneath the gray administrative facade of normalization. The members of the oldest generation, those most responsible for the current malaise, had buried their crimes and repressed their guilt. Therefore, the so-called restoration of order signified a massive cover-up of the extent to which things were not in order. The song offers no solution or respite from its bleak verdict, but rails noisily in the face of meaninglessness, despair, and disgust.

In May 1973, the Plastics again underwent the requalification process to obtain a professional license (though not, of course, with any of the Bondy material) and, surprisingly, were approved for performance. This success was short lived, however, as the committee's decision was overturned by the state booking agency on the grounds that the music was "morbid" and would have a negative social effect. This verdict led the Plastics to finally turn their back on official culture and pursue an independent artistic agenda in the underground, organizing concerts and producing recordings privately, completely outside the state cultural apparatus. The first concert they played with this attitude was a carnivalesque celebration of the marriage of folksinger Charlie Soukup on a steamboat in the river Vltava. The independent scene that developed around the Plastics in their disengagement from official structures marked the beginning of an alternative "second culture" in Czechoslovakia.

However, this disengagement was unilateral, and the implicitly defiant orientation actually provoked increased police intervention. Individual members and fans were harassed and interrogated, and concerts were subject to more intrusive surveillance. In July, Jirous was again arrested for public disturbance and sentenced to ten months in prison. The first large-scale operation against the emergent underground culture—the so-called Bojanovice massacre—took place the following spring in the village of Rudolfov in southern Bohemia. The "massacre" consisted of hundreds of police and paramilitary troops attacking and detaining fans at a rock concert at which the Plastic People were supposed to perform. Trials followed and many students were expelled from school. Although this action was directed primarily against the fans and none of the musicians was directly implicated, the message of intolerance for unsanctioned culture was clear.

Despite the atmosphere of intimidation, the First Festival of the Second Culture, featuring the Plastics and several other bands and performers that had grown up around them, was successfully organized a few months later in the village of Postupice. As private entertainment for a wedding party, it skirted the licensing issue and was permitted to take place without intervention. The success of this festival, the breadth of musical styles it showcased, and the communal atmosphere offered hope for a vibrant and sustainable alternative culture.

The year 1975 was an active one in the underground. Though police interference was common, the scene had developed a momentum, starting to grow and spread beyond the immediate shadow of the Plastics, as several new bands formed and an information and music distribution network developed. Jirous wrote his principal underground manifesto that year, the highly influential "Report on the Third Czech Music Revival," which provided the theoretical basis for a national movement of spiritual rejuvenation through autonomous culture. His lectures on this theme, illustrated by tapes of the Plastic People, met with great success and support in various towns. It seemed as though a truly independent cultural alternative might take root in the barren soil of this "Biafra" of normalization.

The Second Festival of the Second Culture, held as a wedding party for Jirous in the village of Bojanovice in February 1976, was a celebration of the spirit of the second culture, a sustained affirmation of the principles outlined in Jirous's report. This was the largest underground event to date, featuring a wide variety of performers and artists and hundreds of participants. Thanks to a noticeable decrease in police pressure during the preceding months, there was a general feeling of hope, empowerment, and optimism. However, the peaceful atmosphere turned out to be the calm before the storm.

The Trial

A month after the Bojanovice festival, in a coordinated series of raids, security forces detained more than a hundred people who had participated in the events; arrested twenty-seven musicians, including all of the members of the Plastic People; and confiscated a variety of instruments and materials. After spending months in detention, most of those arrested were eventually released, though several would ultimately stand trial on charges of "organized disturbance of the peace."[9] Due to the youth and political innocence of the defendants, the bombastic media campaign against them, and the cynical vehemence of the prosecution, the trial came to the attention of prominent members of the political and literary dissident community. While largely unfamiliar with underground culture, many recognized the government action as a breach of the recently ratified Helsinki Accords on human and civil rights and rallied to the defense of the accused, if only in Voltairean fashion.

The main trial was held in Prague in September 1976, with Plastics artistic director Ivan Jirous, saxophonist Vratislav Brabenec, DG307 front man Pavel Zajicek, and evangelist folksinger Svat'a Karásek in the dock on charges that the vulgar content of the texts and the low artistic standard of the music had a "negative effect on the lifestyle of the young generation." The prosecution's case reiterated the failure of the underground groups to pass the requalification exams and obtain the licenses necessary for public performance, but practically the entire focus of both the indictment and the trial was the "cardinal vulgar expressions, which run against Socialist morality." The indictment read:

> The texts consisted of coarse vulgarity with an anti-Socialist and antisocial effect. The majority extolled nihilism, decadence, and clericalism. It was so bad that members of the audience were roused to indignation by the performance and judicial and social organs were forced to intervene.[10]

Prominent dissident Václav Havel was roused to indignation at the spectacle played out in the courtroom, perceiving in the case against the young musicians a larger existentialist prosecution of "personal and creative integrity" by the posttotalitarian system.[11] Together with several fellow intellectuals[12] he made a private appeal to the president, and then wrote an open letter to the media, but to no avail. Finally, he cowrote a letter to the German writer Heinrich Böll in which he condemned the state's persecution of anonymous individuals "not for their political opinions, activity, or ambitions, but for . . . their aversion to the established values of the world in which they live, to its hypocritical morality, and to its conformity and bureaucratic stupidity, and its consumer style of life." At stake, he opined, was nothing less than "the fate of the freedom of spirit on the European continent."[13] Böll's involvement in the case, as well as the interest of other Western writers and intellectuals, ensured that the proceedings would be closely monitored by Western media and would make the Plastic People something of an international cause célèbre.

After days of absurd and self-contradictory testimony, the prosecution managed to demonstrate only nine instances of vulgarity in the sixty-five songs exhibited, and none of the witnesses could corroborate the allegations of a negative social impact. Despite several irregularities in the prosecution's conduct, and the complete absence of proof, the outcome of the trial was a foregone conclusion. In her ruling, the judge concluded that the musicians had indeed "manifested their disrespect of society and their contempt of the fundamental moral laws." Their activities were "highly dangerous to society" and had an "adverse effect on young people's development."[14] All four of the defendants were found guilty and given unconditional sentences ranging from eight to eighteen months in prison.[15]

The Trial's Aftermath

In the Kafkaesque logic of socialist legality, the trial was not the culmination of the government's campaign against the Plastic People and the underground, but only its opening shot. The period following the trial was characterized by an intensification in both the scope and the character of repression. Surveillance, threats, harassment, and sometimes daily interrogations became commonplace. Paul Wilson's residence permit was revoked and he was abducted from his farewell party and thrown out of the country. The host of the party was sentenced to three months in jail. Although these measures of repression and propaganda did not stop the underground movement, the new climate of fear and intimidation they provoked changed its character. Underground events lost their family-friendly, communal atmosphere and became wilder, gaunt, and self-consciously defiant:

> Gone was the carefree fun, the silliness, merriness, and crazy ideas. Now began a time when the specter of the police hung over everything that had been the least bit normal . . . a time of crazy intrigue and conspiracy. It was a time when the fear of betrayal began to destroy the bonds of friendship.[16]

The experience of the trial finally removed any illusions about the possibilities of cultural autonomy under real socialism. Psychological stress and material insecurity were compounded by a relentless media campaign, which portrayed the underground musicians as hooligans, drug addicts, and mental patients in an effort to intimidate and suppress expressions of independent thought and foster a mood of popular intolerance for nonconformity. Criminalized, slandered in the press, and mocked on the streets, the underground found little sympathy among ordinary Czechs.

But the sympathy and solidarity fostered in the dissident community during the trial had unforeseen consequences. The trial of the Plastic People is generally acknowledged to be the final straw that broke the spell of inertia surrounding resistance to normalization. The collegial efforts of Havel and others to defend the young musicians galvanized the heretofore inchoate dissident community—reform-minded Communists, Catholics, and Protestants; nonaligned intellectuals; and others—and acted as a cata-lyst for the creation of a new civic association dedicated to the monitoring, protection, and promotion of civil and political rights in Czechoslovakia. This organization, Charter 77, would be a thorn in the side of the socialist regime until its collapse, and would form the backbone of the Civic Forum that would eventually overthrow and replace the regime. More than a cat-alyst, however, the cultural underground provided a model of direct action and "living in truth" that would be the cornerstone of Havel's theory of "antipolitical politics." The underground network also provided a bridge to a world beyond the elitist perspective of the dissidents, especially among the young, disenfranchised working class. While Charter 77 (and later, the Civic Forum) never quite shook the stigma of elitism, it did find dispro-portionate support within the underground demographic. Combining the independent spirit and tactics of the underground with a more politically engaged and legalistic agenda represented a new and open form of opposi-tion that threatened the party-state monopoly on civic association.

As the communist regime shifted the focus of its attack from the symbolic threat of underground culture to the more explicitly political threat of the Charter, the underground circled closer to the sheltering orbit of the well-known and connected dissidents. Havel was particularly supportive, hosting the Third Festival of the Second Culture at his country house in Hrádeček on the occasion of Jirous's release from prison. In addition, the Plastics recorded the albums *Passion Play* (1978) and *Leading Horses* (1980) in the sanctuary of Havel's barn. However, the close association with the dissidents presented an identity crisis as well, challenging the underground's apolitical self-conception.

Following the Soviet Union in an antirock crusade, and frustrated by the provocative release and shortwave broadcast of *Passion Play* in Canada, in the early 1980s the Czech government increased its intensity and brutality in the campaign against nonconformist artists, forcing dozens into exile and se-verely curtailing public activities. A live performance of *Leading Horses* in March 1981 proved to be the Plastics' last concert after the police burned down the house where it had taken place. As a result of these and other Dra-conian measures, underground activities tactically retreated into publishing and recording; the underground network developed an impressive distribu-tion network for information in *samizdat* and *magnizdat* but gradually lost its essential spirit of participatory community.

By the mid-1980s, the underground culture was socially isolated and ma-ligned, its members beaten and dispersed, its critical energy suppressed and spent. At this darkest hour, however, the new Soviet premier Mikhail Gorbachev suddenly announced his democratic reformist policies of *glasnost* and *perestroika*, triggering a wave of reform and civic renewal across the region. The Czechoslovak regime was among the most recalcitrant to this return of the repressed, but facing growing demands for democratic liberalization from its citizens on the one hand and the Soviet leadership on the other, it eventually had to concede a loosening of civic control. Dozens of civic initiatives sprang to life and a critical mass of popular disdain would finally bring the regime down in the Velvet Revolution. Ironically, just as the repression was beginning to lift, the Plastic People of the Universe disbanded, riven by discord over how to respond to the new conditions and overtures from the regime.

The rise and fall and rise and fall of the Plastic People of the Universe mirrors, though does not entirely comprise, underground culture as a whole. The group rode a wave of revulsion and hope that upset the tidy, stilted euphemisms of normalization and, through a pragmatic combination of virtue and necessity, helped frame a cultural, philosophical, and moral alternative. It established the textual, musical, and strategic parameters of the second culture, laid claim to the literary and philosophical tradition of subversive tendencies within Czech culture, and functioned as a living model for the abstract principle of "living in truth" that would underwrite Charter 77 and other civic opposition movements, all the while maintaining a keen ear for the rhythm, bleak humor, and the poetic absurdity of life lived under real socialism. It was the first, last, and most productive underground band, leaving a legacy of work as witness and foil to the overarching claims of the regime.

Nearly every society had to negotiate a kind of normalization in the years that followed the cultural paroxysms of the 1960s. Few met the demonstrations of their citizens with tanks or spelled out the restoration of order in such petty and humiliating detail as did the communist governments, but the fundamental issues raised by demands for socialism—and capitalism—with a human face are similar. The way in which the Plastic People strove, and also the ways in which they failed, to maintain a critical distance from an aggressively ideological state is relevant to the practice of democracy and the functioning of civil society in the East and West alike. After 1968, the Czechoslovak emperor had no clothes, and understanding the naked expression of ideological power there can help us see through its thoroughly swaddled postmodern variant in the West. For Havel, the moral of the story is clear:

> With respect to the relation of western Europe to the totalitarian systems, no error could be greater than the one looming largest: that of a failure to understand the totalitarian systems for what they ultimately are—a convex mirror of

all modern civilization and a harsh, perhaps final call for a global recasting of how that civilization understands itself.[17]

"Bylo nebylo," the Czechs begin their fairy tales: "So it was, so it wasn't." Now that a generation has grown up since the collapse of communism in Europe, the bitter absurdity of that misadventure is sometimes lost or forgotten amid the flush of capitalism, the buried humiliation of the older generation, and an emerging integral European identity untrammeled by any Cold War divisions. But there are lessons to be divined in the entrails of that recently vanished world, lives and stories worthy of respect, retelling, and rehabilitation. When the history of that period is written, and the temptations of metanarratives beckon, the historian will have to contend with the Plastic People, men who made their own history, not just as they pleased, nor under circumstances they chose themselves, but still with joy, integrity, and counterpoint.

Notes

1. Louis Aragon's phrase, cited in *A Besieged Culture: Czechoslovakia Ten Years after Helsinki*, ed. A. Heneka, Frantisek Janouch, Vilem Prečan, and Jan Vladislav (Stockholm: Charta 77 Foundation and the International Helsinki Federation for Human Rights, 1985), 15. Similar sentiments were expressed by Heinrich Boll: "Czechoslovakia is today a veritable cultural cemetery" (15); and Milan Kundera: "I am weighing my words carefully: in its duration, extent and consistency, the massacre of Czech culture following 1968 has no analogue in the country's history since the Thirty Years' War" (128).

2. Ivan Jirous, "Report on the Third Czech Musical Revival," booklet accompanying Plastic People of the Universe, *Egon Bondy's Happy Hearts Club Banned*, LP, Boží Mlýn and Scopa Invisible Productions, 1978.

3. Ivan Jirous, *Magorův zápisník* [Magor's notebook] (Prague: Torst, 1997), 244.

4. The band was named after the 1967 Frank Zappa song "Plastic People" from the album *Absolutely Free*.

5. Cited in Tim Ryback, *Rock around the Bloc: A History of Rock Music in Eastern Europe and the Soviet Union* (New York: Oxford University Press, 1990), 141.

6. Jirous, "Report."

7. Jirous, "Report."

8. Egon Bondy, "Dvacet," in *The Plastic People of the Universe*, ed. Jaroslav Riedel (Prague: Globus, 1997), 51.

9. *Vytřnictví*: Art. 202 of the Czechoslovak criminal code. See Václav Havel, "Article 202," in *Open Letters: Selected Writings 1965–1990* (New York: Alfred A. Knopf, 1991), 113–16, for a discussion of the law and its (mis)uses.

10. *Hněda Kniha* [The brown book: Documents of the trial proceedings against Ivan Jirous, Svata Karásek, Pavel Zajíček, and Vratislav Brabenec] (Prague: Samizdat, 1976), 168–70.

11. For a discussion of the term, see Havel, "Power of the Powerless," in *Open Letters*, 131.

12. In addition to Havel, the signers were national poet and future Nobel laureate, Jaroslav Seifert; literary historian Václav Černy; eminent philosopher Jan Patočka; Marxist philosopher Karel Kosik; and internationally renowned writers Pavel Kohout and Ivan Klima.

13. Havel and others, cited in Heneka et al., *A Beseiged Culture*, 22.

14. Cited in H. Gordon Skilling, *Charter 77 and Human Rights in Czechoslovakia* (London: George Allen & Unwin, 1981), 12.

15. Jirous, as a recidivist (he was convicted in 1973 of the same charge), received the longest sentence, eighteen months; Zajíček received twelve months; and Brabenec and Karásek received eight months each.

16. Hlavsa describing the atmosphere after the trial in Mejla Hlavsa and Jan Pelc, *Bez ohňů je underground* [The underground is without fires] (Prague: BFS, 1992), 145.

17. Havel, *Open Letters*, 259.

Suggested Readings

Ash, Timothy Garton. *The Magic Lantern: The Revolution of '89 Witnessed in Warsaw, Budapest, Berlin and Prague*. New York: Random House, 1990.

Dubček, Alexander. *Hope Dies Last*. Translated by Jiři Hochman. New York: Kodansha International, 1993.

Havel, Václav. *Open Letters: Selected Writings 1965–1990*. New York: Alfred A. Knopf, 1991.

Heneka, A., Frantisek Janouch, Vilem Prečan, and Jan Vladislav, eds. 1985. *A Beseiged Culture: Czechoslovakia Ten Years after Helsinki*. Stockholm: Charta 77 Foundation and the International Helsinki Federation for Human Rights, 1985.

Keane, John, ed. *The Power of the Powerless: Citizens against the State in Central and Eastern Europe*. London: Hutchison, 1985.

Konrad, Gyorgy. *Antipolitics: An Essay*. Translated by Richard E. Allen. San Diego: Harcourt, Brace and Jovanovich, 1984.

Kurlansky, Mark. *1968: The Year that Rocked the World*. New York: Random House, 2005.

Michnik, Adam. *Letters from Prison and Other Essays*. Translated by Maya Latynski. Berkeley: University of California Press, 1985.

Ramet, Sabrina. *Rocking the State: Rock Music and Politics in Eastern Europe*. Boulder, CO: Westview Press, 1994.

Riedel, Jaroslav, ed. *The Plastic People of the Universe*. Translated by Olga Zahorbenská. Prague: Globus, 1999.

Rupnik, Jacques. *The Other Europe*. London: Weidenfeld and Nicolson, 1988.

Ryback, Timothy W. *Rock around the Bloc: A History of Rock Music in Eastern Europe and the Soviet Union*. New York: Oxford University Press, 1990.

Skilling, H. Gordon. *Czechoslovakia's Interrupted Revolution*. Princeton, NJ: Princeton University Press, 1976.

Skilling, H. Gordon, and Paul Wilson, eds. *Civic Freedom in Central Europe: Voices from Czechoslovakia*. London: Macmillan, 1991.

Šimečka, Milan. *The Restoration of Order: The Normalisation of Czechoslovakia 1969–1976*. London: Verso, 1984.

Wilson, Paul. "What's It like Playing Rock in a Police State?" *Musician Magazine* (February 1983): 70–76.

Zeman, Z. A. B. *Prague Spring*. New York: Hill & Wang, 1990.

∽

CHAPTER FOURTEEN

Why Not All Germans Celebrated the Fall of the Berlin Wall

East German Jews and the Collapse of Communism

CORA GRANATA

The sudden collapse of communism in the Soviet bloc took the world by surprise in 1989. Scholars in hindsight point to several longer-term pressures and instabilities in the Soviet system. Soviet crackdowns of popular unrest in Berlin in 1953, Budapest in 1956, and Prague in 1968 contributed to disaffection with communism in Western and Eastern Europe. In 1975 Moscow signed the human rights provisions of an international agreement called the Helsinki Accords, and Eastern European dissidents found power in demanding that the Soviets abide by the accords. The Soviet-bloc system did not sit well with nationalism, which grew all over the region as communism collapsed. The most significant catalyst for the collapse was the 1985 appointment of the reform-minded communist Mikhail Gorbachev to head the Communist Party in the Soviet Union. Gorbachev began political and economic reforms that led Soviet-style communism in Eastern Europe to implode.

Revolution first took place in Poland. Massive strikes in 1988 protested government price increases and pressured Communists to negotiate with Solidarity, a labor union that had become a potent opposition movement throughout the 1980s. Unlike Soviet leaders in 1968, Gorbachev did not use force to squash dissent, but instead allowed Eastern bloc states autonomy in reforming communism. Thus, hard-liners could no longer rely on Soviet force to buttress their regimes. After free elections in Poland in August 1989 put in power the first non-Communist leader in the Eastern bloc, other revolutions rapidly followed. In Hungary, which already had a more open, decentralized economy, Communist reformers began to criticize openly the 1956 Soviet invasion. Thousands of Hungarians crowded the streets in the summer of 1989, and multiparty elections soon brought the end of communism. These two revolutions inspired similar protests in East Germany, Czechoslovakia, Bulgaria, and Romania. Given the magnitude of the change, the 1989 revolutions were remarkably peaceful. Substantial violence erupted only in Romania, where the notorious dictator Nicolae Ceauşescu ordered his troops to shoot protesters. Protesters in turn executed him and his wife on television on Christmas Day, 1989. The Soviet Union itself disintegrated soon thereafter. Increasingly under pressure from nationalistic independence movements by Soviet republics, Gorbachev resigned in 1991 as head of the Soviet Communist Party, ending over seventy years of communist rule.

In this chapter, Cora Granata examines the fall of communism in Eastern Europe by focusing on the experiences of East Germany's Jewish community, illustrating both the excitement and the new concerns that the collapse of communism created in the former Soviet bloc. She discusses the revival of Jewish culture in East Germany throughout the 1980s, as well as the anxieties many Jews faced when protest movements came with an undercurrent of nationalism.

On 9 November 1989, East German officials made a fateful decision. For forty years, Germany had been divided into two separate states: communist East Germany, known as the German Democratic Republic (GDR), and capitalist West Germany, the Federal Republic of Germany (FRG). East and West Germany stood on opposite sides of the Cold War that divided much of the world after World War II into competing ideologies of communism and capitalism. The starkest symbol of the Cold War was the Berlin Wall, a mass of concrete, barbed wire, and guard towers that communists built in 1961 through the city of Berlin to stop the millions of East Germans who were fleeing to West Germany. Border guards patrolled the wall with orders to shoot anyone who crossed the Berlin Wall without the rare government permit. By 1989, however, cracks appeared in this menacing border. On that chilly evening in November, East German officials eased travel restrictions between East and West Germany. The communists, under increasing domestic pressure to reform their dictatorship, gambled that a freer border would bolster their weakening government's legitimacy. The strategy backfired. When a Communist Party spokesman offhandedly mentioned at a press conference that the new policy would go into effect right away, masses of East Berliners immediately left their apartments and gathered along the Berlin Wall in the cold night air. They reached the wall before the border guards had learned about the hastily made policy change. The guards glared at the crowds amassing along the wall, and the people stared back. Border guards certainly had shot people before. At least 239 East Germans had been killed attempting to cross the Berlin Wall since its creation. One unlucky man had been killed just a few months prior. But this night was different. As the crowds grew by the thousands, nervous guards did not shoot. After several tense hours, some simply lifted the gates. Other guards followed suit, and a huge party erupted as East and West Berliners popped champagne corks, hugged, waved German flags, and lifted one another on top of the gray concrete wall. No one had imagined that the Berlin Wall would open so suddenly and peacefully. Images of the spontaneous celebration were broadcast globally, and much of the world celebrated with Berliners the opening of the wall that had epitomized Cold War oppression. "Wir sind das Volk" (We are the people) had been the slogan of East German protesters, and that night, the people demonstrated their power.

"For us it was not pleasant," recalled one East German about these events.[1] Despite all the euphoric images broadcast around the world, the events of that evening worried some Germans. Surely, members of East Germany's communist elite were not pleased, as they rapidly lost their monopoly on power. This East German was himself a communist, so his reaction to that evening's events no doubt reflected his uncertainty over whether the system he supported would now crumble around him. Indeed it would, as the entire GDR state collapsed not long thereafter and merged with West Germany to form a larger, united Federal Republic of Germany. But his reaction may also have been shaped by another aspect of his identity: his Jewish background. Many members of the GDR's Jewish community viewed the events of 9 November 1989 with a complex mix of emotions. Most welcomed the end of dictatorial policies, but many also feared a renewed German nationalism. Not long after the fall of the Berlin Wall, the "Wir sind *das* Volk" (We are *the* people) slogans began to change to "Wir sind *ein* Volk" (We are *one* Volk). This linguistic shift changed the meaning of the chant from a focus on the ordinary grassroots population to a call for a united, ethnic-based German community. Nationalistic pressures among the population for unification with West Germany grew. Many East German Jews viewed this nationalism with apprehension. Whether they were Holocaust survivors or descendants of survivors, most had learned from history to react with caution when masses of Germans extolling the *Volk* took to the streets. After all, in a coincidence of history, 9 November was also the date in 1938 when bands of nationalistic Germans roamed the streets to attack Jewish synagogues in the Nazi-organized pogrom of Kristallnacht. Thus, underlying many East German Jewish reactions to 9 November 1989 was a fear of racism.

This chapter focuses on the experiences of East Germany's Jewish community in the period leading up to the fall of the Berlin Wall and collapse of communism in Eastern Europe. Most histories characterize the collapse of Eastern European communism as a period of euphoria in which oppressed people rose up to dismantle the dictatorships that had ruled their societies under Soviet domination since the end of World War II. This story line holds considerable truth, but it simplifies the past. First, it obscures how many ordinary people living in Eastern Europe had managed to construct what they considered to be meaningful, if restricted, lives under communism. The dictatorships were no doubt oppressive, but for many citizens, including many East German Jews, life in these societies had offered some promise. Even many of those who grew disillusioned with dictatorial oppression still hoped in the late 1980s that they could reform rather than abandon German communism. Second, the famous image of the euphoric party at the Berlin Wall on 9 November 1989 ignores the varied reactions many people had to these events. For many members of East Germany's Jewish community, the emergence of a powerful and nationalistic united Germany was not something to celebrate, but to view with caution. As East and West Germany rushed toward unification after 1989, the question on many minds was, would there be a revival of extreme German nationalism and racism?

The Gorbachev Factor and the Fall of the Wall

The events that helped precipitate the fall of the Berlin Wall began in 1985, when Mikhail Gorbachev became the new premier of the Soviet Union. Gorbachev inherited a Soviet Union that was in drastic need of reform. The Soviet bloc's state-planned economies had yielded growing production in the 1950s and 1960s, but by the 1970s they were clearly not serving the needs of ordinary citizens. Families often had to wait years for the right to live in a government-issued apartment, and shoppers endured long lines to buy limited supplies of ordinary groceries. Shortly after coming to power, Gorbachev sought to reform his country by introducing two new principles: *glasnost* (openness) and *perestroika* (restructuring). Glasnost encouraged Soviet citizens for the first time to discuss publicly the problems they had in the workplace, in politics, and in their daily lives. Gorbachev hoped that an open exchange of ideas in the media would encourage people to find ways to improve their country. Perestroika referred to economic restructuring, a policy that allowed some private property ownership to encourage innovation and improve efficiency. Gorbachev's goal was not to abandon communism, but to reinvigorate it through controlled reform. Nonetheless, the Soviet leader became very popular in the West, where observers in the United States and Western Europe nicknamed him "Gorbi" and welcomed him as a charismatic and media-savvy man who was so different from the aged and orthodox leaders who had preceded him.

Gorbachev wanted the Eastern European states that had been satellite states under Soviet control since the end of World War II to reform as well. The populations of Poland, Czechoslovakia, Hungary, Romania, Bulgaria, and East Germany, encouraged by glasnost and perestroika, pressured their own governments to institute similar reforms. Of the Soviet satellite states, the leaders of East Germany were among the most resistant to Gorbachev's reforms. On 7 October 1989, the German Democratic Republic commemorated its fortieth anniversary of statehood with a huge celebration, and Gorbachev came as an honored guest. But tensions ran high between Gorbachev and the hard-line East German leader Erich Honecker. Gorbachev gave Honecker a not-so-subtle warning that East Germany was lagging behind in reforms. In front of a massive crowd, Gorbachev admonished Honecker that "life punishes those who come too late." By the time the East German leaders instituted the open travel policy on 9 November 1989, the communist leaders of Poland and Hungary had already given up power under pressure from popular reform movements, and thousands of East Germans had been rallying in the streets for months.

Survivors of Hitler and Stalin

East German Jews experienced the Gorbachev era in ways that reflected their unique status in German history. After World War II, approximately eight thousand Jews remained in or returned to what became the GDR. They faced difficult prospects. Communist ideology downplayed Jewish suffering under the Nazis and instead granted privileged status to communist opponents of fascism. According to the Marxist view of history, communists, not Jews, had been the primary targets of Nazi oppression. Unlike in West Germany, Jews in East Germany did not receive restitution for property they lost during the Third Reich. The fact that many of the German Jews who had survived the war had done so in exile in such Western countries as England, the United States, and Mexico made matters worse. Like Joseph Stalin's violent rule in the Soviet Union, the East German leadership treated anyone with ties to the West as possible traitors to the people's revolution. It did not matter that many of the exiled Jews who returned to East Germany after the war were committed to communist ideals and hoped to build a better, egalitarian socialist Germany. In winter 1952–1953, over five hundred Jews were forced to flee East Germany after a series of anti-Semitic purges labeled Jews dangerous "cosmopolitans" and made them suspected scapegoats of "Western imperialism."

But not all Jews left the country that winter, and the death of Stalin in March 1953 eased anti-Semitic tensions. Most East German Jews settled into ordinary daily lives. Jews in East Germany were a diverse community. A small number became official members of practicing religious congregations in cities such as Berlin, Leipzig, Erfurt, and Halle. Even though communist ideology called for atheism, the East German state pragmatically offered some financial support of religious institutions such as the Lutheran and Catholic churches and Jewish synagogues. In fact, in 1952, the same year that hundreds of Jews fled East Germany, the state financed in the city of Erfurt the rebuilding of a synagogue that had been damaged during the war. But by the 1960s and 1970s, membership in these religious congregations was aging and dwindling. In general, Jewish culture and history suffered from neglect in this period. The dictatorial state forbade the founding of secular Jewish cultural groups for fear they would be pro-Western. Government censors made sure that historians of the Third Reich gave only marginal attention to Nazi racism against Jews. Jewish cemeteries became overgrown with vegetation. When East Germany, along with most other Soviet-bloc states, allied with Arab states and against Israel in the Arab-Israeli wars of 1967 and 1973, matters grew even more complicated for East German Jews. To be openly Jewish once again brought risk of being labeled pro-Western, pro-Zionist, and bourgeois. For most East Germans with Jewish backgrounds, this atmosphere meant that it was best to downplay their Jewish heritage, assimilate, and focus on constructing successful lives under communism. Most did just that.

Reviving Jewish Culture under Communism

By the late 1970s and 1980s, East Germans cultivated new interest in Jewish culture and history. At first, this revival came from the grass roots, as younger East German citizens grew disillusioned with the promises of socialism and instead embraced a Jewish identity. By the mid-1980s, the party itself cultivated Jewish culture in an effort to bolster its declining legitimacy. The lives of a few individuals highlight this transformation and help us understand East German Jews' complex reactions to the fall of the wall in 1989.

In 1981, Barbara Honigmann wanted to have a Jewish wedding. Since there was no rabbi in all of East Germany in 1981, she tried to get a rabbi from West Berlin to travel east to conduct the ceremony. East German officials denied the rabbi's travel request. Frustrated by the state's efforts to block his daughter's wedding plans, Georg Honigmann wrote a letter to the powerful state secretary for church questions. Georg told the official that "I myself have no understanding for the efforts to revive the Jewish world," but he still supported his daughter's religious hopes. He explained to the state secretary, "Recently my daughter . . . has discovered her Jewishness, and she is under the impression that her life would miss something essential if she were to remain estranged from Jewish tradition—as is the case in her family."[2]

The contrasting perspectives of this father and daughter illustrate the growing interest in Jewish culture in the decade before the fall of the wall. As was the case for many Jews who had constructed reasonably successful lives in East Germany, Jewishness had little salience for Georg. Born in 1903, he survived World War II in British exile, returned to Soviet-occupied Germany in 1946, joined the East German Communist Party, and built a reputation as a prominent journalist.[3] After Barbara's birth in 1949, he and his wife placed no emphasis on Jewish culture in her upbringing. In the view of many individuals like Georg, a system that in theory claimed to move beyond ethnic categories to unite people under universal socialist ideals represented a relief after the Third Reich's obsession with racial hierarchy.

Barbara, on the other had, was part of a younger generation that was increasingly disillusioned with life in East Germany. While her parents enjoyed what they saw as good lives for themselves in East Germany, Barbara's increased interest in her Jewish heritage coincided with her growing distance from the GDR. As an artist and author, Barbara became part of an emerging dissident writers' scene in Berlin, and this underground community provided a forum for her to cultivate her alternative Jewish identity. Small groups of artists and intellectuals in Berlin and Dresden began to craft their own pamphlets and makeshift journals. Barbara published in one such Berlin-based underground journal.[4] After frustrations such as the state's efforts to derail her Jewish wedding, Barbara decided that she had no future in East Germany. She left the country in 1984 for Strasbourg, France, home to a large Jewish community. She had become drawn to Orthodox Judaism, for which she felt there was no place in East Germany. Later she described her emigration as a move "out of assimilation into the middle of Torah-Judaism."[5] Rather than fitting into the socialist mainstream as her parents had done, Barbara expressed Jewish cultural difference as a way to voice her political discontent.

Irene Runge similarly became interested in her Jewish background, but she chose to stay in East Germany, eventually creating a vibrant community for secular East German Jews who had for decades kept Jewish culture on the periphery of their lives. When Runge formed a Jewish culture club in 1986 named *Wir für uns* (For Ourselves), she was surprised at how many people came "out of the closet" to join. She recalled, "Jews came who never had any-thing to do with the religious Jewish Community. . . . These were all people whose parents had been politically active in the GDR, Communists, in the [party], completely integrated. . . . They had their positions as teachers, at the universities, everywhere. They hadn't married according to Jewish tradition, their children knew nothing about it, their parents hadn't spoken with them about it, and suddenly there was an opportunity to get together."[6]

Unlike Barbara Honigmann, Irene Runge could hardly be described as a dissident. Of the same generation as Honigmann, Runge gave little attention to her Jewish heritage as a child and young adult, focusing instead on fitting in with mainstream East German society. In fact, she had integrated so com-pletely into East German political culture that she became a part of the coun-try's notorious secret police, the Ministry for State Security (Stasi). As a smart and very sociable young woman, she served the Stasi as a useful IM, or "unofficial informer"—part of the vast network of ordinary citizens the Stasi employed to keep tabs on the East German population.

However, Runge's relationship with the Stasi began to weaken at the same time that she became increasingly active in Jewish cultural activities. Runge first became a Stasi informant in 1962, and the information she pro-vided the secret police led to the arrest of at least four people.[7] At the same time, the Stasi, ever paranoid about maintaining East German stability, kept close watch on her. When she once doubted the objectivity of the coverage of the Middle East in the East German press in 1973, the Stasi noted it in her personnel file.[8] Continuing the long tradition of linking Jewishness with the West, the Stasi was suspicious of Runge's new involve-ment in Jewish circles. In 1981, the Stasi put a concerned note in her per-sonnel file alerting officials that she had "pronounced Zionist views" and "intensive contact with the Jewish Community and in the USA."[9] Runge became increasingly uncooperative, and in 1985, Stasi officials filed their concluding report explaining that the relationship between Runge and the secret police had definitively ended: "In the first years of working together the IM reliably fulfilled her duties. . . . While the source generally had a positive perspective of GDR politics and represented those views in her cir-cles, she became less and less willing to report openly to the MfS [Ministry for State Security] over problems that would be of interest. In addition, the source became deeply involved with the Jewish Community."[10] Officials re-ported that in recent years Runge had often engaged them in intense po-litical discussions. Insisting that all her contacts were "progressive people," she had become unwilling to recognize "enemy activities."[11] In the eyes of the Stasi, Runge was no longer a reliable informer.

A decade after the wall fell, Runge explained in an oral history interview how she first became involved in Jewish activities. At first, some friends brought her to Jewish Community events, which initially did not particularly appeal to her. "Then," she recalled, "at some point they asked me if I would be more active in the Board [of the Jewish Community of Berlin]. I thought that wouldn't be a bad idea, as I had just broken off with the Stasi pretty dramatically. That ran consecutively. . . . I figured why not, and then I tried to fulfill my dream of a 'coffee house Jewry' [*Kaffeehaus Judentum*] and founded Wir für uns."[12] One day in early 1986, she sat down and drew up a list of about fifty friends and acquaintances she knew to be of Jewish background but who were not members of Berlin's religious Jewish Community.[13] It was from this initial list that she built up her club. Having become disillusioned because of the Stasi's efforts to find enemies everywhere, Runge found new meaning in her life by organizing a secular, urban, intellectual Jewish culture club. Indeed, the same social skills that at one time made Runge an appealing Stasi informer now served her well in her work organizing a new club. For Runge, Jewishness was a social identity, or, as she put it, "To be Jewish to me meant eating, drinking, trying things out."[14]

Despite growing up with parents and a government that discouraged Jewish identity, Wir für uns members still shared a history of common experience. Most were children of Jews who had been émigrés during World War II and, as committed socialists, had returned to communist-controlled Germany. Many of these returnees had even settled in the same neighborhoods. Runge recalled, "We were children of émigrés. We all more or less knew one another, or everyone knew someone who knew someone."[15] The organization created a structure under the rubric of Jewish culture for informal connections that had already existed among children of émigrés in Berlin, yet previously these people had not viewed these connections through a Jewish lens. While a Jewish identity had not been salient for their parents as they built lives under socialism, members of the younger generation, becoming less invested in the East German state, began to find meaning in a collective Jewish identity. Wir für uns became an important part of revived Jewish life—a place to celebrate Jewish holidays, to put on theater pieces, or discuss history. "For me it was all the things that we had never gotten at home," Runge said.[16] By September 1987, when the Jewish Community of Berlin held an informal gathering for nonmembers, over three hundred people came. Partly as a result of organizing efforts such as Wir für uns, well over half of the people who came to the gathering were newly interested nonmembers.[17]

At first suspicious, the East German government by the mid-1980s began to support this revival of Jewish culture. The communist leadership's shift resulted from a combination of international and domestic circumstances. State officials watched with concern the growing political and economic unrest in other Eastern bloc countries, in particular the Solidarity labor movement in neighboring Poland. In addition, when Mikhail Gorbachev came to power in the Soviet Union in 1985 and began to allow more free expression under his policy of glasnost, East German officials feared for the stability of their own regime. While East German leader Erich Honecker resisted Gorbachev's reform policies, party leaders also realized that East Germany's survival depended on some openness with the West. Plagued by the economic problems facing Eastern bloc states, and confronting a discontented populace, GDR leaders believed that some measured gestures toward openness might attract Western economic aid.[18] A new acceptance of Jewish culture became a way to forge new Western ties and guarantee the stability of the regime. East German Jews' ties to the West, once a burden, now took on a more positive meaning.

One of the most visible gestures by East Germany to revive Jewish culture was its support of the reconstruction of Berlin's Neue Synagoge. Built in 1866 as Berlin's second synagogue for the city's growing Jewish population, the Neue Synagoge had been a grand structure. Its elaborate golden dome helped define Berlin's skyline and symbolized the city's status as the center of Jewish life in pre-Nazi Germany. Albert Einstein, a member of prewar Berlin's Jewish community, gave a violin concert in the Neue Synagoge in 1930. But damaged by Allied bombing in 1943, the synagogue lay in rubble for over forty years. The East Berlin Jewish Community unsuccessfully petitioned the state in 1961 and 1967 to reconstruct it as a museum.[19] But as East German officials sought to nurture new ties to the West, the interests of Berlin's Jewish Community and those of the state coincided in 1986. Party officials now for the first time envisioned "a monument to Jewish victims" that would have exhibits on Jewish tradition. It would house "representations of Jewish contributions to German and cultural history and a center to research these contributions."[20]

With the Neue Synagoge as a new center for the celebration of Jewish culture, East German officials in 1988 also organized a large-scale commemoration of the fiftieth anniversary of the 9 November Kristallnacht pogrom. East Germany had occasionally commemorated Kristallnacht in the past, but the fiftieth anniversary became a forum to demonstrate to the outside world the GDR's altered perspective on the past and on Jewishness. As officials from the State Secretariat for Church Questions explained to the Stasi in May 1988, "this commemoration will not be narrow, but rather will be understood as a part of our history."[21] By describing Kristallnacht as part of East German history, state officials signaled a new definition of national identity. Rather than focusing on the progressive heroism of communist resistance, they showed a new willingness to recognize the power of racism in Germany's past.

Many East German Jews viewed all this new attention with optimism and a touch of anxiety. Encouraged by the government's new support for Jewish culture, Irene Runge, no longer a Stasi informer, began telephoning high-level party officials to request the renaming of streets that had lost Jewish names after Kristallnacht.[22] Some reacted with mixed feelings. A Stasi report meant to gauge opinion within Berlin's Jewish Community captured this ambivalence. The report found that Jewish Community members "greeted the increased value the state granted [them]." Yet some were concerned that the attention might be "exaggerated" and feared an anti-Semitic backlash from the general population. Some reasoned that since many East German citizens were dissatisfied with their material conditions, they might begin to voice their unrest in anti-Jewish terms.[23] Indeed, East German Jews had reason to fear anti-Semitic backlash. In the town of Fürstenwalde, officials planned to unveil a memorial plaque in the Jewish cemetery to commemorate the fiftieth anniversary of Kristallnacht. The day before the event vandals desecrated the new plaque with three swastikas. After an urgent scrubbing, the ceremony went on.[24] In May 1988, a staff member of the Jewish Community in Erfurt received a disturbing phone call. A voice on the other line told her, "Jews. Do they still exist? Are they still here? Must have forgotten about you. The ovens are still warm and are calling for you."[25]

This anti-Semitic backlash and right-wing nationalism became a way for some ordinary Germans to voice their protest against the East German regime. Just as many East German Jews turned toward a Jewish identity as an alternative to socialism, others turned toward German nationalism or skinhead groups as an alternative way to view the world and themselves. In an internal 1989 report, Stasi officials expressed their concern about skinhead actions and counted 188 investigations against "fascist, racist, and militaristic" activities since 1 January 1988.[26] Police and other state officials counted judicial processes against more than four hundred skinheads in the same time frame.[27] In December 1988, the Jewish Community of Berlin received a letter that blamed Jews for the Russian occupation of East Germany and claimed, "Jews pray that the Russians will stay in Germany a long time." Foretelling the German nationalism that would help catapult East Germany toward unification, the letter was titled "Jews Are Not Germans."[28]

By the late 1980s, East German Jews found themselves in a curious position. The communist dictatorship, no matter how repressive, had also become openly supportive of expressions of Jewish culture. Meanwhile, the growing popular protest against the government, while largely peaceful and tolerant, also brought a disturbing growing undercurrent of anti-Semitism. The end of communism brought with it an upsurge in ethnic-based nationalism. In this revival of ethnic nationalism, East Germany marched alongside other Eastern European countries. Ethnic nationalism led to the 1993 separation of Czechoslovakia into two states: the Czech Republic and Slovakia. Most violently, Yugoslavia for much of the 1990s fell into a bloody ethnic civil war.

"The More German Germany Becomes . . . "

In May 1989, communist officials in Hungary cut down the barbed wire of their border with Austria. A small number of East Germans traveled through Hungary to escape to the West. After the Hungarian government formally opened its borders in September 1989, fifty thousand more East German citizens fled for West Germany within a month. Among those who stayed in the East, dissident gatherings grew each week. In October 1989, between 300,000 and 500,000 protesters rallied in Leipzig. Protesters marched for diverse causes, including nuclear disarmament, environmentalism, and gay rights. Some called for free elections. Others called for an end to the state's repression of punk rock clubs. Chanting the now-famous slogan "We are the people," demonstrators put increasing pressure on the East German regime, which had been told by Gorbachev that it could not rely on Soviet military force to maintain stability. On 18 October, a more moderate Communist, Egon Krenz, replaced the hard-line Honecker. Exactly one year after the fiftieth-anniversary Kristallnacht commemorations, state officials opened the Berlin Wall.

Most East German Jews were not among those leaving in the fall of 1989.[29] The Jewish Community of Berlin, which had the largest population of religious Jews, felt newly encouraged by state support of the Neue Synagoge's reconstruction and likely wanted to see it through.[30] Younger secular intellectual Jews active in Irene Runge's Wir für uns group were more likely to try to reform socialist East Germany than give up on it altogether. Those who had no investment in the country anymore, like Barbara Honigmann, had left years earlier. When the "We are the people" slogans began to change to "We are one Volk" many East German Jews viewed this new German nationalism with apprehension. Irene Runge remembers that as people started chanting, "We are one Volk," members of her Jewish culture club wondered how they fit into the picture.[31] A month after the Berlin Wall toppled, a racist letter blaming Jews for the postwar division of Germany was passed on to the librarian of the Jewish Community of Berlin. "Up until now we never had to face anything like this, but maybe we have to get used to it. The thought scares me," the librarian wrote.[32]

Ultimately, for East German Jews, the events of 1989 and 1990 brought both positive and negative effects. The fall of the Berlin Wall led to new freedoms. After the official unification of East and West Germany in October 1990, the revival of Jewish culture that had begun in the mid-1980s continued. Since April 1990, tens of thousands of Jews from the former Soviet Union have settled in eastern Germany, radically altering the makeup of Jewish Communities in former East German towns and cities. Irene Runge continued her work organizing secular Jews, turning her Wir für uns group into the Jüdischer Kulturverein (Jewish Cultural Club), which remains a forum for left-leaning East German Jews. Down the street from the Jüdischer Kulturverein, the reconstructed Neue Synagoge now stands near the new capitol buildings of the united Germany in the heart of a bustling Berlin neighborhood that showcases to visitors from all over the world the resurgence of Jewish culture in Germany.

Along with a flourishing of Jewish cultural activities, however, former East German Jews also face disillusionment as East Germans in a united Germany. Facing high unemployment unknown to them during GDR times, many have had to completely restructure their lives. In addition, the fears of anti-Semitism that became visible with the upsurge in German nationalism during the collapse of the GDR have continued. While they do not miss dictatorial rule, some fondly remember growing up in an East German state whose ideology theoretically privileged a universalistic socialist collective identity over ethnic categories. Contrasting the GDR with united Germany a decade after the fall of the wall, one man recalled with a hint of nostalgia, "What you were didn't matter in the GDR."[33] The way some former East German Jews like this man see it, they are forced to live as Jews in a united Germany that is becoming ever more conscious of its Germanness. He explained,

> Even today I still have difficulties when I have to decide what I'm supposed to write down for country or nationality. . . . Let me put it this way. In the past ten years, the more German Germany becomes, the more Jewish I become.[34]

Notes

I am grateful to the Alexander von Humboldt Foundation for providing the fellowship support to make this research possible.

1. Walter S., interview by the author, tape recording, 29 August 2000.

2. Honigmann an den Staatssekretär für Kirchenfragen, 8 June 1981, Bundesarchiv Berlin (henceforth BA-Berlin), Staatssekretariat für Kirchenfragen, DO/4/448, 138.

3. Bernd-Rainer Barth, Christoph Links, Helmut Müller-Enbergs, and Jan Wielgohs, ed., *Wer war Wer in der DDR: Ein biographisches Handbuch* (Frankfurt, 1996), 322.

4. Wolfgang Emmerich, *Kleine Literatur Geschichte der DDR* (Leipzig, 1997), 407–8.

5. Emmerich, *Kleine Literatur Geschichte*, 431.

6. Irene Runge, interview by the author, tape recording, 4 August 2000. This essay uses the capitalized term "Community" for the German term *Gemeinde*, referring to a religious Jewish congregation affiliated with a synagogue.

7. Ministerium für Staatssicherheit (henceforth MfS), AIM 11422/85, Band I. Runge, Irene, 25.

8. MfS, AIM 11422/85, Band I. Runge, Irene, 71.

9. MfS, AIM 11422/85, Band I. Runge, Irene, 95.

10. MfS, AIM 11422/85, Band I. Runge, Irene, 123.

11. MfS, AIM 11422/85, Band I. Runge, Irene.

12. Runge, interview.

13. For more on Runge's work organizing secular Jewish culture, see Robin Ostow, *Jews in Contemporary East Germany: Children of Moses in the Land of Marx* (New York, 1989), 59.

14. Runge, interview.

15. Runge, interview.

16. Runge, interview.

17. Robin Ostow attended this meeting and reported on it in her 1989 book. See Ostow, *Jews in Contemporary East Germany*, 149.

18. On East Germany's economic situation in its final decade, including its reliance on Western loans, see Charles S. Maier, *Dissolution: The Crisis of Communism and the End of East Germany* (Princeton, 1997).

19. Jüdische Gemeinde von Gross Berlin to Hans Seigewasser, 3 January 1967, BA-Berlin, Staatssekretariat für Kirchenfragen, DO/4/1051, 31, and Jüdische Gemeinde von Gross-Berlin to Kusch, 7 March 1961, BA-Berlin, Staatssekretariat für Kirchenfragen DO/4/1051, 32.

20. Konzeption zum Wiederaufbau der "Neuen Synagoge," Berlin, Hauptstadt der DDR, 17 March 1986, BA-Berlin, Staatssekretariat für Kirchenfragen, DO/4/1051, 5.

21. Information über das Gespräch mit Dr. Heinz Galinski in der Dienstelle, 16 May 1988, MfS-HA XX/4-2183, 12.

22. Information über ein Anruf von Frau Dr. Irene Runge an Staatssekretär Gysi, 9 February 1988, MfS HA-XX/4-2183, 51.

23. Information zu Meinungen/Reaktionen unter Mitgliedern der Jüdischen Gemeinde Berlin bezüglich der Würdigung der jüdischen Opfer des Faschismus anläßlich des 50. Jahrestages der Pogromnacht, 10 November 1988, MfS-HA XX/4-2183, 192.

24. Anbringung faschistischer Symbole in Zusammenhang mit dem 50. Jahrestag des faschistischen Pogromnacht, MfS-HA XX/4-2183, 437.

25. Jüdische Landesgemeinde Thüringen to Klaus Gysi, 12 May 1988, MfS-HA XX/4-2183, 455.

26. Mitteilung der Pressestelle des MfS, n.d., MfS HA-XX/4-2181, 64.

27. Mitteilung der Pressestelle des MfS, 66.

28. Juden sind keine Deutsche, October 1988, MfS-HA XX/4-2181, 107.

29. Zu aktuellen Problemen innerhalb der jüdischen Gemeinden in der DDR, 19 October 1989, MfS-HA XX/4-2181, 20.

30. Zu aktuellen Problemen innerhalb der jüdischen Gemeinden in der DDR, 19 October 1989, MfS-HA XX/4-2181, 20.

31. Runge, interview.

32. Jüdische Gemeinde Berlin to Heinz Galinski, 5 December 1989, MfS-HA XX/4-2181, 51.

33. Andreas P., interview by the author, tape recording, 16 August 2000.

34. Andreas P., interview.

Suggested Readings

Brenner, Michael. *After the Holocaust: Rebuilding Jewish Lives in Postwar Germany.* Princeton, NJ: Princeton University Press, 1997.

Gay, Ruth. *Safe among Germans: Liberated Jews after World War II.* New Haven, CT: Yale University Press, 2002.

Jarausch, Konrad. *The Rush to German Unity.* New York: Oxford University Press, 1994.

Ostow, Robin. *Jews in Contemporary East Germany: Children of Moses in the Land of Marx.* New York: St. Martin's Press, 1989.

Peck, Jeffrey. *Being Jewish in the New Germany.* New Brunswick, NJ: Rutgers University Press, 2006.

Stokes, Gale. *The Walls Came Tumbling Down: The Collapse of Communism in Eastern Europe.* New York: Oxford University Press, 1993.

Index

Note: Page numbers in italics indicate illustrations.

~

About the Editors

Cora Granata is associate professor of history and director of the European Studies Program at California State University, Fullerton. Her work has appeared in *German Studies Review* and in *Zwischen Politik und Kultur: Juden in der DDR*, edited by Moshe Zuckermann. She received her PhD from the University of North Carolina at Chapel Hill. She is currently writing a book on nationalism and cultural minorities in East Germany, entitled *Celebration and Suspicion: Jews and Sorbs in the Soviet Occupied Zone and the German Democratic Republic*.

Cheryl A. Koos is associate professor of history at California State University, Los Angeles, where she teaches courses on modern European and French history. She has published articles and anthology chapters on gender, the family, and early twentieth-century right-wing French politics. She received her PhD from the University of Southern California and is currently working on a book manuscript about the intersection of gender and right-wing politics in the pronatalist and profamily movement in interwar France.

About the Contributors

Karin Breuer is assistant professor of history at Ithaca College. She received her PhD from the University of North Carolina at Chapel Hill, in 2002. Her dissertation, "Constructing Germanness: The Student Movement from the *Burschenschaft* to the *Progress*, 1815–1848," examined the intersection between student activism, nationalism, and democratization in the German states in the first half of the nineteenth century.

Helen Harden Chenut received her PhD from the University of Paris VII and teaches in the History Department at the University of California, Irvine. She is the author of *The Fabric of Gender: Working-Class Culture in Third Republic France* (2005), and of numerous articles in English and French on gender and work. She recently translated and wrote a historical introduction to *Breaking the Silence: French Women's Voices from the Ghetto* (2006).

John Cox earned his master's degree at Brandeis University and his PhD at the University of North Carolina at Chapel Hill. His dissertation, "Circles of Resistance: Intersections of Jewish, Leftist, and Youth Dissidence During the Third Reich, 1933–1945," examined the Baum groups and other similar resistance operations within Berlin. Cox is currently assistant professor of history at Florida Gulf Coast University, where he is director of the Center for the Study of Judaism, the Holocaust, and Human Rights.

Stephen P. Frank is associate professor of history at the University of California, Los Angeles; he teaches Russian and European history, criminal justice history, and the history of popular culture. He received his PhD from Brown University. In addition to two edited anthologies, he has published *Crime, Cultural Conflict, and Justice in Rural Russia, 1856–1914* (2000), and is currently working on a book that explores popular culture and social reform in rural Russia.

Maura E. Hametz received her PhD from Brandeis University in 1995 and is currently associate professor of history at Old Dominion University. Her research focuses on Italy and Central Europe. She is the author of *Making Trieste Italian, 1918–1954* (2005). Her work has appeared in *Austrian History Yearbook, Names, Holocaust and Genocide Studies*, and the *Journal of Modern Italian Studies*. She is currently working on a book examining the Signora's case and the status of women in Fascist Italy.

Michael Kilburn is associate professor of political science and international studies at Endicott College in Beverly, Massachusetts, and director of the Endicott Oral History Center. His research interests include democratization and post-Communist transition, human rights, Cold War culture and history, and the politics of art and music. He received his PhD from Emory University in 2001 with a dissertation on the Plastic People entitled "The Merry Ghetto: The Czech Underground in the Time of Normalization." He is currently revising this research for publication and cowriting a book on human rights and victimology.

Robert A. McLain was born in Chillan, Chile, and raised in Mississippi. He earned his MA in history at the University of Southern Mississippi (1996) and his PhD at the University of Illinois, Urbana-Champaign (2003). He specializes in the "New Imperial" history of the British Empire, emphasizing the roles of race, gender, and sexuality in ideologically undergirding and protecting colonial power, particularly in India. He is currently assistant professor of history at California State University, Fullerton.

Karen Petrone is associate professor of history at the University of Kentucky. She received her PhD from the University of Michigan. She is the author of *Life Has Become More Joyous, Comrades: Celebrations in the Time of Stalin* (2000). She has also published articles on masculinity and heroism in World

War I posters and in imperial and Soviet military-patriotic cultures. Her book in progress is tentatively entitled "World War I Remembrance and the Culture of Soviet Military Mobilization."

Paolo Scrivano is assistant professor of history of modern architecture in the Art History Department of Boston University. He received his PhD in the history of architecture and town planning from the Politecnico di Torino in 1997. Between 1997 and 2001 he taught at the Politecnico di Milano. He has served as visiting scholar at the Massachusetts Institute of Technology (1995), visiting scholar at the Canadian Centre for Architecture (2002), and Ailsa Mellon Bruce Visiting Senior Fellow at the Center for Advanced Study in the Visual Arts of the National Gallery of Art (2003). His publications include *Tra Guerra e Pace: Società, Cultura e Architettura nel Secondo Dopoguerra* (1998, as coeditor), *Storia di un'idea di architettura moderna: Henry-Russell Hitchcock and the International Style* (2001), and, with Patrizia Bonifazio, *Olivetti Builds: Modern Architecture in Ivrea* (2001).

Alyssa Goldstein Sepinwall received her PhD from Stanford University. She is associate professor of history at California State University, San Marcos. She is the author of *The Abbé Grégoire and the French Revolution: The Making of Modern Universalism* (2005). Her research interests include the Enlightenment and the French and Haitian revolutions.

Matthew G. Stanard is assistant professor in the Department of History at Berry College, where he teaches modern European history, world history, African history, and a course on imperialism, colonialism, and nationalism. Working with the late William B. Cohen and then James D. Le Sueur (of the University of Nebraska, Lincoln), Stanard received his PhD in modern European history from Indiana University, Bloomington, in 2006. Stanard has been a Belgian American Educational Foundation fellow in Brussels, a future faculty teaching fellow at Indiana University-Purdue University Indianapolis, and a chancellor's fellow at Indiana University.

Michele Strong is assistant professor of history at the University of South Alabama, Mobile, where she teaches courses in Western civilization, Great Britain, and empire. She received her PhD at the University of North Carolina at Chapel Hill. She is currently writing a book-length manuscript on British working-class "study abroad" between 1840 and 1914.

Patricia Tilburg is assistant professor of history at Davidson College where she teaches modern European and French history as well as gender and cultural history. She received her doctorate from the University of California, Los Angeles. Her publications on late nineteenth- and early twentieth-century French popular culture have appeared in *French Historical Studies* and *Radical History Review*. She is currently completing a cultural history of Belle Époque France through the prism of the life, work, and reception of Colette.